D0838501

PS
3537
H384
Z673
1991

136070

N.L. TERTELING LIBRARY
THE COLLEGE OF IDAHO
CALDWELL, IDAHO

PURCHASED WITH NEH
ENDOWMENT FUNDS

IRWIN
SHAW

A Study of the Short Fiction

Also available in Twayne's Studies in Short Fiction Series

Twayne's Studies in Short Fiction

Gordon Weaver, General Editor
Oklahoma State University

Irwin Shaw.
Photograph by David Morris.

IRWIN SHAW

A Study of the Short Fiction

James R. Giles
Northern Illinois University

TWAYNE PUBLISHERS • BOSTON
A Division of G. K. Hall & Co.

PS 3537
H384
Z673
1991

Twayne's Studies in Short Fiction Series No. 21

Copyright 1991 by G. K. Hall & Co.
All rights reserved.
Published by Twayne Publishers
A division of G. K. Hall & Co.
70 Lincoln Street
Boston, Massachusetts 02111

Copyediting supervised by Barbara Sutton.
Book production by Gabrielle B. McDonald.
Book design by Janet Z. Reynolds.
Typeset in 10/12 Caslon by Compset, Inc., Beverly, Massachusetts.

First published 1991.
10 9 8 7 6 5 4 3 2 1

The paper used in this publication meets the minimum requirements
of American National Standard for Information Sciences—Permanence
of Paper for Printed Library Materials, ANSI Z39.48-1984. ∞™

Printed and bound in the United States of America.

Library of Congress Cataloging-in-Publication Data

Giles, James Richard, 1937–
    Irwin Shaw : a study of the short fiction / James R. Giles.
        p.   cm.—(Twayne's studies in short fiction ; no. 21)
    Includes bibliographical references and index.
    ISBN 0-8057-8331-8 (alk. paper)
    1. Shaw, Irwin, 1913–   —Criticism and interpretation.   2. Short
story.   I. Title.   II. Series.
PS3537.H384Z673   1991
813'.52—dc20
                                                            90-22101
                                                            CIP

136070

To Morgan

N. L. TERTELING LIBRARY
THE COLLEGE OF IDAHO
CALDWELL, IDAHO

Contents

Preface

During the last three decades of his career, Irwin Shaw was increasingly known as a best-selling novelist. The broad public acceptance of his three epic novels, *The Young Lions* (1948), *Rich Man, Poor Man* (1970), and *Beggarman, Thief* (1977), tended to overshadow his achievements in short fiction. Yet Shaw had published three collections of stories before his first novel appeared, and throughout his career his short fiction was generally well received, even by those critics who disliked his novels. "The Girls in Their Summer Dresses," "The Eighty-Yard Run," and "Act of Faith" have been praised by influential and perceptive critics such as Cleanth Brooks, Robert Penn Warren, Lionel Trilling, and William Peden. The 1978 publication of *Short Stories: Five Decades*, a collection of 63 of his 85 published stories, stands as conclusive evidence of Shaw's lasting contribution to American short fiction.

The critical reception of Irwin Shaw's novels and plays has been decidedly mixed. While his first two novels, *The Young Lions* (1948) and *The Troubled Air* (1951), were well received by critics, his subsequent long fiction was generally dismissed as superficial and commercial. In contrast, his short stories have been consistently praised for their craft and powerful realism. In fact, he is generally recognized as one of the best American practitioners of modernist, existentialist short fiction, and he is certainly one of the most frequently anthologized. Yet his short fiction has received surprisingly little serious critical attention, perhaps because the decline of his reputation as a novelist resulted in his work being ignored by much of the critical establishment.

In this study I focus on the social relevance of Shaw's stories. Certainly, the corrupt and collapsing American capitalism of the 1930s, Hitler and European fascism, American anti-Semitism, and 1950s McCarthyism provided obvious and relatively unambiguous targets for a writer of social protest. Moreover, as an American of Jewish descent whose father had gone bankrupt, as one who served in Europe during World War II and saw firsthand the devastation of Hitler's legacy, and as a writer who was then blacklisted in the 1950s, Shaw had direct and personal knowledge of these economic, social, and political evils. Still, in his best early stories he avoids a kind of artistic oversimplification common to much protest fiction. His exploited characters are not one-dimensional martyrs—they are fully realized human beings with complex emotions and motivations. Especially in the McCarthyism stories, the characters' very complexity often contributes to their victimization.

Still, the total body of Shaw's short fiction cannot be approached exclusively as social protest, especially since critics have charged that the expatriate fiction of his 25 years in Europe reflects a weary cynicism rather than an involvement with American social and political issues. While it is true that the central characters in these later stories generally come from a decidedly upper-class, rather than a proletarian, background, Shaw's sojourn in Europe is not the main reason for the shift in narrative emphasis or for the inadequacy of limited sociological approaches to his work.

A quite personal concept of decency underscores virtually all of Shaw's writing. Shaw's fiction depicts a fallen, secular world controlled by accident and dominated by seemingly limitless manifestations and abuses of the flesh. The inevitability of accident and death are the only certainties in Shaw's fictional world. As a result, the inhabitants of Shaw's universe must develop and strive to remain faithful to personal ethical codes. Shaw believed, however, that such codes must center around the traditional values of loyalty, compassion, courage, and devotion to justice, virtues that he cumulatively labeled as "decency."

In the expatriate stories, then, Shaw is no longer primarily concerned with protest against external injustice and oppression. His focus, instead, is on the inherent difficulties of creating an ethical center for the Self. His young expatriates are not struggling against forces as clear and as obviously evil as Nazism or anti-Semitism—they are fighting for ethical survival in a chaotic, accident-dominated world. Instead of discussing Shaw's short fiction collection by collection, I have used a thematic structure, in part to detail Shaw's evolution from a writer concerned with protesting clear social injustice to one devoted to exploring ethical ambiguity in an uncertain world. It must be emphasized that the importance of individual human decency is a central consideration in all his short fiction.

It should be said that critics have not always seen the ethical concerns underlying Shaw's fiction. In part, this oversight results from Shaw's mastery in capturing the surface reality of American life, and especially New York City life. Like F. Scott Fitzgerald, Shaw depicts the rich, glittering surface of materialistic urban America. But, also like F. Scott Fitzgerald, he investigates the ways in which material comfort can undermine the integrity of the twentieth-century American.

In a 1980 interview at his home in Southampton, New York, Shaw told me that he believed the values of decency still had more meaning in America than anywhere else in the world. While he believed that American decency had survived the Great Depression, World War II, and McCarthyism, he saw it fundamentally threatened by Vietnam and the turmoil of the 1960s. I have therefore concluded my study of his short fiction with an extended analysis of "God Was Here but He Left Early," an angry and despairing late story. In summary, I see Shaw's short fiction as a body of work inspired by, but ultimately transcending, the social and political turmoil and upheaval of the last five decades of American life.

In addition to Irwin, I want to thank Willie Morris, Marian Shaw, Gloria Jones, and Wanda Hancock Giles for their contributions to this study. I am also indebted to Cheryl Fuller for typing the manuscript from my handwriting.

Acknowledgments

Previously published material is reprinted by permission of the following:

Willie Morris and Lucas Matthiessen, "The Art of Fiction IV: Irwin Shaw," in *Writers at Work: The Paris Review Interviews, Fifth Series*, ed. George Plimpton. © 1981 by the Paris Review, Inc. Reprinted by permission of Viking Penguin, a division of Penguin Books, USA Inc.

James R. Giles, "Interviews with Irwin Shaw, Summer 1980." *Resources for American Literary Study*. Reprinted by permission of *Resources for American Literary Study*.

William Peden, "Best of Irwin Shaw," *Saturday Review*. Reprinted by permission of Omni Publications International Ltd. and William Peden.

Bergen Evans, "Irwin Shaw," *English Journal*. Reprinted by permission of *English Journal* and National Council of Teachers of English.

Hubert Saal, "Disenchanted Men," *Saturday Review*. Reprinted by permission of Omni Publications International Ltd. and Hubert Saal.

William Startt, "Irwin Shaw: An Extended Talent," *Midwest Quarterly*. Reprinted by permission of *Midwest Quarterly* editor-in-chief Dr. James B. M. Schick.

Chester E. Eisinger, "Fiction and the Liberal Reassessment," in *Fiction of the Forties*. Reprinted by permission of the University of Chicago Press and Chester E. Eisinger.

Ross Wetzsteon, "Irwin Shaw: The Conflict Between Big Bucks and Good Books," *Saturday Review*. Reprinted by permission of Omni Publications International Ltd. and Ross Wetzsteon.

Part 1

THE SHORT FICTION

The Evolution of a Career

Decency and the Common Man

Irwin Shaw's first published story collection, *Sailor off the Bremen and Other Stories*, appeared in 1939 to favorable reviews. Several of its 20 stories exemplify Shaw's socially committed, or engaged fiction. The title story, which depicts the revenge carried out by a group of American leftists against a sadistic German Nazi, is brutal and angry in tone and execution. To a lesser degree, four other stories in the collection—"I Stand by Dempsey," "Second Mortgage," "Residents of Other Cities," and "Borough of Cemeteries"—are also designed to shock the reader into an awareness of injustice. "Sailor off the Bremen" and "Residents of Other Cities" gave Chester E. Eisinger, usually a perceptive critic, a largely misleading impression that Shaw was a violently militant writer. Although protest against the socioeconomic injustice of the Great Depression runs throughout this first collection, it is generally subdued and often quite indirect.

Like his 1939 play *The Gentle People, Sailor off the Bremen* illustrates Shaw's commitment to ordinary people struggling to retain their dignity in an impersonal and frequently oppressive society. Shaw was a firm believer in the unique strength of character of the American common man and woman. In an unpublished 1980 interview Shaw discussed the capacity for resilience inherent in citizens of modern Western democracies, and especially America. Speaking about the "ordinary American," Shaw said, "He's slow to move. He gets dragged into doing some good things. Reluctantly. But then he comes through."[1] A bemused awareness of the archetypal American's reluctant strength characterizes the authorial tone of several of the stories in *Sailor off the Bremen*.

The device of placing his ordinary Americans, his "gentle people," in situations that threaten their dignity and sense of decency emerges in this first collection and recurs throughout Shaw's fiction. His most perceptive critics agree that the theme of decency underscores all his best work—novels, plays, and stories. He is concerned with the necessity and the difficulty of the individual preserving an integrated moral center in an increasingly complex era. Moral struggle, then, is central to Shaw's aesthetic.

Clearly, in most of Shaw's stories commitment to a code of decency is the basis of an integrated sense of self and is thus the necessary foundation of individual dignity. Shaw is not, however, a didactic writer, and he is rarely specific about precisely what his concept of decency entails. This ambiguity has resulted in some critical misunderstanding of the ethical code central to his work. For instance, in *Fiction of the Forties* (1963), Eisinger dismisses the moral and intellectual content of Shaw's fiction as superficial. Although he states accurately that "an affinity for the general propositions of democracy, summed up perhaps in the idea of the value and dignity of man, marks every phase of [Shaw's] fiction,"[2] he adds a condemnation, variations of which would be sounded by later critics: "Shaw can resent neither the deadly lure of what passes for metropolitan sophistication nor the comfortable corruption of bourgeois materialism" (Eisinger, 106). To Eisinger, Shaw's concept of decency is nothing more than 1930s "old liberalism" diluted by an attraction to material comfort. Eisinger judges Shaw "of inestimable value" for his realistic depiction of the surface of American life, but asserts that "he has not developed the skepticism and the provisionalism of the new liberalism. He has not stared unblinkingly at the power of evil, but has turned his back upon its magnitude" (Eisinger, 110). Shaw, in Eisinger's view, never outgrows the limitations of the old liberalism, which rested on a simplified vision of evil capitalists, fascists, and anti-Semites victimizing the good common man. Eisinger believes that Shaw's concept of decency is so dangerously old-fashioned that it prevents a meaningful investigation of morality, and further, that its sincerity is compromised by the novelist's attraction to material indulgence.

Seven years earlier Leslie Fiedler had condemned Shaw even more harshly. Fiedler, too, sees the early Shaw as a writer devoted to the values of 1930s liberalism. Unlike Eisinger, Fiedler believes that by the 1950s Shaw had recognized the limitations of the old liberalism and had abandoned it for fictional investigations of adultery: "The marriage relationship has become the last politics of those who have lost their politics, the subject of the subjectless, the one area in which 'liberalism' of the vintage of the thirties or even the twenties can still swagger smugly before its glass."[3] Fiedler sees Shaw's alleged abandonment of politics as symptomatic of a deeper problem. He writes that "the whole body of Shaw's work is precisely what the soul-weary liberal writer of bad movie scripts imagines he might produce if he were only 'free': the sort of work in which slickness and sentimentality are turned from the service of entertainment and name brands to social awareness and 'human understanding'" (Fiedler, 72). Clearly, Fiedler believes that Shaw began as a 1930s proletarian writer but he quickly surrendered his commitment to the oppressed, which was never strong, to the temptation of commercial "success" (Fiedler, 72). The implication of this attack is that Shaw's emphasis on decency was always superficial, never more than a shallow leftist response.

Although there is an unmistakable proletarian emphasis in *Sailor off the Bremen* and the early plays *Bury the Dead* (1936) and *The Gentle People*, Shaw's concept of decency was, from the first, too amorphous and personal to be equated with 1930s liberalism. Eisinger's and Fiedler's attacks contain their own simplifications. Shaw was never *only* a social protest writer—he is concerned with more than external economic and political forces. In the earlier stories and plays loyalty to social class is important, but finally not as important as loyalty to family and self. Emphasis on the doctrines of elemental fairness and humanistic concern for others runs throughout Shaw's work. Although Eisinger and other critics correctly perceive that Shaw sanctions violent retaliation against fascists and anti-Semites in "Sailor off the Bremen" and "Residents of Other Cities," they fail to acknowledge that in a later story, "Act of Faith" (1946), revenge is overtly displaced by something akin to New Testament forgiveness.

More than political dogma, Shaw's decency derives from an unmistakably American sense of fair play. In the 1980 interview Shaw said that although he was blacklisted in the 1950s and saw the careers of other writers ruined, he always knew that McCarthyism "wouldn't last" because the inherent fairness of the American people would win out in the end. His belief in this native sense of fair play, originating in the tenets of Jefferson and the legacy of the frontier (see Giles interview in part 2), was shaken by his experience of McCarthyism. Still, Shaw also saw himself as a product of the twentieth century, an age in which Jeffersonian and frontier values were increasingly challenged and threatened. He lived and wrote in a secular age in which God was indifferent, if not completely absent. Shaw wrote, then, out of a tension resulting from his idealistic and determined faith in innate American decency and fairness and a clear-eyed awareness that, in fact, indecency and injustice often prevail in American society. Yet he believed that specific historical indecencies in America would always be of temporary duration.

Shaw perceives the twentieth century as an age dominated by the obsession with, and perversion of, the flesh. Modern society, tormented by old beliefs in the preeminence of the soul, is painfully aware of the absence of a moral center to the universe. Random accidents, rather than a benevolent god, control us. For Shaw, belief in humanity is all that is possible in such a fallen world: "believe in man, and take the accidents as they come" (see Giles interview in part 2).

Shaw's vision of a fallen twentieth century can best be illustrated by two central passages from two of his novels. In *Lucy Crown* (1961) Oliver Crown learns that his wife has been unfaithful to him. He seeks some understanding of her infidelity through reflection and reading Shakespeare. Instead, he finds these lines in *The Winter's Tale:*

> "Should all despair," . . .
> "That have revolted wives, the tenth of mankind
> Would hang themselves. Physic for 't, there's none;
> It is a bawdy planet."[4]

Crown feels he is a "twisting, stubborn inhabitant of the bawdy planet (*LC*, 159). Likewise, Jack Andrus, the central character in *Two Weeks in Another Town* (1960), is stunned by an even more grim epiphany. While visiting the Sistine Chapel with his ex-wife, Jack stares up at the magnificent ceiling and, far from being comforted, realizes that "he could believe in Michelangelo . . . but he could not believe in God. . . . Man is flesh, God is flesh, man makes man, man makes God, all mysteries are equal. . . . Salvation was the caprice of the usher who made out the seating plan on the last day."[5] Abruptly, Michelangelo's nudes evoke images in his mind "of thousands of naked women being paraded before SS doctors in the German concentration camps" (*TW*, 317). Briefly, Jack considers the possibility that "God is an SS doctor, and Michelangelo had advance information" (*TW*, 317).

Jack Andrus rejects this nihilistic vision for belief in an imperfect god unconcerned with man. In contrast, the atheism of Shaw seems to have been more complete. In the 1980 interview Shaw discussed his use of accidents as the central structural device in much of his fiction. Accidents are central to his work, he said, simply because he believes in them—the universe is controlled not by any coherent system of cause and effect, but by random accident.

The existentialist overtones of Shaw's vision complicate, but do not negate, his commitment to a concept of decency based on the traditional American values of loyalty and fair play. The characters of his fiction, threatened by economic, political, and personal accidents, struggle to be faithful to themselves and decent to others. Constantly reminded of "the various uses and manifestations of the flesh,"[6] they are constantly challenged to remain faithful to internal beliefs for which no external verification is possible. Not surprisingly, they sometimes fail. Even in the early proletarian story "Second Mortgage" Shaw's concept of decency is too complex to be reduced to 1930s old liberalism.

Fiedler's charge that Shaw replaced the political emphasis of his early work with explorations into the politics of adultery constitutes another critical simplification. From the first, Shaw explored problems of loyalty as experienced in political *and* sexual spheres of relationship. His most famous adultery story, "The Girls in Their Summer Dresses," appeared in *Sailor off the Bremen*. A late story, "God Was Here but He Left Early," depicts a world in which all bonds between sexual partners are distorted by preoccupations with "the various uses and manifestations of the flesh." It was almost inevitable that Shaw would explore the subject of marital infidelity in his fiction. It is clearly related to his more general concern with the necessity, and the difficulties, of personal loyalty in a flesh-obsessed universe that seems to deny the soul.

Lionel Trilling has described the unifying focus of Shaw's early fiction much more perceptively than Eisinger and Fiedler. In an analysis of the novelist's work up to the early 1950s, Trilling writes,

> He has undertaken the guidance of the moral and political emotions of a large and important class of people, those whom he once called "the gentle people." These are men and women usually of a middling position in our society. . . . They are likely to be quiet, even passive, until aroused by the violence of those who are not gentle. To these people as his audience and by means of these people as his characters he has tried to represent the social and political actualities of our time, setting forth in terms of the private life what economic depression, commercial corruption, fascism, xenophobia, and war really mean, and to suggest the right responses of feeling and action to these grim commonplaces of danger.[7]

When qualified by the observation that the "private" lives of Shaw's characters are also complicated by internal (largely sexual) pressures, Trilling's evaluation is accurate. A gentle Everyman, reluctant but finally not unwilling to act on an internal moral code, is the dominant figure in Shaw's stories, novels, and plays of the first two decades especially.

New York, World War II, and Europe

Shaw's second collection, *Welcome to the City and Other Stories*, appeared in 1942. In general, its twenty titles repeat the thematic concerns and narrative patterns of *Sailor off the Bremen*, though, as indicated by its title, New York City as a setting receives a fuller and more varied emphasis. Two distinct images of New York emerge from *Sailor off the Bremen*—lower-class Brooklyn and the cornucopia of luxuries that is Manhattan. Shaw reverts to these images in *Welcome to the City*, while also depicting New York as the center of political radicalism and artistic sophistication. In "The Eighty-Yard Run" Christian Darling, after his migration to New York from a bucolic Midwest, is as baffled by leftist political ideology and aesthetic sophistication as he is tempted by material luxury.

Shaw also brings an absurdist sensibility to his treatment of New York in a few of the more comic stories in this second collection. In "Welcome to the City," "The House of Pain," "The Indian in Depth of Night," and "Lemkau, Pogran and Blaufox" New York is treated with bemused nostalgia as a place where wonderfully implausible things regularly happen. In these stories Shaw depicts the city as a natural haven for the writer because of the stimulation afforded by the astonishing variety of its inhabitants. Yet a dark undercurrent usually runs beneath the surface absurdity of these stories.

In the three years between 1939 and 1942 Nazism changed from an abstract and distant concern to a real and immediate threat to the security of the United States. Several stories in *Welcome to the City* focus, with anger, on America's complicity in the worldwide outbreak of fascism and anti-Semitism. In "Free Conscience, Void of Offence," "The City Was in Total Darkness," and "Select Clientele" the enemy is drawn with considerably more complexity than in "Sailor off the Bremen." Drunken, crude American businessmen, bored and cynical intellectuals, and physically brutal rural Americans are portrayed as contributing to the rise of fascism, illustrating that the threat to world peace and human justice was too complex and too pervasive to personify in the character of a sadistic German sailor.

Shaw's third published collection, *Act of Faith and Other Stories*, containing 12 stories focusing on World War II and the traumas attendant upon the creation of a Jewish sanctuary in the Middle East, appeared in 1946. Not surprisingly, since he saw no combat himself, Shaw's war stories treat character in situations outside the combat zone—especially weary GIs on temporary leave from battle, endangered but courageous members of the French Resistance, and embittered Germans in retreat. A tone of moral indignation at Allied hypocrisy and bad faith in the creation of Israel dominates "Medal from Jerusalem." With considerable anger, this story points out that Allied anti-Semitism did not diminish after the war.

In 1950 Random House, Shaw's hardback publisher for most of his career, issued *Mixed Company*, a collection of 37 stories, most of which had appeared in *Sailor off the Bremen*, *Welcome to the City*, and *Act of Faith*. This omnibus collection also contains a few new titles, the most memorable of which is an absurdist satire of McCarthyism, "The Green Nude." In an important sense, *Mixed Company* is a summing up of the first stage of Shaw's career as a short story writer. Containing such often anthologized stories as "The Girls in Their Summer Dresses," "The Eighty-Yard Run," "Act of Faith," "Main Currents of American Thought," and "Gunners' Passage," it depicts, in various guises, Shaw's Everyman struggling to retain inner decency.

For some critics, Shaw's next two collections, *Tip on a Dead Jockey* (1957) and *Love on a Dark Street* (1965), represent a disturbing shift in focus and emphasis. In 1951 Shaw moved to Paris, where he lived for much of the next 25 years. Increasingly, his novels and stories began to treat Americans in Europe. It has become a commonplace to assert that in leaving America Shaw turned his back on the cultural roots essential to the vitality of his writing. A related charge is that the post-1951 American-in-Europe is a more affluent, less representative creature than the troubled Everyman of the earlier stories. In reviewing *Tip on a Dead Jockey*, Hubert Saal first praises the moral integrity of the early stories: "[They] show him to be a man of moral values, aware of evil wherever he found it, aware of all the injustices and discrepancies within man or without him which cause him to suffer. Against wrong, Shaw spoke up. Again and again, with true tragic dignity, his characters rose up at the last, refused to submit, protested, did something."[8] But, Saal continues, "a gap that cannot be measured by time alone" exists between these early stories and the titles in the 1957 collection. He finds the "amorality" of the title story "astonishing" and is disturbed by the tone of cynical weariness that he feels is dominant throughout the collection (Saal, 12).

Although Shaw's American expatriates might seem more at home in F. Scott Fitzgerald's world than in that of Clifford Odets, they have hardly escaped the challenge of creating and maintaining an ethical center. The American protagonists in the comic stories "Tip on a Dead Jockey" and "Love on a Dark Street" are bewildered, as well as tempted, by a pervasive European hedonism and cynicism, yet they long for a secure and familiar ethical center. In his best expatriate fiction Shaw approaches the theme of decency from a new, more complex direction. Stories such as "A Year to Learn the Language," "Then We Were Three," and "The Man Who Married a French Wife" contain variations on Henry James's "international theme": "innocent" Americans undergo formative experiences in sophisticated Europe. In each case initial pain ultimately leads to necessary self-awareness. In these stories, Shaw's Everyman has moved to Europe and is no longer troubled by questions of social injustice, but he still faces the challenge of creating and remaining faithful to an individual ethical code.

It should also be said that some of the most memorable stories in *Love on a Dark Street* are set in the United States. The two dark and brooding stories "Noises in the City" and "Circle of Light" depict a pervasive paranoia in New York City and in suburbia; "Wistful, Delicately Gay," a portrayal of an obsessed and slightly demented actress, is one of Shaw's most powerful character studies; and "Goldilocks at Graveside" is his most angry treatment of 1950s McCarthyism. Blacklisted himself, Shaw detected a new and troubling irrationality in the American character. As a result, his optimistic faith in American fair play was momentarily shaken, and despite the comic title story, *Love on a Dark Street* is his most pessimistic collection.

An entirely different mood dominates his last collection, *God Was Here but He Left Early* (1973), which focuses almost exclusively on American settings. *God Was Here* is an experimental work of two parts. Part 1 consists of two of Shaw's best stories, the brutally realistic title story and an evocative mingling of tragedy and lyricism, "Where All Things Wise and Fair Descend." Three comic novellas treating, in Shaw's words, "three of the major preoccupations of our age—Science, Sport and Sex," constitute part 2.[9] Though an awareness of such grim social and political realities as Vietnam and the antiwar protests of the

1960s underscores the entire volume, the mood, except in the title story, is not nearly so dark and pessimistic as that of *Love on a Dark Street*. To a significant degree, Shaw's faith in a fundamental American decency has returned.

Shaw: The Storyteller

For *God Was Here but He Left Early,* Shaw wrote a preface describing the advantages and disadvantages of being a short story writer in America. Granting that "there has been an appreciable decline in the *appreciation* of short stories in the past forty years," he asserts that "that decline is not the consequence of a corresponding falling-off in quality" (Shaw's italics; *GWH,* 9). He says that while in recent years markets for short stories have declined, financial rewards for the writer of short fiction in America have, in fact, never been great. He received $25 from the *New Republic* for his first published story and his "rate went up" to $75 when he "finally broke into *The New Yorker*" (*GWH,* 9). Still, the short story form does have its rewards for the writer: "There is the reward of the storyteller seated cross-legged in the middle of the bazaar, filling the need of humanity in the humdrum course of an ordinary day for magic and tales of distant wonders, for disguised moralizing which will set everyday transactions into larger perspectives, for the compression of great matters into digestible portions, for the shaping of mysteries into sharply-edged and comprehensible symbols" (*GWH,* 11).

Two implications of this passage should be noted. Shaw always considered himself a traditional "storyteller"; and this self-definition, combined with his "disguised moralizing" about "everyday transactions," makes him seem old-fashioned to those critics devoted to postmodernist fiction. While Shaw emphasized in the 1980 interview that his fictional moralizing is quite a different thing from overt didacticism, it can seem outdated to those committed to a narration in which the author is invisible or morally transparent.

Finally, Shaw comments that the luxury of self-fragmentation is unique to the short story writer: "In a novel or a play you must be a whole man. In a collection of stories you can be all the men or fragments of men, worthy and unworthy, who in different seasons abound within you. It is a luxury not to be scorned" (*GWH,* 11–12). The novel form rarely seems as comfortable to Shaw as the story form. His talent was always best suited to the discipline of the short, controlled fictional entity. At times, his novels, even *The Young Lions*, seem to disintegrate into separate and barely connected fictional units. One feels that, in this preface Shaw is acknowledging, between the lines, that he turned to the novel primarily out of economic necessity.

The *New Yorker*

In technique, Irwin Shaw typifies the Hemingway-inspired modernist short story writer. He was a friend and something of a disciple of Hemingway's until the older man cruelly attacked *The Young Lions* as a dishonest and cowardly war novel. In their emphasis on compression, narrative indirection, and the occasional omission of key detail Shaw's stories recall the narrative technique found in Hemingway's "first forty-nine stories." A summary comment on Shaw's modernist technique should note that he generally uses variations of Henry James's "scenic" method of plot development. The influence of the theater on Shaw can be seen in his fondness for building stories around key dramatic speeches by central characters. "The Girls in Their Summer Dresses," for instance, is essentially a "confession story"; its climax comes when Michael explains at length the attraction anonymous New York City women hold for him. Early in his career Shaw was also strongly associated with the *New Yorker;* his modernist technique, combined with a distinctly eastern-seaboard, urban sophistication, often make him seem the archetypal *New Yorker* writer.

In a 1979 *Paris Review* interview Shaw discussed his association with the *New Yorker.* He quit writing for the magazine in 1952, he says, because "I just didn't feel that I belonged there anymore.[10] At the first of his career, though, the *New Yorker* was a "very hospitable" place for him because of four "great editors . . . Woolcott Gibbs, William Maxwell, Gus Lobrano and above all—Harold Ross" (*Paris Review,* 258). Shaw also takes some credit for helping change the magazine's direction. He says that although its editors were "against violence," "they did publish 'The Sailor Off the Bremen' [*sic*], which is the first long story they ever published and the first politically serious story they'd ever accepted" (*Paris Review,* 259). It was primarily Ross, Shaw says, who was receptive to the political story: "He could learn to change, which is why the *New Yorker* is still going strong after its dilletantish beginnings. When you think its first cover was the fop with the monocle looking at a butterfly, and they wound up publishing *In Cold Blood* by Truman Capote and *Hiroshima* by John Hersey, you can see the ability to grow that made Ross and made the magazine" (*Paris Review*, 261). Similarly, Shaw's responsiveness to major sociopolitical issues is one of the traits that distinguishes him from many modernist writers and from recent *New Yorker* mainstays such as Donald Barthelme.

It seems appropriate to let Shaw speak for himself before concluding this introduction to his career as a short story writer. In the Preface to the 1978 omnibus collection *Short Stories: Five Decades*, the most important single book of his long and prolific literary career, he emphasizes the political dimension of his fiction:

> I am a product of my times. I remember the end of World War I, the bells and whistles and cheering, and as an adolescent I profited briefly from the boom years. I suffered the Depression; exulted at the election of Franklin D. Roosevelt; drank my first glass of legal 3.2 beer the day Prohibition ended; mourned over Spain; listened to the Communist sirens; sensed the coming of World War II; went to that war; was shamed by the McCarthy era; saw the rebirth of Europe; marveled at the new generations of students; admired Kennedy; mourned over Vietnam. . . . All these things, in one way or another, are reflected in my stories, which I now see as a record of the events of almost sixty years, all coming together in the imagination of one American. (*FD*, xi)

It is certainly valid to approach Shaw's stories as a cumulative fictional record of much of the twentieth century. But his stories have an even deeper value as an examination of the American character struggling to retain a sense of national decency. The threats to this unique brand of decency are internal as well as external; and fidelity to self is as much a concern as loyalty to groups and causes.

The Great Depression and New York

The End of Innocence

Several of Shaw's early stories reflect the economic desperation of victims of the Great Depression. Though its central characters are from the middle class, "Second Mortgage" is one of the most pessimistic of these stories. Its seventeen-year-old narrator recounts the consternation produced in his family by a visit from Mrs. Shapiro, a widow who holds a second mortgage on their house. The narrator's father, already in full retreat from bill collectors, tells his son not to answer the doorbell because it might be a summons, but after reminding his father that a summons cannot be served on Sunday, the son opens the door. Shaw's technical mastery is evident in the manner in which he quickly establishes the father's weakness and creates dramatic tension and reverses. The brief opening dialogue, in conjunction with the story's title, produces the expectation that a one-dimensional representative of capitalism will be waiting outside the house; Mrs. Shapiro is instead a lonely, desperate figure, as much the victim of a failed economy as the narrator's family.

Once inside the house she tells the family about how a shady financial adviser, Mr. Mayer, put her life savings of $8,000 into second mortgages after her husband died of cancer. The eight thousand dollars represents the hard work of a lifetime: "I had a vegetable store. It's hard to make money in vegetables nowadays. Vegetables are expensive and they spoil and there is always somebody else who sells them cheaper than you can" (*FD*, 30). Hearing her story, the weak father promises Mrs. Shapiro that he will have the money "next Sunday," but his stronger, more realistic wife contradicts him, "We can't give you anything! Next Sunday or any Sunday! We haven't got a cent" (*FD*, 31–32). Hearing the truth, Mrs. Shapiro faints. The narrator's family revives her, and the mother recommends "a doctor who would wait for his money." Mrs. Shapiro then leaves, "her fat, shabby stockings shaking as she went down the steps" (*FD*, 32).

The narrator's family and Mrs. Shapiro are representatives of Shaw's "gentle people" who want to lead decent, honest lives. Either poverty or internal weakness or both have reduced the father to a prisoner cow-

14

ering inside a house he does not own. Mrs. Shapiro is not yet beaten and returns "the next Sunday and two Sundays after that" (*FD*, 32). Still, her fainting and mounting desperation indicate the impending end of her futile quest for salvation and justice. The mother's strength is the strength of an essential and limiting self-protection. Giving Mrs. Shapiro tea and the name of a potential doctor constitute a passing moment of generosity, which is all the mother can afford. There is no possibility of unified resistance for these victims of a bankrupt economic system. Although the family feels compassion for Mrs. Shapiro, the family does not let her in the house again. One assumes that the son learns from the experience because he does not argue that she be asked inside "the next Sunday" or "two Sundays after that."

Shaw's craft is especially evident in the treatment of Mr. Mayer. An exploiter of widows, Mayer might easily have become the stereotypical "heartless capitalist" so often found in proletarian protest fiction; instead, Shaw keeps him a shadowy, vaguely menacing figure outside of the narrative frame and thus represents more effectively the evils and failures of capitalism. Moreover, the distance between Mayer and the story's setting corresponds to the distance between the controllers of the economic system and Mrs. Shapiro and the narrator's family.

In "Borough of Cemeteries" Shaw utilizes a very different kind of setting to paint an even more despairing picture of economic desperation. Containing allusions to Mussolini, Mayor Fiorello La Guardia, and 1930s Brooklyn Dodgers pitcher Van Lingle Mungo, the story takes place at the cocktail hour in Lammanawitz's Bar and Grill in Brooklyn. The clientele of Lammanawitz's Bar and Grill is distinctly working class; and an unsuccessful effort at unionization by a character named Geary serves as one of the story's unifying threads.

Geary's unionization pitch is primarily directed at two cabdrivers, Elias and Palangio. A tone of barely repressed anger is established in the opening dialogue in which Elias Pinsker attempts to badger Pinky the bartender into selling him a beer on credit and trades ethnic insults with Geary, an Irishman, and Palangio, an Italian-American. In addition, Palangio pronounces a harshly negative judgment on Brooklyn: "Brooklyn stinks. . . . The borough of cemeteries. This is a first class place for graveyards" (*FD*, 13).

The story treats Brooklyn, embodied in Lammanawitz's Bar and Grill, as a graveyard of working-class dreams and aspirations. For Elias Pinsker the dreams of love and pride have died. He remembers proudly owning the "biggest pigeon flight in Brownsville" in 1928, but he irrationally associates two events of 1929, his marriage and the stock market crash, and blames them for the destruction of his happiness: "I got fifteen pigeons left. Everytime I bring home less than seventy-five cents, my wife cooks one for supper. All pedigreed pigeons. My lousy wife." Pinsker concludes that "a woman is a trap" (*FD*, 15). The economic system has made it impossible for Elias Pinsker to protect his beloved pigeons, and rather than confronting his helplessness directly, he blames and hates his wife. For him, marriage has come to represent the end of love and individual freedom. He cannot then listen to Geary's arguments for a union. Shaw creates an ironic effect through the radio that plays "I Married an Angel" in the background as Pinsker proclaims his resentment of his wife. At one point, he turns on Geary and says, "An' I should be a bachelor. Geary, can you organize *that?*" (*FD*, 17).

The story's climax occurs when Pinsker and Palangio try to escape their frustration by going outside and destroying their taxis in a game of "chicken." Afterward, they decide to go to the movies to see Simone Simon. The concluding paragraph effectively underscores the story's bitter irony: "Walking steadily, arm in arm, like two gentlemen, Elias and Angelo Palangio went down the street, through the lengthening shadows, toward Simone Simon" (*FD*, 19). The phrase "like two gentlemen" contrasts with the senseless violence of the game of "chicken." Throughout Shaw's writings about the 1930s the movies function as an illusion of escape for characters trapped in dead-end prosaic lives. For Elias Pinsker, the remote and shadowy screen figure of actress Simone Simon serves as a fantasy of the romantic love he cannot find. Pinsker and Palangio are trapped in "the lengthening shadows" of economic despair. The story holds out even less hope than "Second Mortgage" for unified resistance to socioeconomic injustice; Geary, the voice of reason, is ridiculed.

A tone of hopelessness also dominates "Santa Claus," an extended confession story in which Sam Koven confesses to his wife that he has been pretending for four weeks to go to work at a job he does not have. He has really been going in the afternoons to the public library to read about the days before the 1929 stock market crash: "Those were good days. . . . I should've died in 1929."[11]

Sam's life, like Elias Pinsker's, did, in a real sense, end in 1929. He lost comfort, security, and pride and now he is reduced to taking money from his brother-in-law to support his family. Still, he clings to some hope and tells his wife, Annie, "I'll pay him back. Things'll get better. . . . Once I had sixty thousand dollars in the bank. In cash." Annie laughs bitterly and responds, "Once the Indians owned the United States. For God's sake, Santa Claus has stopped visiting the Bronx" (*SS*, 61). Throughout the story, Santa Claus represents lost innocence, a mythic time of generosity and good will. Sam's main hope is that things simply must improve, that people cannot tolerate unlimited suffering. He tells Annie, "You can only go so far down," to which she ironically responds, "Santa Claus . . . Santa Claus" (*SS*, 62).

"Second Mortgage," "Borough of Cemeteries," and "Santa Claus" are set in New York and represent Shaw's most pessimistic response to the despair of the 1930s. The characters in all three are bewildered that the American economic system, ostensibly based on fair play and free competition, has collapsed. Commitment to others has become an unaffordable luxury—Elias Pinsker does not even feel a sense of loyalty to his wife. Because of the degree to which economic suffering has diminished these characters, Shaw's decency is simply not within reach for them.

Other Shaw stories set in New York City during the 1930s do not focus on class struggle. While a sense of poverty dominates "Welcome to the City," the story nevertheless conveys, until the ending, a comic tone. Shaw enhances the mock seriousness of most of the story by juxtaposing allusions to T. S. Eliot's poems "The Waste Land" and "Gerontion" and MGM's 1932 "all-star" film *Grand Hotel*. "Welcome to the City" takes place not in a grand hotel, but in the Circus Hotel, which offers "the odor of sin and age, all at reasonable rates" (*FD*, 51). In capturing the ambiance of the Circus Hotel, Shaw exercises his gift for absurdity, a quality in his writing infrequently noticed by critics. The story focuses on Enders, an actor who has fled Davenport, Iowa, for the excitement of New York City.

The story opens with Enders returning to his "home" in the Circus and abruptly finding himself in the middle of an absurd debate between Wysocki, the hotel manager, dressed "in his gray suit with the markings of all the cafeteria soup in the city on it," and Josephine, a prostitute, about whether the English eat herring (*FD*, 52–53). Bishop, the hotel owner, enters the lobby from his office and tries to sell Enders "a dead, wet chicken," which he proudly displays. Enders is further disconcerted by Josephine's solicitation of him.

A woman who resembles Greta Garbo is sitting on a chair near the stairway. Wysocki informs Enders that her name is Bertha Zelinka and that she had checked into the hotel that afternoon. The woman's legs

17

offer "a promise of poetry and flowers, past the grime and gloom of the hallway," and Enders yearns to protect her from the ugliness of Bishop's and Josephine's propositions (*FD*, 54–55). Instead, he retreats to his room and T. S. Eliot.

His reading of "Gerontion" is interrupted by Josephine's voice from the hallway: "What a night! . . . The river will be stuffed with bodies in the morning" (*FD*, 55). Josephine's proclamation echoes Eliot's famous warning in "The Waste Land" to fear "death by water" and, in conjunction with the absurdity of the Circus Hotel, recalls the poem's allusions to the "unreal city" in which "death had undone so many."

The specific lines from "Gerontion" Enders reads also emphasize the failure of heroism in the modern age, and Enders feels acutely his failure to undertake a heroic act for Bertha Zelinka. Still, the comic mood of most of "Welcome to the City" is quite different from Eliot's poetry, and as Enders puts down his book he reflects that "it was hard to read T. S. Eliot in the Circus Hotel without a deep feeling of irony" (*FD*, 55).

Enders cannot get Miss Zelinka out of his mind, and he dreams of taking her to "a night club lit by orange lamps, where no dish cost less than a dollar seventy-five, even tomato juice," dancing with her, and quoting Eliot to her (*FD*, 56). The reference to orange lamps and the popular association of the words "dish" and "tomato" with alluring women underscore Enders's sexual excitement over Bertha Zelinka and undercut his conscious idea of a heroic rescue of, and an intellectual conversation with, her. When he returns to the lobby, his idealism is further challenged. An embittered Josephine warns him that he should have stayed in Davenport, Iowa, and that he will end up as a suicide floating in the river: "I come from Fall River [Iowa], . . . I should've stayed there. At least when you're dead in Fall River they bury you. Here they leave you walk around until your friends notice it. Why did I ever leave Fall River? I was attracted by the glamor of the Great White Way" (*FD*, 56–57). Besides further echoing Eliot, Josephine's speech emphasizes one of the story's central motifs—the popular legend of the innocent midwesterner attracted to, but unsuited for New York City. Enders turns away from Josephine only to be told by Wysocki that Bishop finds the chickens he sells dead by the railroad tracks.

Undaunted, Enders asks Miss Zelinka if he can buy her a cup of coffee. Two hours later in his room, she intensifies Enders's sexual excitement by informing him that she is a specialty dancer and is "as supple as a cat" (*FD*, 58). His attention is focused even more on her body since, over coffee, she had opened her mouth, which she had carefully kept closed in the hotel lobby, to reveal "the poor, poverty-stricken, ruined teeth jagged and sorrowful in the mouth" (*FD*, 58). Like the Circus Hotel lobby, Bertha Zelinka's ruined teeth intensify the note of 1930s desperation that underlies the dominant comic absurdity of "Welcome to the City." Despite this handicap, Bertha momentarily creates an alluring fiction for Enders, telling him that while her resemblance to Greta Garbo has destroyed her in Hollywood, she "has done very well" and lives in a luxurious suite on East 75th Street (*FD*, 59–61).

Her pretense abruptly crumbles, however, when, in tears, she tells Enders about performing at a convention in January 1936 in Miami, Florida. On that occasion, as she finished her specialty dance with a backbend, a conventioner, inspired by a cartoon in a magazine, put an olive in her exposed navel and sprinkled it with salt. She still feels "the humiliation": "It's funny in a magazine, but wait until it happens to you" (*FD*, 60). Bertha's confession underscores the absurdist tone of the entire story—the likelihood of another person being humiliated by a salt-sprinkled olive placed in the navel is, after all, remote. Yet Shaw conveys that her pain is real—she was treated contemptuously by the conventioner as an "other," a being less than human, as women in such situations usually are. The ridiculousness of the situation does not prevent the reader from responding to her tearful cry, "I want to be treated with respect" (*FD*, 60).

Bertha's cry for respect does not, however, evoke a purely altruistic response in Enders; and the story's ending represents a sharp departure from the earlier comic tone. Miss Zelinka concludes her confession by admitting that she has no suite on East 75th Street and professionally is not doing well at all: "Why do I lie, why do I always lie?" (*FD*, 61). Enders, "knowing that he was going to have this woman," finally feels at home in New York City: "He kissed her, feeling deep within him, that in its own way, on this rainy night, the city had put out its hand in greeting, had called, in its own voice, wry and ironic, 'Welcome, Citizen'" (*FD*, 61). By consciously taking advantage of Miss Zelinka's pain and loneliness, Enders truly becomes a citizen of the cynical and sophisticated city. Josephine's earlier prophecy turns out, in a sense, to be true: the innocent Enders of Davenport, Iowa, does drown in the cosmopolitan eastern capital. Knowingly surrendering to the temptations of the flesh, he chooses, on this night, to surrender his decency.

The comic absurdity of most of "Welcome to the City" significantly dilutes this concluding cynicism, and there is even an element of absurdity in Enders's seduction of Miss Zelinka. Grateful that the city can produce a woman who, at least with her mouth closed, looks like the popular ideal of female beauty, the would-be actor is last seen "hating himself, his hands shaking exultantly," kneeling before the specialty dancer to remove her shoes (*FD*, 61).

In contrast, no comedy of any kind mitigates Shaw's treatment of the motif of lost midwestern innocence in "The Eighty-Yard Run," one of his most frequently reprinted stories, which in theme and mood recalls *The Great Gatsby*. (In the 1980 interview, Shaw expressed his admiration for F. Scott Fitzgerald [see Giles interview in part 2]; and his fiction frequently echoes Fitzgerald's.) Like Tom Buchanan, Christian Darling spends his adult life "seeking . . . for the dramatic turbulence of some irrecoverable football game."[12] Darling's story also recalls Nick Carraway's analysis that *Gatsby*'s five central characters "were all Westerners, and perhaps . . . possessed some deficiency in common which made us subtly unadaptable to Eastern life" (Fitzgerald, 212). Christian Darling is unable to adapt to New York City's political and artistic sophistication and to an American society dramatically changed by 1929.

In "The Eighty-Yard Run" the Great Depression serves as a metaphor for the loss of native American innocence and optimism. A tone of bitterness and loss dominates the story from the beginning. In the present tense of the early 1940s Christian Darling exhibits, in his face and thoughts, the painful disillusionment he experienced in "the years between 1925 and 1940" (*FD*, 2); most of "The Eighty-Yard Run" is an extended flashback. Working as a tailor's representative, he has returned to the midwestern college where, fifteen years earlier, he had seemed to be destiny's darling. On returning to the college football stadium he is initially shown walking "slowly over the same ground in the spring twilight" (*FD*, 2) on which, at the age of twenty, he had made an eighty-yard touchdown run in practice. Now in the twilight of his once bright dreams, Darling attempts to relive in memory his golden youth. Ultimately, however, his memories evoke only pain and bitterness.

After his moment of triumph in practice, Darling had played for two years on the football team, primarily as a blocking back for Diederich, "everybody's All-American" who carried the ball "three times out of four, keeping everybody else out of the headlines." Darling "had never broken away"—his longest run in an actual game was "thirty-five yards, and that in a game that was already won" (*FD*, 3–4). Shaw's prose is richly evocative throughout this story; at no point in his life has Darling really broken away from his own weaknesses and the limitations imposed on him by social change. Attempting to recapture a golden past, he is unable to escape his own awareness that such an idyllic time never truly existed.

Still, while never a star on the football field, Darling had been popular and widely recognized while at college. In his relationships with women, and especially with his fiancée, Louise, Christian had triumphed, as a football dreamer might believe. He remembers being with Louise after the 80-yard run and knowing "for the first time, that he could do whatever he wanted with her" (*FD*, 3). Louise had in truth been completely devoted to him: "Louise loved him and watched him faithfully in the games . . . and drove him around in her car keeping the top down because she was proud of him and wanted to show everybody that she was Christian Darling's girl. She brought him crazy presents because her father was rich" (*FD*, 4–5). During their courtship, Louise had seemed to exist primarily as a satellite of Christian's glory, and, certain of her, he had engaged in a few "casual and secret" affairs with other women (*FD*, 5).

After college, Christian and Louise had married and moved to New York where her father, an ink manufacturer, has set Christian up in an office. For a time in New York they had luxuriated in the good life of the late 1920s when "everybody was buying everything" (*FD*, 5). Shaw emphasizes Christian's bewilderment at the "prints of paintings by Dufy, Braque, and Picasso" hanging in their apartment to show his alienation from Eastern cosmopolitanism (*FD*, 5). The alienation had intensified in 1929, when Louise's father committed suicide after going bankrupt. Out of work, "Darling [had] sat home and drank" while Louise had obtained a job with a fashion magazine. Through crisp dialogue, Shaw demonstrates the subsequent deterioration of their relationship:

[Christian] "I like paintings with horses in them. Why should you like pictures like that?"
[Louise] "I just happen to have gone to a lot of galleries in the

last few years. . . . That's what I do in the afternoon."
[Christian] "I drink in the afternoon." (*FD*, 6)

Darling had also been bewildered by his wife's growing interest in radical leftist politics. In their only real fight, she had turned on him in frustration when he insisted on voting for Alf Landon: "Oh Christ . . . doesn't *anything* happen inside your head? Don't you read the papers? The penniless Republican!" (*FD*, 10). He is incapable of moving intellectually beyond a vanished midwestern ideal of stability and clear, "Republican" values. Louise's habit, acquired in New York, of calling him "Baby" had begun to bother him, and he had asked her to stop calling him that. Darling feels profoundly diminished but he can see no way to regain lost stature. He can neither bear nor change his new role as Louise's satellite; in the Midwest of his youth, wives were clearly subservient to husbands. In a pathetic attempt to deny the new reality in which he found himself, he had refused to go with Louise, a radical lawyer for the longshoremen named Flaherty, and Flaherty's girl to see a production of *Waiting for Lefty*. Odets's play effectively symbolizes the world of artistic innovation and left-wing politics from which Darling feels so estranged.

The *Waiting for Lefty* episode had been Christian's last attempt to assert and define himself. After that "he [had been] good, completely devoted, ready at all times to go any place with [Louise], do anything she wanted" (*FD*, 10–11). He had even allowed her to decide whether he should take the tailor's representative job. Having so completely surrendered his pride, Darling is overwhelmed by bitterness—learning that the all-American Diedrich broke his neck playing pro football and is paralyzed, he had thought "that, at least, had turned out well." Constantly aware that Louise feels "a kind of patient, kindly, remote boredom with him," he had been relieved to find that his new job required travel and frequent separation from her (*FD*, 10–11).

After recounting Christian's past, the story returns briefly to the opening scene in which Darling attempts to relive the glory of the eighty-yard run. Recognition of the hopelessness of his attempt begins to overwhelm him: "That was the high point . . . an eighty-yard run in practice, and a girl's kiss, and everything after that a decline. . . . He hadn't practiced for 1929 and New York City and a girl who must turn into a woman. . . . [H]is wife was in another city having dinner with another and better man [Flaherty], speaking with him a different, new language nobody had ever taught him" (*FD*, 11). Christian's youth had been only practice for a boy's game, and he has been unable to grow beyond it. He had been the "darling" of a pastoral Midwest, but merely a "baby" in cosmopolitan New York City. He is a boy-man like Fitzgerald's Tom Buchanan, lacking Tom's coarse brutality and protection of wealth. No one had taught him the "new language" of the 1930s and adulthood, and he has made no sustained effort to learn it himself.

Desperately trying to flee self-recognition, Darling, wearing a double-breasted suit, abruptly repeats the 80-yard run only to discover that he has been watched by a boy and girl sitting together beside the field. He turns to them in embarrassment and attempts to explain, but can only say, "I—once I played here" (*FD*, 12).

"The Eighty-Yard Run" is one of Shaw's most powerful and evocative stories. He effectively dramatizes the exuberance of the 1920s and the depression of the 1930s to communicate the end of American innocence. Always attentive to the national obsession with sports, Shaw uses the game of football to symbolize a peculiarly American brand of arrested development. Finally, Christian Darling emerges as a pathetic character—a pampered child of a doomed and artificial world who attempts to return to the fields on which he once played.

Ambition and Economic Reality

The Great Depression functions as an underlying motif in another of Shaw's best stories, "Main Currents of American Thought." One of Shaw's most overtly autobiographical stories, it is set in Brooklyn and focuses on the struggles of a young writer who wants to escape the demand of producing hack radio scripts and the pressures from his family and fiancée long enough to write a serious play. Shaw, who wrote adventure serials for the radio before his early success with *Bury the Dead*, acknowledged the story's parallels to his own life:

> First of all, the character writes for the radio. And I, in fact, have a long paragraph in which he dictated something very much like what I used to dictate. . . . And he lives on the street where I lived with my mother and father and my brother. I played football in the field—baseball and football in the field opposite. I was in love with a girl like that one—and I didn't want to marry. Because I knew I'd have to support another family, and then I'd be committed to writing for money all my life. (see Giles interview, part 2)

The tone of "Main Currents" is an effective blending of cynicism and nostalgia. The story opens with Andrew, the young writer, finishing the dictation of an adolescent escapist radio script and telling his stenographer to "put it next to Moby Dick on your library shelf" (*FD*, 20). Wanting to return to his play, Andrew is distracted by the everyday sounds of the house and the neighborhood. He is initially drawn to the sounds of "the tall trees outside, as old as Brooklyn, [when they] rustled a little from time to time as little sprints of wind swept across the baseball field" (*FD*, 21). Abruptly, less pastoral sounds assault him—a little neighbor girl quarreling with her French governess who had "the only unpleasant French accent Andrew had ever heard" (*FD*, 21–22), a call from the bank informing him that his checking account is overdrawn, his mother running the vacuum cleaner, and a call from his agent, Herman, complaining that his radio scripts are "too slow": "you're not writing for the *Atlantic Monthly*" (*FD*, 23).

Andrew's accelerating desperation results, in large part, from his knowing very well for whom he writes and for whom he wants to write. The notes to his projected, but constantly postponed, serious play have begun to haunt him. Andrew's attention is further diverted by his checkbook. Examining the record of his vouchers he feels even more trapped in the grind of writing juvenile adventure stories. Shaw effectively communicates Andrew's sense of entrapment in an extended passage in which he juxtaposes Andrew's mental composition of a "Dusty Blades" radio script with the realities evoked by the checkbook:

> Eighty dollars rent. The roof over his head equaled two Ronnie Cook's and His Friends. Five thousand words for rent.
> Buddy was in the hands of Flacker. Flacker could torture him for six pages. Then you could have Dusty Blades speeding to the rescue. . . .
> Spain, one hundred dollars. Oh, Lord.
> A hundred and fifty to his father, to meet his father's payroll. . . .
> Flacker is about to kill Buddy out of anger and desperation. In bursts Dusty, alone. (*FD*, 24)

Allusions to the "Dusty Blades" and "Ronnie Cook" scripts function as an ironic countertext in Shaw's story. Intended as escapist fiction for adolescents, they constitute an unescapable reality for Andrew. The demands of the adult world make the continued production of the scripts and the resulting postponement of Andrew's serious ambitions necessary. His life has become serialized, and no heroic figure waits outside the door to rescue him. Even the few pure pleasures and altruistic gestures he allows himself contribute to his desperation. His social conscience demands that he contribute one hundred dollars that he does not have to the loyalists in the Spanish Civil War. In the checkbook he finds a record of payments for his sister's piano lessons ("He would have to support her for life, a sister who would only buy her dresses in Saks" [*FD*, 24]) and for a present to his girlfriend, Martha, who is demanding that he marry her ("If you married you paid rent in two places" [*FD*, 25]). A reminder of his purchase of V. L. Parrington's famous critical study of American literature, *Main Currents of American Thought*, intensifies his awareness of the ephemeral nature of Dusty Blades and Ronnie Cook and His Friends ("How does Dusty Blades fit into the *Main Currents of American Thought?*" [*FD*, 25]).

The future seems to promise only more and different pain: "Martha was Jewish. That meant . . . you never could escape from one particular meanness of the world around you; and when the bad time came there you'd be, adrift on that dangerous sea" (*FD*, 26). When his mother interrupts him to demand $50 for a new dress for his sister Dorothy, he hesitates, having just discovered that his bank account is already more than $400 overdrawn. Andrew's mother argues that Dorothy needs the dress for a party at which she hopes to catch a man. Andrew responds, "She won't get him, dress or no dress. . . . Your daughter's a very plain girl" (*FD*, 27). Intensified by a feeling that, like anti-Semitism, his sister's needs will have to be accommodated forever, Andrew's frustration finally explodes and he yells at his mother to leave him alone: "Everybody comes to me! . . . Nobody leaves me alone! Not for a minute!" (*FD*, 27).

Almost immediately after this outburst, Andrew apologizes and writes a check for his sister's new dress. In an effective ending, he hears, as in the opening of the story, echoes of a neighborhood baseball game outside the window. In an attempt to escape the unbearable pressures of the present, he joins the game. He is not a character in a "Dusty Blades" or a "Ronnie Cook" script, though, and he can find no lasting escape even on the field. "The sun and the breeze felt good on the baseball field, and he forgot for an hour, but he moved slowly. His arm hurt at the shoulder when he threw, and the boy playing second base called him Mister, which he wouldn't have done even last year, when Andrew was twenty-four" (*FD*, 28). Shaw has said that the concluding reference to the second baseman calling Andrew "Mister" cements the success of "Main Currents" as a story (see Giles interview in part 2). There is, of course, little real difference between being 24 and being 25; but the boy's salutation reminds Andrew of the passing of time and, thus, evokes the reality that he is trying to forget: a year has passed, during which he has made little progress on his play.

Still, the ending of "Main Currents of American Thought" is far from the despair of the end of "The Eighty-Yard Run." Andrew's retreat to the baseball field is a momentary, isolated event, not an attempt, like Christian Darling's re-creation of his touchdown run in practice, to wake a heroic past. The young writer is, in fact, committed to the struggles of the present by his own decency. He cannot deny his sister a new dress any more than he can turn his back on his other responsibilities to his family or his sense of obligation to the Spanish loyalists. Fundamentally, Andrew is not a self-centered individual. Despite his outbursts of cynicism and anger, one feels that he will not turn his back on the demands of the present. A native of Brooklyn, Andrew is not handicapped by an unrealistic midwestern innocence. The concluding reminder of the passing of time creates, then, a tone of bittersweet irony.

Virtually excluded from the surface of the story, the Great Depression functions as an important subtext in "Main Currents of American Thought." The pressures on Andrew are, of course, exacerbated by the economic suffering of the 1930s. Leonard Kriegel and Abraham H. Lass classify "Main Currents" as a tale of the depression in their anthology *Stories of the American Experience*.[13] Still, this story is not primarily a socioeconomic study, but a representative of the familiar story of the struggles of the young artist. This story was one Irwin Shaw knew quite well. In an interview he talked about his family pressures as a young writer: "I had a father who'd never worked since 1928, a mother, a brother who was under age and had to be put through law school" (see Giles interview, part 2). Like Andrew, he was too decent to avoid personal responsibilities.

The Deceptive Atmosphere of Art

A number of Shaw's New York stories merely evoke, and sometimes celebrate, the city as a capital of human diversity and potential romance. Because these stories portray New York City's diverse culture, their tone and mood range from gentle comedy to unrelieved seriousness.

"Lemkau, Pogran and Blaufox" recounts an amusing crisis in the relationship of the three owners of "Lemkau, Pogran and Blaufox, Knit Goods, Girdles, Brassieres, Corsets of All Descriptions." The story focuses on an emergency meeting that the respectable and proper Lemkau and Pogran have called with their less conventional partner, Blaufox. Blaufox, it seems, is something of a ladies' man, and his romantic exploits have awakened jealousy in his partners. As he does with the description of the firm, Shaw simultaneously evokes and undercuts a hint of eroticism in his description of Blaufox: "He was only five feet five inches tall, but standing next to his partner, Maurice Blaufox was a large man, full of juice and confidence" (*SS*, 584).

Lemkau and Pogran exemplify Shaw's concept of the gentle people. Literally little men, they faithfully carry out the insignificant responsibilities of their dull, respectable lives while dreaming of exotic romance. They have called the meeting to ask Blaufox if they might have dinner once a week with their dashing partner and his "theatrical" girlfriend, Annie Gerenson. The prospect of such an arrangement is almost too much for Lemkau: "It would be pleasant . . . to make the acquaintance of a person we would not normally make the acquaintance of. A lady of the theatrical profession, for example, who—oh, my God!" (*SS*, 587). Pogran's reasons for wishing to make the acquaintance of the glamorous Miss Gerenson originate in feelings of inadequacy occasioned by his family life. Describing his wife, he says, "She attends lectures, she is on committees, she reads new books. Frankly, she is ashamed of me. . . . Also, my daughters. They go to New York University" (*SS*, 588). Pogran needs to prove to himself that he is not the dull, boring man his family perceives him to be.

Blaufox generously agrees to his partners' proposal, and the first dinner with the theatrical Miss Gerenson is a success. The future stability of the company is assured.

The story is a good example of Shaw's scenic method of storytelling. "Lemkau, Pogran and Blaufox" could easily be a one-act comic play, and one suspects a textual joke in the author's repeated stress on Anne Gerenson's background in the theater.

The New York theater is also central to "It Happened in Rochester," a comic treatment of the deceptive nature of truth in art. Sundstrom, a retired vaudeville juggler, and his wife ask Robert McCleary, a desperate New York stage director, to direct Sundstrom's play, *It Happened*

27

in Rochester. McCleary is so desperate for something to direct that he accepts the Sundstroms' offer without reading the play. In addition, he is swayed by the former juggler's conviction about his play: "It's a true story. . . . It happened to me. . . . The girl is a young woman I knew in Rochester" (*SS*, 559). Sundstrom continually asserts that his play has "the ring of an absolutely true story" simply because it really happened.

After reading *It Happened in Rochester* and staging a dress rehearsal, McCleary is forced to admit to himself and to the author that the play is a hopelessly clichéd melodrama. Sundstrom is undaunted and decides to direct the play himself, with predictable results: "The reviews were very bad. The *Times* said: '*It Happened in Rochester* opened last night at the Jackson Theater. It was written, produced and directed by Leon Sundstrom.' That was all it said. It was the kindest review" (*SS*, 565). McCleary naturally assumes that this is the end of *It Happened in Rochester* until he encounters Sundstrom strolling along Broadway wearing sandwich boards advertising the play: "See *It Happened in Rochester* . . . It is an absolutely true story. Now playing at the Jackson Theater" (*SS*, 565).

The playwright then informs the director that he has gone bankrupt keeping the play going for two weeks: "The critics didn't understand. . . . They wrote about it as though it was impossible. I've written them. They won't believe that it actually happened to me. I could introduce them to the girl" (*SS*, 565). In this story Shaw comically treats what Henry James called "the deceptive atmosphere of art"— the phenomenon that what is real in external reality can seem totally false in art. McCleary knows, as Sundstrom does not, that artistic realism involves much more than the literal reproduction of events. The story's last lines are a concluding comment on the theme of truth in art. Sundstrom comments about the message on the sandwich boards he is wearing: "It's not a bad sign, is it?" When McCleary responds "It's a very good sign," the playwright once again insists, "It's the truth" (*SS*, 566).

The story's ending represents a sophisticated modification of the "snapper," Mark Twain's device for ending his tall tales with a joke. Sundstrom informs McCleary that he plans to return to juggling so that he can save enough money to write another play. The former vaudevillian has become helplessly addicted to the allure of the theater and is not discouraged by the considerable evidence of his lack of talent.

The reader's sense that the intoxication of Broadway is a very real phenomenon gives the story's ending a mood of bittersweet comedy. Sundstrom would not be the first person to be seduced and destroyed by the great white way.

The motif of the writer in New York also receives a comic treatment in "Prize for Promise." The story opens with six struggling writers waiting together in an office to receive their $1,000 prizes from a foundation. The backgrounds of three of the "promising" playwrights parallel aspects of Shaw's early career. Dowd, a short story writer from Brooklyn, remarks, "'I work very carefully. . . . It takes me a long time to finish anything.' He had had two stories in *Story*. They had taken three months apiece and he'd got twenty-five dollars for them and his brother-in-law had grimly figured this out on a weekly basis" (*SS*, 578).

In the preface to *God Was Here but He Left Early* Shaw recalls receiving $25 for his first published story and he discusses the deliberate manner in which he worked (*GWH*, 10). Schwartz is a playwright who, like Shaw, has had three failures in the theater after an initial success. (After the successful *Bury the Dead*, Shaw's New York–produced plays were commercial failures.) As a playwright Midkiff is even less successful than Schwartz: "Twice producers had bought plays from Midkiff and nearly put them on" (*SS*, 579). There is clearly an autobiographical impulse at work in the characterizations of Dowd, Schwartz, and Midkiff.

The three remaining playwrights represent deliberate stereotypes familiar to any student of American literature. Johnny Marble is a stage manager who desires to be seen as a creative presence: "he left his collar open to show that he was not really a stage manager, but a poet" (*SS*, 580). In contrast, Miss Tittle is a painfully shy librarian who giggles nervously throughout the story. Gentling, a flamboyant southern playwright, is the most satirically drawn of the three: "his long dirty coat capelike and romantic on his shoulders. . . . He came from Mississippi and his speech was very dramatic" (*SS*, 580). An alcoholic, Gentling blames his drinking and his failures as a writer on New York: "'No good writing can come out of New York City,' said Gentling. Nobody asked him to explain this. . . . 'I'm leaving for Natchez tomorrow,' he announced. . . . He wasn't going to drink in Natchez" (*SS*, 581).

The story's climax occurs when Van Meter, the representative of the benevolent foundation, arrives to distribute the prize money. After proclaiming that artists and writers are "talented, wonderful children. Especially about money," Van Meter announces that the foundation has decided to disburse the prize money in weekly $25 installments: "[the officers of the foundation] have decided that . . . on twenty-five dollars a week it is possible to live comfortably and do your work" (*SS*, 583). Van Meter's news abruptly forces the meeting and the story to a close. Midkiff encourages the six "promising" writers in a pride-salvaging gesture. He sarcastically comments, "I don't know what you bastards're going to do with your money, but I'm going out to buy a Packard," offers Van Meter a defiant "little bow," and leads the other five in a march past the foundation representative and out of the office (*SS*, 583).

"Prize for Promise" clearly has a serious, even angry, undertone, reflecting Shaw's belief that aspiring writers in America are often reduced to the status of "talented, wonderful children" by economic dependency upon patronizing bureaucracies. The six "promising" playwrights may save face by walking out on Van Meter, but they will almost certainly not turn down the $25 a week. Though they will hardly be able to "live comfortably" on it, they all need it. Still, dialogue and characterization in "Prize for Promise" are sufficiently exaggerated and comic to minimize the story's anger. Moreover, Shaw's broad satire in his portrayals of Gentling and Marble especially leaves us with the question of how much real talent the group has. One feels that Dowd, the character closest to Shaw, is probably the real thing.

Another aspiring playwright undergoes an experience that challenges his morale in "The House of Pain." Before the story opens, Philip Bloomer has submitted his play, *The House of Pain*, to a famous but aging actress, Adele Gerry, in the hope that she will agree to play the lead. Two months pass without Bloomer hearing from Miss Gerry. During this time, the Theater Guild expresses an interest in seeing the play. The story opens with Bloomer paying a visit to the actress's hotel room to retrieve *The House of Pain*. His interview with the actress goes well until he describes the character he wants her to play: "a slatternly, tyrannical, scheming harsh woman" of 45 who runs "a low, dreary, miserable boarding house with bad plumbing and poor devils who can't pay the rent" (*FD*, 325). Abruptly, Miss Gerry picks up the phone and calls Wilkes, her former director, to abuse him for destroying her career by having twice cast her as an unglamorous, aging woman. By overhearing one end of the conversation, Philip learns that the actress and

Wilkes have been lovers. He realizes that he has inadvertently provoked another round in an ongoing lovers' quarrel. Finally, Miss Gerry
dismisses Bloomer with instructions to pick up his play at Wilkes's
office: "You're a nice, clean, stupid boy, . . . I'm glad to see there's a
new crop springing up. Go" (*FD*, 327). Later, Wilkes returns the play
and gives Philip one bit of advice: "Young man . . . in the theater you
must learn one thing. Never tell an actress what type of part you think
she can play" (*FD*, 327). Wilkes's advice is unnecessary because Miss
Gerry has already forcefully brought the point home to the naïve young
man.

As in "Prize for Promise," the potential seriousness of "The House
of Pain" is undercut. Adele Gerry might well have dominated the story
and transformed it into a painful study of a once-beautiful leading lady
too proud to face the necessity of redirecting her career, but Shaw focuses instead on the embarrassment experienced by Philip when he is
permitted an up-close look at the less than glamorous reality of the
world behind the stage of the New York theater.

In "Wistful, Delicately Gay," one of his darkest stories, Shaw's treatment of another troubled New York actress is dramatically different.
Its narrative focus is Drake, a New York businessman who receives, as
the story opens, a phone call from Carol Hunt, an actress he had once
hoped to marry. Carol Hunt's request to see him for the first time in
two years sets off a sequence of memories that constitute most of the
story. Drake had first known her as a promising actress: "her quality
. . . was one of frailty, wistfulness, pathos, adolescence, romance. . . .
She was wary and fastidious with men and was, in male company, frail,
wistful, pathetic, delicately gay, adolescent, romantic. And only part of
this was cynical."[14] From the first her deliberate strategy has been to
achieve success as an actress through capitalizing on her innate ability
to project a delicate vulnerability. She has even cultivated the role of
patient victim when trying out for parts—each time she has narrowly
missed getting a major role, she has been careful to appear stoic and
resigned. From the first, Drake recognized that Carol's surface serenity
masks something darker than simple cynicism; what drives her always,
he knew, is a "hard, sexless obsessiveness of an artist cleaving to his
art" (*LDS*, 197).

Still, he had persisted in asking her to marry him, and she had
agreed, with the provision that she would pursue her acting career.
When he had asked her what would happen if she failed, she had re-

plied "I'll be disappointed for the rest of my life" (*LDS*, 204). Drake had been so much in love with Carol that he had succeeded in denying the truth about her—that her surface vulnerability only disguised a cold obsessiveness to succeed—until her big break had apparently come. One morning he had picked up the paper to read a scandal involving Carol Hunt—a prominent financier, married and a father, had been found dead of a heart attack in her hotel room. Drake's first thoughts had been that the scandal would irrevocably destroy Carol's chances of success and that she had been unfaithful to him. Before the story is over Drake and the reader learn that he had been wrong on both counts.

Instead, precisely because of the scandal Carol had been a sensational success in the play when it was produced; and Drake had reluctantly acknowledged that they were through. Her obsessive need to succeed as an actress would prevent her from having a true and lasting relationship with any man. Ironically, though, Carol has been unable to capitalize permanently on her breakthrough. Her first lead, "a young girl who was sweet and pathetic for two and a half acts and turned out to be a bitch," had not "quite come off" (*LDS*, 209); and after one more failure, public notice of her had dropped off.

When Drake meets with Carol, he discovers that she wishes to tell him the truth about the hotel room incident. Her belated "confession" provides Shaw's story with a surprise ending: the financier had actually suffered his fatal heart attack in the room of the show's star, Eileen Munsing. Terrified of scandal, Miss Munsing had come to Carol's room searching for someone to help her move the body. The panicked Miss Munsing had remarked that a scandal would destroy her at this point in her career, although it would have helped had it come earlier in her career. Hearing this, Carol had known instantly what she had to do: "This is the moment. Who would have ever thought it was going to come like this?" (*LDS*, 217). She and Miss Munsing had then moved the body to Carol's room.

After finishing her story, Carol tells Drake that she wanted him to know the truth so that he would no longer believe her guilty of infidelity—she wants him to have "a good opinion" of her. Then Drake watches her walk away, "youthful, delicate, beautiful, demented" (*LDS*, 218).

"Wistful, Delicately Gay" is a dark study of obsession. Carol Hunt is no Sundstrom comically wearing sandwich boards that fervently proclaim the truth of a hopelessly bad play. The obsessive degree of her ambition initially making her calculating and cynical and finally causing her to dissociate herself from the sustaining values and mores of society lead Drake to the conclusion that she is demented. She proves this assertion in that she actually believes that telling Drake about deliberately using a man's death to further her career will convince Drake to regain a "good opinion" of her. Shaw touches on, but does not stress, the idea that this specific form of insanity is one to which the artist is particularly susceptible.

A central irony in the story is Carol's failure to be convincing in her final lead—playing a girl who seems at first "sweet and pathetic" but is finally revealed to be cruel and cynical. The actress has so perfected a public veneer of soft delicacy that she is no longer capable of conveying her inner hardness. Thus Shaw is again treating the theme of the deceptive atmosphere of art.

Stories of Ethnic Diversity

The theater is not the only source of excitement and diversity that Shaw examines in his New York City stories. An appreciation of the city's rich ethnic diversity underscores much of this fiction and is emphasized in a handful of stories. "The Lament of Madame Rechevsky" memorably unites a theatrical motif with an investigation of Jewish-American identity. It is an unusual kind of story to come from Shaw. The overriding concern of the bulk of his fiction focusing on Jewish-Americans is protest against anti-Semitism. "The Lament of Madame Rechevsky" is one of two Shaw stories devoted to the kind of amused but loving examination of Jewish-American culture that one frequently finds in the fiction of Saul Bellow and Bernard Malamud.

The story reflects Shaw's background as a playwright in that it is primarily a soliloquy delivered by 73-year-old Madame Rechevsky at the grave of her husband, Abraham. She and Abraham were once prominent figures in New York's Yiddish Theater, but now he is dead and she is forgotten. The story opens with their daughter, Helen, receiving a 9:00 A.M. phone call from Madame Rechevsky, who demands to be taken to visit Abraham's grave: "I woke up this morning and a voice spoke to me. 'Go to Abraham's grave! Immediately! Go to the grave of your husband!'" (*FD*, 111–12). Helen reluctantly capitulates to her mother's demand, and on the trip to the cemetery finds herself arguing with her mother about her life-style. An actress herself, she is forced to explain why she is not at present in a play. Her defense that she is waiting for "the right part" only provokes Madame Rechevsky further: "The right part! . . . In my day we did seven plays a year, right part or no right part." When Helen patiently responds that "it's different now. This isn't the Yiddish Theater and this isn't 1900." her mother snaps back, "That was a better theater, . . . And that was a better time" (*FD*, 112–13).

After they reach the cemetery and the grave of Abraham, Madame Rechevsky directs her anger at her dead husband. The language of her preliminary exhortation to him evokes the Old Testament: "Abraham! . . . Abraham, listen to me!" (*FD*, 114–15). She then purges herself of the grievances of a lifetime:

> You gave diamonds and rubies and strings of pearls to enough women to make up three ballet companies! Sometimes you were paying railroad fare for five women at one time crossing the country after you, on tour. You ate and drank and you always had a baby daughter in your lap till the day you died, and you lived like a king of the earth, in all respects. . . . And I. Your wife? . . . Only one thing left—children! (*FD*, 115)

She is especially bitter that although "relatives are dying in Germany," she has no money left to help save them. Her outburst produces the desired catharsis for Madame Rechevsky: "Then she shrugged, stood up, her face more relaxed, confident, at peace, than it had been in months" (*FD*, 116).

Madame Rechevsky's soliloquy is a variation of the ritual quarrel motif found in several of Shaw's stories about married couples. Her long list of grievances, one feels, was recited more than once before Abraham's death. Throughout Shaw's fiction married couples frequently substitute ritual quarrels for meaningful communication. Now that Abraham is dead, his widow knows no other way to talk to him.

"The Lament of Madame Rechevsky" is closer to being a memorable character sketch than a fully developed story; Shaw simply establishes a frame for the widow's soliloquy of resentments. It is, though, a successful character sketch because both Madame Rechevsky and the dead Abraham emerge as powerful characters. The reader senses that like his acting career, Abraham's philandering has taken on mythic proportions since his death.

"The Boss" is also an investigation of a troubled Jewish-American marriage. The narrator recounts the disintegration of the marriage of his family's landlords, the Goldsteins, an American immigrant couple. Mr. Goldstein, a tailor, is initially content with quite modest success in America. His troubles begin when his wife's ambition becomes more intense and focused. Mrs. Goldstein is, in fact, another of Shaw's victims of obsession. The narrator remembers that "We were all more than a little afraid of Mrs. Goldstein. . . . The light of a Cause burned intensely in Mrs. Goldstein's eyes—and like other persons with a Cause that is bigger than they, she had her way with people. Money was Mrs. Goldstein's Cause" (100–101).

Initially, Mrs. Goldstein's obsession is satisfied by relentless collecting of rents and "savage haggling" in the marketplace (*SS*, 100). Soon, however, she starts her own poultry stand where she conducts her business "in the manner approved alike by Pennsylvania Avenue and Wall Street" (*SS*, 102). Unable to run his tailor shop without her help, Mr. Goldstein is reduced to plucking chickens for his wife. At his home Mrs. Goldstein's female employees constantly ridicule him, accusing him of being less than a man. He silently broods as he hears his wife addressed as "Boss." Finally, he challenges Mrs. Goldstein, "I am your husband and the master of your household . . . always must the man be the head of the house—and so shall it be here! . . . *I'm de boss!*" (*SS*, 106–7). When she ignores his assertion of dignity, he snaps, tearing the house apart and assaulting his wife. When he is led away to the county asylum two hours later, he goes "docilely, saying, 'I am de boss'" (*SS*, 107).

"The Boss" is a powerful study of the failure to assimilate. Mr. Goldstein, tied to the customs and traditions of the old country, cannot adjust to life in the New World. In contrast, his wife's latent ambition is so stimulated by American capitalist opportunity that she is transformed into a terrifying creature. Unique among Shaw's stories, "The Boss" evokes the twentieth-century Jewish-American urban ghetto in a manner comparable to that of Michael Gold's *Jews without Money* and the short stories of Bernard Malamud. Its power is lessened somewhat by the one-dimensional characterization of Mrs. Goldstein, who is never more than a frightening harridan.

The City and Suburbia

In three quite different comic stories, Shaw depicts New York as a place of danger and romance. "Material Witness" is masterful black humor, a story of a man whose life is destroyed because one day "he'd turned down Columbia Avenue, instead of Broadway" (*FD*, 310). Lester Barnum's wrong turn brings him face-to-face with a gangland murder. One of Shaw's "gentle people," Lester initially finds his notoriety as a "material witness" a glamorous departure from the dullness of his life: "It seemed to Barnum nearly a thousand people must be congregated around him, all with their eyes fixed eagerly on him, who never, even in his own home, could get three people at one time, even his wife and two children, to listen to him for as long as a minute without interruption" (*FD*, 311–12). Lester is so caught up in his sudden status as celebrity that he ignores the "small man" who warns him that he is about to get in trouble.

The small man's prophecy indeed proves correct. Lester is taken into protective custody and "for a whole year the murderer was not caught, and he sat in jail and lost his wife and children and a bearded Rumanian took his job and highwaymen and forgers beat him with mop handles and slop buckets" (*FD*, 313). Shaw gives the story an effective concluding snapper. After he is finally released, Lester walks "aimlessly down the street . . . childless, jobless," and witnesses a traffic accident. Quickly, he rushes away, protesting that he "didn't see anything" (*FD*, 313). "Material Witness" has the feel of an urban tall tale written in a tone of absurdist black humor.

Absurdity also dominates "Small Saturday," one of the three long stories that make up part 2 of *God Was Here but He Left Early*. Shaw says that the story is about "sex," one of the three "major preoccupations of our age" (*GWH*, 12). It is a light-hearted satire of sexual maneuvering in New York City. The focal character, Christopher Bagshot, is tormented because he is so short: "He was a small man, five feet six, but fit. . . . In another age, before everybody looked as though he or she had been brought up in Texas or California, his size would not have bothered him" (*FD*, 618). The story opens after he has heard a voice in a dream: "You must make love to a woman at least five feet, eight inches tall tonight" (*FD*, 618). A subtextual joke throughout the story is that Bagshot's obsession with his lack of height is related to a concern about the size of his penis. The inherent ridiculousness of a male obsessed by the sexual hunt determines the tone of "Small Saturday."

Bagshot, the manager of "a book-and-record store," keeps a carefully coded address book devoted exclusively to the names of girls: "One Star meant that she was tall and pretty or even beautiful and that, for one reason or another, she seemed to be a girl who might be free with her favors" (*FD*, 622). At the store he proceeds to call the most promising names in the book in order to fulfill the command of the voice in his dream.

After rejections by *"Anderson, Paulette**"* and *"Stickney, Beaulah**,"* Bagshot tries *"Toye, Dorothea**,"* who looks "like a child who has been splashed out of the sea to be dried with a rough towel by her mother" (*FD*, 637). Miss Toye turns out to be quite available indeed—she is a prostitute. Seemingly, Bagshot's last hope is the "politically advanced" *"Marsh, Susan**":* "The reason Christopher knew she was politically advanced was that the only books she ever showed an interest in were written by people like Fanon and Marcuse and Cleaver and LeRoi Jones and Marshall McLuhan. She had beautiful legs. It was unsettling to sell books of that nature to a girl with legs as beautiful as that" (*FD*, 641). Susan Marsh, in fact, is a 1960s revolutionary who is interested in using Bagshot's bookstore as a place to store explosive materials. She tells him that she cannot say for certain that she is free, but she may drop into the store later.

Bagshot is almost reconciled to failure when Anna Bukowski walks in off the street: "She was beautiful, in a strange, haunted way, like some of those movie actresses in Swedish pictures who have affairs with their brothers or sisters" (*FD*, 654). Miss Bukowski abruptly confesses to Christopher that she is broke and almost faints from hunger. She adds one other piece of information: "I'm up for a part off-off-Broadway. One of those naked plays" (*FD*, 655). When she quickly and gratefully accepts Bagshot's offer of dinner, "he [knows] that voice in his dreams hadn't spoken for nothing" (*FD*, 656). Overcome with hubris, he sends her on to the restaurant to wait for him. His sense of power is intensified when Paulette Anderson and Beulah Stickney appear to offer belated acceptance of a date. Thinking that Anna Bukowski awaits him, Bagshot haughtily dismisses both of them. Yet Miss Bukowski has already been picked up by a "nice" 40-year-old man.

The story then concludes by informing us that some time later, Bagshot marries June, his loyal, if small, girlfriend. This ending is effectively ambiguous—the reader does not know if Christopher has given up his quest because his moment of power with Paulette Anderson and Beulah Stickney in the bookstore was enough for him or because he has learned a lesson about fidelity.

Despite its length, though, "Small Saturday" is slight, if entertaining. The beautiful women who appear in it recall the masterful early Shaw story "The Girls in Their Summer Dresses." The story's direct or indirect references to young, middle-class revolutionaries, the films of Ingmar Bergman, and "off-off-Broadway" "naked shows" communicate a feel for the chaotic experimentation of the American 1960s. Still, a determinedly sexist tone and one-dimensional characterization make taking "Small Saturday" ultimately very seriously impossible for the reader. In that way, its length works against it.

Shaw is much more successful at evoking the excitement of New York in an earlier and shorter absurdist story, "The Indian in Depth of Night." The story opens with O'Malley walking slowly through Central Park: "[He] looked around him at the city slumbering magnificently past the trees of the park and was glad to know his home was there, his work, his future" (*FD*, 304). His peace of mind is not deeply disturbed when he is forced to reject the advances of a homosexual—he is "ready, with the drinks and the sweetness of the air, and the feeling of living in, and, in a way, owning the great city of New York, to pass on a kind word to every living thing" (*FD*, 305). A more serious threat to his calmness materializes in the form of Billy Elk, "a penniless Creek Indian prizefighter astray far from home in Central Park" (*FD*, 306). When O'Malley refuses Billy Elk a dollar because he has no money with him, the displaced young Indian threatens to report him to the police "for talking to a fairy" (*FD*, 306–7).

Before O'Malley knows what is happening, Billy Elk goes up to a policeman who is soliciting advice from a cabdriver about his sexually promiscuous teenage daughter. Instead of reporting O'Malley's "transgression" with the homosexual, Elk simply asks the police officer if there is an Indian reservation nearby. Surprised at the question, the officer is nevertheless "grateful that no murder had turned up, no entry, rape, arson, assault, double-parking committed" (*FD*, 307). Not surprisingly, in the mood that Shaw has established for the story, the cabdriver knows of a reservation just "up the river" (*FD*, 307).

Satisfied with this information, Elk returns to O'Malley and says, "See . . . I'm not such a bad guy" and then disappears "expertly among the trees, like Tecumseh's braves and the slippery, valiant red defenders of Kentucky's bloody ground" (*FD*, 307–8). Relieved, "O'Malley walked slowly home, breathing deeply the clear morning air, pleased to be in a city in which Indians roamed the streets and went to great lengths to prove their friendliness and goodness of heart" (*FD*, 308).

"The Indian in Depth of Night" works the way good absurdist fiction should. The story establishes its own inverted logic in which such improbabilities as the hostile appearance of a prizefighting Indian in Central Park, a policeman openly discussing his teenage daughter's sexual adventures with a New York cabdriver, the cabdriver actually knowing a nearby Indian reservation, and the Indian suddenly wanting to be remembered as "not such a bad guy" assume probability.

Shaw's prose, moreover, effectively communicates a sense of danger underlying the calm surface of New York City. When Billy Elk approaches him, the policeman instinctively anticipates hearing about a violent crime. One evocative passage almost hidden in the middle of the story describes O'Malley "looking up at the towers of the city rearing dark and magnificent against the clear soft sky, with here and there the scattered lights, lust and illness, keeping the city from total sleep in the depths of night" (*FD*, 306). Still, "The Indian in Depth of Night" is primarily light and comic in tone and mood. The reader soon shares O'Malley's intoxication with the city.

Finally, in two of his most brooding stories, Shaw emphasizes the pain and sickness hidden beneath the surfaces of the city and suburbia. The narrative focus of "Noises in the City" is a married man named Weatherby who stops at a restaurant in the early evening for a drink. At the restaurant bar, he is engaged in conversation by Sidney Gosden, an interior decorator whom he vaguely remembers having met once before. Through the somewhat personal questions Gosden asks Weatherby, Shaw effectively creates a sense of something ominous lurking in the sanctuary of the restaurant. The reader suspects a possible homosexual approach by the strange Gosden until he abruptly announces that he had proposed to his wife in the restaurant and then asks Weatherby a startling question: "have you ever killed a man?" (*FD*, 297). Alarmed, Weatherby confesses that he did serve in the artillery during the war and undoubtedly participated in killing someone. Gosden responds, "There must be a moment of the utmost exaltation when you take a human life, . . . followed by a wave of the most abject, ineradicable shame" (*FD*, 298). The bartender Giovanni soon intercedes and Gosden goes away to make a phone call. Because of Shaw's skill in building suspense, the reader understands that the strange man's questions about killing portend something darker and more frightening than a homosexual advance.

Finally, Giovanni explains to Weatherby that Gosden's wife had been raped and murdered and that the killer is being electrocuted that night. When Gosden returns from his phone call, he talks openly about the rape and murder:

> My wife was a virgin when I married her, . . . [b]ut we had the most passionate and complete relationship right from the beginning. . . . At eleven-o-eight, . . . they pulled the switch. The man is dead. . . . The city is full of wild beasts, it is ridiculous to say that we are civilized. She screamed. Various people in the building heard her screams, but in the city one pays little attention to the noises that emanate from a neighbor's apartment. (*FD*, 301–2)

"Noises in the City" is an important Shaw story because it completes Shaw's vision of the city: beneath the surface materialism and glamor and as a dark corollary to its promise of romance and excitement the city harbors an undercurrent of savage brutality and cruel indifference. "Noises in the City" demonstrates that people in the city are alienated and thus vulnerable to unseen danger. Gosden's wife died in part because she was inherently trusting and refused to lock her apartment door securely. To a degree, the story undercuts the vision of decency that dominates most of Shaw's fiction; instead trust and openness lead to horrible death.

Nonetheless, Gosden remains one of Shaw's "gentle people," for he is deeply concerned about the ethical implications of the execution of his wife's murderer and has even sent money anonymously to the man's wife. Gosden is struggling to prevent his grim vision of the city from completely absorbing his soul. After hearing the little man's story, Weatherby quickly hurries home to his wife. That night, in bed with her, he does not immediately fall asleep: "He lay awake for a while, holding her gently, listening to the muffled sounds from the street below. God deliver us from accidents, he thought, and make us understand the true nature of the noises arising from the city around us" (*FD*, 303). Shaw believed that accidents control all human destiny; Weatherby, the reader assumes, will learn that there is finally no way to prepare for, or guard against, them.

Increasingly, Americans who can afford the move have fled the ominous noises of the city for the apparent sanctuary of suburbia. In "Circle of Light" Shaw demonstrates that fleeing the city does not necessarily ensure escape from humanity's dark impulses. The story opens with Martin Brackett visiting his sister Linda and her husband, John Willard, in their upper-class suburban New York home. Initially,

Linda and John appear to be what Martin has expected—a perfect married couple. Abruptly, though, the security of the Willard home and marriage is threatened when Martin observes, at 1 A.M. a Peeping Tom outside the house, but he is unable to identify the man beyond saying that he looks "solid" (*FD*, 742).

The incident inspires a quarrel between the Willards. John accuses Linda of walking around inside the house undressed, and she responds that "he prefers to live in a vault" (*FD*, 740–41). Martin begins to wonder whether they are as happily married as they appear to be in public. The shocking episode prompts an even more disturbing realization for him—in attempting to give the police a more helpful description of the prowler, Martin understands "that the remembered face was being simplified, intensified, becoming heraldic, symbolic, a racial, dangerous apparition staring out of dark and dripping forests at the frail safety of the sheltered circle of light" (*FD*, 743). Civilized society, he comprehends, is a thin, easily shattered veneer of protection and humanity's attempt to lock out the inexplicable evil that constantly threatens it. A subtext of "Circle of Light" is that the conspicuous wealth of the upper classes serves primarily as an illusion of protection against the dangers of "dark and dripping forests." Still, the tension that has surfaced in the Willard marriage makes Martin wonder whether the mysterious threat might not come from within suburbia.

At the story's climax the three protagonists attend a cocktail party given at the home of a man named Bowman. At the party, the story of the Willards' prowler inspires a series of reminiscences of intruders:

> All these solid, comfortable people, in their cosy and orderly community shared a general fear, a widespread uneasiness, and . . . the face outside the Willard window had made them all remember that there were obscure and unpredictable forces always ready to descend upon them in their warm homes and that, with all their locked doors and all their police and all their loaded .45's, they were exposed and vulnerable to attack. (*FD*, 744)

Truly, Shaw's suburbanites have moved a long way beyond Gosden's tragic wife—they have learned the fallacy of trust. In their specific accounts of intrusion the suburbanites commonly remember the perpetrators as Puerto Rican or black—because they very much want to believe that the threat lives outside their warm "circle of light." But as he is leaving the party, Martin recognizes Bowman, his host, as the man outside Linda's window. Bowman is no outsider; indeed, he is truly "solid": "the sort of man, pushing a robust forty, you might see at the reunion of a good college or behind a vice-president's desk of one of those polite businesses where everybody has a deep rug on the floor and where money is only mentioned in quiet tones and behind closed doors" (*FD*, 745).

Later, in the car, Martin remembers that Bowman kissed Linda good-night in a "familiar, habitual way." As renewed tension between Linda and her husband surfaces, Martin becomes increasingly suspicious of his sister: "Linda was his sister and he loved her, but how well did he know her, after all these years? He remembered his own sensuality and the regrettable things he had done, himself, because of it . . . and the same blood ran in both of them" (*FD*, 746). Now he wonders if the threat to the "circle of light" is simply sexuality, a force truly difficult to lock outside.

The next evening Martin returns with the Willards to Bowman's house for an outdoor barbecue. Privately he confronts his host, who makes a lengthy confession. Bowman initially defends himself by saying that he only watches: "I never hurt anyone" (*FD*, 752). When Martin presses for a further explanation, Bowman provides it: "I watch the happy ones. . . . Sometimes I make love to my wife and it doesn't mean anything. One animal falling on another animal in the jungle. One driven, the other—what shall I say—resigned. No more than that. I get up from her bed and I go to my bed and I'm ashamed of myself, I don't feel like a human being" (*FD*, 752). Still, Bowman says, he is an "optimist" and believes that some people "*are* happy": "Only you have to catch them by surprise, boy, when they don't know you're watching them, to find out the secret" (*FD*, 753). Bowman clarifies that he is an "explorer" searching for the "secret" of sexual happiness in America. The story's subtheme of suburban racism receives an ironic twist when Bowman tells of spying on a black couple in bed: "Our colored population. . . . Closer to the primeval push. Simpler, I thought, less inhibited" (*FD*, 754–55). Here, Bowman is simply making explicit an assumed formula that is implicit in the stories about prowlers at the first party: sexuality is animalistic, blacks are atavistic throwbacks to prehistory, thus black sexuality should be primitive. Bowman, however, had been disappointed—the black couple had been reading in bed, she Simone de Beauvoir's *The Second Sex* and he the Bible. Shaw effectively satirizes the historic obsession of white

Americans with the sexuality of blacks. James Baldwin, one feels, would have enjoyed this part of the story.

Bowman concludes his confession by saying that he spies on the Willards because they are his "last hope": they are two people who seem "*pleasurable* to each other" (*FD*, 755). Perhaps, he suggests, he has been wrong. Martin now realizes that his suspicions of Linda's infidelity and his fears about the Willard marriage have been groundless. Relieved, he answers Bowman, "No, . . . you're not wrong" (*FD*, 755–56). The ending of "Circle of Light" is effectively balanced: Martin learns that the threat to the peace and security of suburbia is internal and derives in part from the sexual sickness of one of its inhabitants. Still, Linda is not afflicted by the illness, and he need fear no taint of shared blood.

The inhabitants of "the circle of light" are largely transposed New Yorkers hoping to escape the dangers of the city. Despite its frightening undercurrent of sexual perversion and random violence, New York City, with its magnificent theater, its ethnic diversity, its material abundance, and its legions of attractive women was, for Irwin Shaw, the American capital of romance and excitement.

Protests against Fascism and Anti-Semitism

Fascism

For Shaw, New York's beauty was clouded by the forces of history during the late 1930s and early 1940s. He could not ignore the rise of fascism in Europe and anti-Semitism at home. A number of Shaw's stories, most of them still set in New York, focus directly on these interrelated threats to American peace and stability. The threat of Hitler directly inspired a number of stories in *Sailor off the Bremen* and *Welcome to the City.* These stories sometimes make him appear susceptible to charges of oversimplification made by Chester E. Eisinger and other critics on two counts: in "Sailor off the Bremen" his answer to nazism's senseless violence seems to be more violence, and the surface of his protest fiction implies that essentially "the good life" of the American middle class was endangered in the late 1930s and early 1940s. A superficial reading of "Weep in Years to Come," for instance, might lead one to assume that a triumph by Hitler would simply mean that the economically secure American male could no longer enjoy listening to good music, looking at impressionist paintings, and enjoying the company of pretty women. There is, however, considerably more depth and complexity in both stories and in most of Shaw's protest fiction.

"Sailor off the Bremen" was an unusual story for the early *New Yorker.* It is an unflinchingly realistic account of the brutal revenge taken by four of Shaw's "gentle people" against a sadistic German. Before the narration begins, Ernest had been beaten during an anti-Nazi Communist party demonstration aboard a German ship docked in New York. The beating had been so savage and prolonged that Ernest had lost several teeth and one eye. The story opens with Ernest's wife, Sally, his brother Charley, and Preminger and Dr. Stryker, two fellow members of the Communist party, planning retaliation against Lueger, the Austrian ship steward who had repeatedly hit Ernest while two other men had held him. The climax of the story is Charley's equally brutal beating of Lueger. Shaw's obvious problem in writing the story lay in describing the assault on Lueger while retaining the reader's sympathy for the characters who first carefully plan the beating and then carry it out. Through a number of fictional devices, he largely succeeds in doing so.

The opening scene emphasizes the premeditated savagery of Lueger's beating of Ernest. Lueger is described as virtually subhuman, a sadistic womanizer. His name recalls a weapon, an instrument of violence. In sharp contrast, Ernest, Charley, Sally, and Dr. Stryker emerge as "innocents," representatives of Shaw's "gentle people," and a German Communist, Preminger, is sickened by his people's capacity for brutality and violence. Because they live in a state of undeclared war passivity becomes a form of suicide for the characters who seek retribution.

Preminger, a shipmate of Lueger's, essentially provides background information about the Nazi: "He is twenty-five years old, very dark and good-looking, and he sleeps with at least two ladies a voyage. . . . His name is Lueger. He spies on the crew for the Nazis. He has sent two men already to concentration camps" (*FD*, 34). Juxtaposed to this virtual personification of sadism and treachery is the victimized Ernest, a painter who argues against revenge: "It is not a personal thing. . . . It is the movement of Fascism. You don't stop Fascism with a personal crusade against one German" (*FD*, 35). Shaw has thus drawn the contrast sharply—evil, one-dimensional Nazi versus gentle, artistic American Communist.

Nevertheless, Ernest is outvoted by the other "innocents." Charley, a nonpolitical football player who personifies another form of American innocence, responds angrily to Ernest's plea for nonviolence: "I am disregarding the class struggle, I am disregarding the education of the proletariat. . . . I am acting strictly in the capacity of your brother" (*FD*, 36). The ironically named Dr. Stryker is described as an almost ethereal being: he weighs "a hundred and thirty-three pounds and it was almost possible to see through his wrists, he was so frail" (*FD*, 35). Still, after announcing that he is "not the type for violence," he endorses retaliation against Lueger. The key voice in the decision and the most memorably drawn character in the story is Ernest's wife, Sally. A gentle, loving woman sickened by the savage assault on her husband, she provides a crucial, if understated, endorsement of the planned retaliation.

The specific plan calls for Sally to function as "bait"—to go out with

Lueger in order to lure him to a secluded part of the city where the assault can take place. Charley intends to administer the beating with his bare fists: "I want it to be a very personal affair" (*FD*, 37).

In his account of Sally's "date" with Lueger, Shaw adds to the picture of the Austrian as a one-dimensional sadist. Walking down the street with Sally, he repeatedly pinches her arm. When she complains that it hurts, he laughingly says, "It does not hurt much. . . . You don't mind if it hurts, nevertheless. . . ." To further distance the American reader from Lueger, Shaw describes his speech: "His English was very complicated, with a thick accent" (*FD*, 37). He also makes it clear that Lueger prefers the company of women who he believes like being hurt: "He pinched her hard and laughed, looking obliquely into her eyes with a kind of technical suggestiveness he used on the two ladies a voyage on the *Bremen*" (*FD*, 38).

Shaw then cuts to Charley and Dr. Stryker waiting in ambush. Stryker is talking nervously about the man Ernest was before the beating: "He used to be a very merry man, . . . always laughing. . . . Before he was married we used to go out together all the time and all the time the girls, my girl and his girl, no matter who they were, would give all their attention to him" (*FD*, 38). Ernest's "merry" laughter and normal, healthy sexuality contrasts with Lueger's menacing sadism. Irony is added to the contrast when Shaw switches back to Sally and Lueger. The Austrian expresses his enjoyment of the movie they have just seen: "That was a very fine film tonight. . . . I enjoy Deanna Durbin. Very young, fresh, sweet. Like you. . . . A small little maid. You are just the kind I like" (*FD*, 39). Deanna Durbin, the embodiment of American female innocence and virginity, appeals to him as an imagined victim of abuse. After this speech, he forces his body against Sally's and attempts to kiss her. Because sexual symbolism is central to the story, Shaw has evoked an image of a bestial Nazi raping a pure and innocent America. Like most protest fiction, "Sailor off the Bremen" has unashamedly propagandistic overtones.

At this point the story moves quickly to its climax. Sally suddenly feels that she cannot go through with the plan and attempts to warn the Austrian to flee. She does so "not because she liked him, but because he was a human being and thoughtless and unsuspecting and because her heart was softer than she had thought" (*FD*, 39). Sally's abrupt change of mind is, in one way, problematic in the story, because Lueger hardly seems a human being. In fact, his only human moment is his expression of admiration for Deanna Durbin, and that in itself is uglier and more complicated than it appears on the surface. In this moment Shaw attempts to have it both ways—he wants the reader to accept and even endorse what will soon happen to Lueger, while releasing Sally from full complicity in the event. Sally, like Ernest and even Charley, is one of Shaw's "gentle people," decent and innately gentle.

Similarly, Shaw next provides a long, brutal description of Charley repeatedly hitting Lueger, but sobbing uncontrollably while doing so. The story's concluding brutality is conveyed verbally. In a hospital Preminger identifies Lueger to a detective: "He was a very popular boy. Especially with the ladies." The detective's response is, "Well, . . . he won't be a very popular boy when he gets out of here" (*FD*, 41). Like his victim Ernest, Lueger has been disfigured in an enactment of a kind of Old Testament revenge.

"Sailor off the Bremen" has troubled critics because it advocates violence against the violent and because its narrative has an implicit hint of racism. Although Lueger is identified as Austrian, the story appears to contain anti-German, as opposed to anti-Nazi, sentiments. In fact, Preminger, the German Communist, makes this overt in a speech in the opening scene: "But my people, the Germans. You must always expect the worst from them" (*FD*, 34). The story's subtext seems to tell us that by 1939 it was clear to anyone willing to see that Hitler and the Germans could only be stopped by violent, organized resistance. The plot against Lueger can be taken as an allegorical call for American military action against the Nazis. In the 1980 interview, Shaw said, "We could have stopped Hitler . . . if we had known that eventually we were going to have a fight, as Roosevelt did, but enough people in this country didn't believe him. And if we'd gotten together with England and France and got *them* to move, we could've unseated Hitler without losing a man (see Giles interview in part 2). In 1939 Shaw was less sanguine about American casualties in a military conflict, but like Roosevelt, he knew that "eventually we were going to have a fight."

As happens to much protest fiction, "Sailor off the Bremen" by now seems somewhat dated. It advocates a response to totalitarianism that is simplistic, if not unthinkable, in the nuclear age. The story is also intensely melodramatic in execution. Its central incident, the largely one-dimensional characters, and the political-sexual symbolism inevitably lead to melodrama. Still, the story retains undeniable power in its depiction of "gentle people" forced to fight an as yet undeclared war.

Brutality and melodramatic incident do not appear in "Weep in Years to Come," which also appeared in Shaw's first collection; in fact, very little "happens" in the story. It opens with Paul and Dora, an attractive middle-class couple, exploring the area around New York's Fifth Avenue. Their observations focus on the world of wealth and pleasure surrounding them: "Couples strolled slowly down from Fifth Avenue . . . appreciating the Rockefeller frivolity and extravagance which had carved a place for hydrangeas and water and saplings and spring and sea-gods riding bronze dolphins out of these austere buildings, out of the bleak side of Business" (*FD*, 145). It is precisely "bleak Business" that supports the city's display of material abundance, but Paul and Dora have little difficulty in remaining oblivious to this reality. Nor are they bothered that they cannot possess all the riches they see advertised: Dora says, "It's nice to know things like that exist . . . Even if you can't have them" (*FD*, 145). Later Paul asks Dora, "Do you think God walks up Fifth Avenue?" and then comments, "We are princes of the earth, . . . All over the world men slave to bring riches to these few blocks for us to look at and say, 'Yes, very nice' or 'Take it away, it stinks.' I feel very important when I walk up Fifth Avenue" (*FD*, 146). In this part of the story, as elsewhere in his fiction, Shaw seems to be praising uncritically the power of American consumerism to make the middle class feel like "princes of the earth." Yet, this effect is minimized by the rest of the story.

The mood abruptly shifts when Paul and Dora pass a window advertising a German vacation, and Paul comments, "I'll be there soon" (*FD*, 146). The remainder of the story is essentially a debate between the two attractive young people as to whether he should participate in a war when it comes. Paul does not challenge Dora's central point that the Americans who fought in World War I were "gypped": Paul says, "That's right . . . They were killed for six-per-cent interest on bonds, for oil wells, for spheres of influence" (*FD*, 147). A recognition that material abundance does indeed demand a price beyond money now enters the story through Paul. Despite this awareness, Paul insists that when the war comes, he will enlist "the first day" (*FD*, 147). Frightened and puzzled, Dora tells him that in such a war, "You wouldn't kill Hitler, . . . You'd just kill young boys like yourself" (*FD*, 148). Again, Paul largely agrees with her. After clarifying his motivation (he does not want to kill Hitler but wants to stop "the idea he represents for so many people"), he says that the enemy will undoubtedly comprise young boys like himself: "I'm sure they'd love to go to bed with you tonight. I bet they'd love to walk along the fountains with the bronze statues in Rockefeller Plaza, holding hands with you on a spring Saturday evening and looking at the sports clothes in the windows. I bet a lot of them like Mozart too." Still, he says, he would kill them "gladly . . . Their bodies protect an idea I have to kill to live" (*FD*, 148).

The story never really clarifies this "idea," and one assumes that German nazism and totalitarianism in general really threaten a cluster of ideas: Mozart's music and the material abundance of Fifth Avenue, implying individual freedom and personal comfort. The ambiguity in the story results from the manner in which Shaw uses symbolic counterparts for this set of abstractions. One problem is that the logic of the story does, at times, suggest that Hitler primarily threatens American material abundance (to which Paul again uncritically responds), male sexual enjoyment of attractive women, and art and music. But when asked what he hopes might result from war with Germany, Paul says, "Maybe some day the world'll be run for people who like Mozart" (*FD*, 148).

In the conclusion of the story, Paul and Dora first stop to admire a reproduction of Renoir's *Luncheon of the Boating Party*, and Paul analyzes the painting: "It's settled, happy, solid. It's a picture of a summertime that vanished a long time ago" (*FD*, 149). Then the couple decides to settle for immediate pleasure and rushes away to make love in his apartment.

Paul's analysis of Renoir's painting seems to postulate something like a political and social "golden age," a time of stability and simple sensuality. The reader must wonder whether it is this concept that Hitler most threatens and how this concept precisely relates to "people who like Mozart." Shaw's fondness for transcribing the surface of American urban sophistication becomes a problem in this story, since one of its implicit values seems to be the material luxuries displayed on Fifth Avenue. Still, the story effectively evokes one aspect of the American mood of the late 1930s. Young men like Paul were reluctantly realizing the destructive fallacy of American isolationism and the inevitability of global destruction. At such a time, a philosophy of carpe diem must have had its strong attractions. Shaw's skill as a storyteller is also evident in the story. It opens with a newsboy calling, "Hitler! . . . Hitler!" as Paul and Dora exit from a movie theater. Momentarily, the fictional couple ignores him; but the logic of "Weep in Years to Come" is that the newsboy has proclaimed the future. He is a truly ominous foreshadowing device.

Despite its grim message of warning, the story contains a strong element of innocent optimism. It encourages the 1939 reader to imagine a future world "run for people who like Mozart." In addition, its assurance that the German army in the impending war will be comprised of young men like Paul negates. to some degree at least, the charge that Shaw harbors prejudice against the German people. Except in "Sailor off the Bremen," one does not find in his fiction any anti-German sentiment totally isolated from warnings against or outrage at Hitler and nazism.

A similar kind of optimism underlies "Night, Birth and Opinion," which is unusual among Shaw's fictional protests against nazism in its use of a distinctly proletarian setting, a working-class bar. First collected in *Welcome to the City*, the story examines, in allegorical fashion, the common American's reluctant agreement to make the sacrifices necessary to fighting fascism.

The story's initial mood is one of disharmony and dissent. It opens with Lubbock, a physically large, belligerent anarchist, loudly proclaiming his unwillingness to have any part of the army: "Yuh join the army, yuh sit in a tent and freeze yer tail all winter. I'm a civilized man, I'm used to steam-heated apartments." Patiently, Cody, the bartender, attempts to answer Lubbock: "Everybody has to make certain sacrifices" (*FD*, 162). After complaining about the army and the inevitability of a catastrophic world war, Lubbock begins berating Sweeney, an Irish man who announces that he has two cousins in the British Air Force. In a manner reminiscent of Hemingway's *A Farewell to Arms*, Lubbock uses the word *patriot* to insult Sweeney and anyone else in the bar who suggests that fighting Hitler is desirable or inevitable. He says to Sweeney, "One war after another, . . . One after another, and they get poor sons of bitches like you into tents in the wintertime, and yuh never catch on" (*FD*, 165). According to Lubbock, wars are nothing but capitalistic tricks to exploit the naïve patriotism of the lower classes for the greater profit of the upper classes. He asserts, "They are dividing up the world. . . . I got eighty-five cents to my name. No matter which way they finish dividing, I'll be lucky to still have eighty-five cents when it's all over. . . . We get trouble. The workingman gets trouble" (*FD*, 165–66).

Unable to refute Lubbock, Sweeney begins berating Di Calco, an

Italian-American, about Mussolini. In self-defense, Di Calco asserts his patriotism. Sweeney soon interrupts by announcing that he hates the English, the French, and the Americans. When asked whom he does like, Sweeney answers, "The Italians. You can't get them to fight. They're civilized human beings. A man comes up to them with a gun, they run like antelopes. I admire that" (*FD*, 164). Before he quite realizes what is happening, Di Calco, the Italian-American patriot, begins defending the Italian army. When the bartender, absurdly named William Cody, periodically tries to stop the bickering among his customers, Lubbock turns on him, derisively calling him "Buffalo Bill." Finally Lubbock's anger turns to rage. Grabbing Sweeney and Di Calco and shaking them, he asserts "If I get shot it's your fault! . . . I oughta kill you. I feel like killin' every drunk slob walkin' the streets" (*FD*, 167).

At this point, only a deus ex machina can bring peace to the bar, and one enters in the form of a thin, tired-looking girl. The girl explains that her 19-year-old sister had married a sailor who has deserted her. Her sister is in the hospital after hemorrhaging while giving birth. Her sister will die, the girl says, if she does not receive blood: "My blood's the wrong type" (*FD*, 167). Lubbock, Sweeney, Di Calco, and Cody lay aside their differences and rush to the hospital to save the sister. Lubbock turns out to have the needed blood type. After the transfusion is over, he walks out to find the three other men and the girl waiting for him. Proudly, he announces that "everything's fine. . . . My blood is singing in her system like whiskey" (*FD*, 168). Sweeney then hesitantly asks Lubbock to share a drink with Di Calco, Cody, the girl, and himself and then tensely awaits the anticipated attack. But the anarchist accepts, while embracing the girl: "Sure. . . . It'll be an honor" (*FD*, 168).

The allegorical implications of "Night, Birth and Opinion" are obvious. The story's emphasis on the ethnic backgrounds of its central characters communicates the American melting-pot ideal, while Lubbock's cynicism reflects a working-class disillusionment with all political systems. For most of the story, unified national resistance to European fascism seems an impossible goal. Still, despite his nihilistic stance, Lubbock has the right type of blood, and his instant willingness to share it with the dying woman inspires a spirit of community among the other characters. His willing sacrifice of blood, of course, symbolically foreshadows the incalculable bloody sacrifices that the impending war will demand of the American and international proletariat.

Lubbock is a distinctly proletarian example of Shaw's "gentle people." Finally, the birth in the story prefigures a renewal of hope and dedication in America and throughout the world. The structural logic of "Night, Birth and Opinion" implies Lubbock's realization of the selfishness of his nihilistic stance: the necessity of defeating fascism demands that strictly proletarian concerns be, at least for the moment, put aside.

In two stories set outside New York City Shaw is not so sanguine about America's potential for national sacrifice. Both "Free Conscience, Void of Offence" and "The City Was in Total Darkness" emphasize the selfishness of the prewar upper middle classes.

The first story takes place in the autumn of 1938 at Trent's Inn, a historic New England restaurant-bar. The title is derived from a sign on the lawn outside the inn: "Free conscience, void of offence, 1840." Its narrative focus is Margaret Clay, a thoughtful 20-year-old college woman, and her playboy father. When Mr. Clay comments to Trent about the unusual sign, the proprietor significantly responds: "It came with the place, . . . I didn't have the heart to take it down" (*FD*, 138). Trent has no idea of what the sign might have once meant.

Margaret has asked her father to meet with her at the inn so she can tell him that she wants to leave the exclusive girls' school she attends. The overheard conversation of other people, especially a group of sophisticates at the next table praising Neville Chamberlain and a party of middle-aged people celebrating a football victory by Columbia over Yale, functions as an ironic background for Margaret's debate with Mr. Clay.

Much of the story simply characterizes Margaret Clay and her father through their dialogue. When Margaret announces that she wishes to leave school, her father automatically assumes that a boy is involved. He adds that Margaret can tell him all about it since he has "been around." Her response indicates a long-standing practice of reluctant acceptance of her father: "I know my father's been around, . . . The headwaiters' delight. . . . I don't mind it, . . . In fact, I like it. It makes me feel I come from durable yet light-footed stock. Every time I see your picture with one of those girls in a mink coat, I feel proud. Honest" (*FD*, 138).

There is, in fact, no boy involved; instead, in the world of 1938, Margaret's girls' school simply seems irrelevant to her: "The French novel, Elizabethan poetry, *exclusive* of the drama—remote, remote, the world's racing by" (*FD*, 139). Her father does not understand her and insists that she should stay in school because it offers protection. Looking out at the sign, Margaret answers, "I don't want to be afforded protection, . . . I want to be easily swayed. . . . 'Free conscience, void of offence, 1840.' That's the nicest thing about this whole place" (*FD*, 139). Margaret understands, as her father cannot, that the gathering storm in Europe makes 1938 a time for "conscience" and commitment, not protection and hedonistic selfishness.

The story's background conversation emphasizes the degree to which Margaret is isolated in her awareness. As the story opens a woman named Mrs. Taylor is at the bar drinking a toast "To my good friend Neville Chamberlain" (*FD*, 136). Earlier Mrs. Taylor had been in with another man, but she is now holding hands with her husband. The Taylors are with a party of celebrants, most noticeably a man named Oliver who seems more "confident" than the other men he is with, "as though he had more money in the bank than any of his friends" (*FD*, 137). Increasingly, Margaret notices the faces of the other men in the restaurant, "the faces of her friends' fathers. . . . The mouths, assured, arrogant, superior, because the men had never found a place in the last forty years of their lives where they hadn't made themselves at home, felt themselves superior. They were the faces of businessmen ready to assume responsibility, give orders, watch machines run for them, money be counted for them" (*FD*, 140). Soon Margaret cannot help being aware of the homage to Chamberlain coming from the Taylor-Oliver table, and she is further distracted by the entrance of a new party "loudly celebrating Columbia's 27–14 football win" over Yale.

Her feelings of isolation and despair are soon intensified when a "fat man" from the football party begins loudly singing "Heigh-ho, heigh-ho, I joined the CIO, I pay my dues to a bunch of Jews, heigh-ho, heigh-ho!" and the other middle-aged males at the inn, including her father, join him (*FD*, 142). Now she carefully examines her father's face, which is "like the faces of the fathers of her friends, the men who had graduated from the good colleges around 1910 and had gone on to stand at the head of businesses, committees, charity organizations, lodges, lobbies, political parties, who got brick red when they thought of the income tax, who said, "That lunatic in the White House" (*FD*, 142). Abruptly, Margaret realizes that there is no possibility for meaningful conversation with her father and stands up to leave, saying "I don't feel like eating here" (*FD*, 142–43).

The effectiveness of the story comes from Shaw's subtle paralleling of Margaret's isolation, the result of awareness and conviction, with the self-centered, mindless isolationism of the American middle class. The smug, self-centered American middle class is willfully ignorant of the destruction into which the world is about to be plunged. American anti-Semitism, capitalistic selfishness, and middle-class drunken hedonism prevent these people from any meaningful exercise of conscience. As the references to the CIO and FDR indicate, "Free Conscience, Void of Offence" is written from a distinctly leftist perspective. The element of hope that slightly ameliorates its dominant pessimism parallels the optimism that emerges at the end of "Night, Birth and Opinion": a new generation of integrity and conviction, personified by Margaret Clay, may rescue America from the corruption of its middle-aged middle class. Margaret's insistence upon leaving Trent's Inn may signal a new birth of honest conviction.

Margaret's identification with the intriguing sign on the lawn with its 1840 date indicates that she is more truly representative of American traditions than are her father, Mrs. Taylor, Oliver, and "the fat man." The sign recalls the legacy of American intellectual commitment to social justice represented by such mid–nineteenth-century figures as Emerson, Thoreau, and Whitman. Still, the story's concluding paragraph brings the reader jarringly back to the cynicism of the years just prior to World War II: "This was in the autumn of 1938, the year Columbia beat Yale 27–14 in the first game of the season" (*FD*, 143). Two of America's greatest academic institutions are playing football and producing arrogant, self-centered businessmen while Europe is engulfed in injustice and brutality.

A comparable tone of anger and pessimism dominates "The City Was in Total Darkness," a story focusing on characters involved in the motion picture industry. Its focal character is a bitter, disillusioned Hollywood writer named Dutcher, who is strongly reminiscent of *The Young Lions'* Michael Whitacre. The central incident of the story is a trip from Los Angeles to Tijuana that Dutcher makes with another writer named Machamer, Machamer's girl, Dolly, and an "actress" named Maxine. Machamer convinces Maxine to be Dutcher's "companion" on the trip. As in "Free Conscience, Void of Offence," Shaw uses background conversation for ironic emphasis of the story's thematic concerns.

The first part of the story emphasizes Dutcher's boredom and self-contempt. He is initially shown drinking at a bar and listening to the conversation of those around him. One voice repeatedly asserts that Hitler will not be able to start a war because "he has no oil" (*FD*, 150).

Wishing to escape such global concerns, Dutcher accepts Machamer's Tijuana invitation because he wants a "startling adventure" (*FD*, 151). He is, in fact, attempting to flee a recurrent vision of a young German bomber pilot who is about to attack a heroic Polish cavalryman. Until Machamer arrives, Dutcher attempts to distract himself from this troubling vision by staring at a woman at the bar "who had long black hair and tremendous full breasts that jutted out like pennants in front of her" (*FD*, 151). This attempt, however, only serves to intensify Dutcher's self-contempt: "I ought to be ashamed, Dutcher thought. The reader of Spinoza, the admirer of John Milton, the advocate of moral and economic reforms, a sufferer from general and indiscriminate lust ten times daily at the sight of a face, a ruffle, at the sound of a woman's laugh." Without conviction, he attempts to justify his contradictory natures: "We live on two planes" (*FD*, 152). He tries to convince himself that his superficiality is the result of his environment and remembers the absurdly trite and superficial film he is working on, *Murder at Midnight:* "Hollywood, you could always blame everything on Hollywood. That was the nicest thing about Hollywood" (*FD*, 152). A writer, he lapses into a triteness quite appropriate for *Murder at Midnight* when trying to block out the haunting image of the German bomber pilot and the Polish cavalryman, an image that represents the only "sacred" element in Dutcher's overwhelmingly "profane" consciousness. Still Dutcher, knowing that Hollywood cannot serve as a scapegoat for his own failures, returns to the "two planes" concept: "Sacred and profane, . . . [t]hat's the whole explanation" (*FD*, 152).

Dutcher makes a ludicrous attempt to merge the "sacred" and "profane" by imagining the face of the "actress" Machamer has found for him: "A face for the weekend . . . a face tragic and tortured by the guilt of a slaughtering and slaughtered world" (*FD*, 153). It is only appropriate, then, that Maxine's face looks "as though it had been created in God's mind with a careful smear of lipstick already on it" (*FD*, 154). The girl's empty, superficial face provokes another trite, "Hollywood" reaction in Dutcher: "Tonight I want to be everything . . . mean, angry, noble, gracious, lordly, docile, everything. I want my emotions to be engaged. I can't love her, I can't make her love me, but I can make her angry at me and then win her over, then . . ." (*FD*, 155). He then deliberately insults and provokes Maxine.

During the drive to Tijuana, Dutcher luxuriates in a mood of self-centered despair that is intensified by the voice from Berlin broadcast over the car radio, which announces that "[t]he city is in total darkness. . . . There is constant troop movement at the Berlin radio stations and trains are pouring toward the Polish frontier." The announcement is followed by a band playing "Begin the Beguine" (*FD,* 155). External reality is now beginning to conform to Dutcher's consciousness. Imminent world-scale tragedy and horror are momentarily suppressed by triteness—the profane subdues the sacred. A national mood of suicidal illusion is again stressed when Dutcher and his companions make a brief stop at a bar in San Diego, where they encounter a young sailor from Arkansas who has the "guarantee" of his congressman that America will not enter the war (*FD,* 156). The sailor's unrealistic faith in his congressman exemplies the mistaken belief that America can simply ignore the war in Europe.

After leaving the bar, they go to the Square Deal Waffle Shop, where Maxine learns in the women's room that England has just declared war on Germany: "That's how I found out, Dutcher thought. In the ladies' room in a waffle shop in San Diego, a woman told an actress from Republic, who drank too much wine in New York, that the English declared war on Germany, and that's how I found out" (*FD,* 157). After her stunning announcement, Maxine begins loudly berating the waitress for giving her a dirty fork: "They'll get away with murder . . . if you let them" (*FD,* 157). The pathetic, shallow woman cannot realize that she has just brought news of the beginning of a time of large-scale real murder and technological slaughter beyond human comprehension. The tragic is almost engulfed in profane superficiality and triteness.

For Dutcher, there is now no escape from the presence of death, from the image that haunts him: "The cavalryman in Poland now lay across the dusty Polish road, his mouth open in surprise and death and his dead horse beside him and the boy in the German bomber flew back to Warsaw saying to himself, 'One more time. I came back one more time'" (*FD,* 159). In Tijuana, the presence of death becomes immediate when Machamer tells Dutcher that he has planned the whole trip just for Dolly, who is dying of Bright's disease: "I don't love her. . . . I tell her I do, but . . . I like other girls. . . . I tell her I do. She doesn't want to lose an hour" (*FD,* 160). Although Machamer is capable of generosity to Dolly, he, like Dutcher, lacks the capacity for the kind of commitment on which love must rest. In him, too, the profane is stronger than the sacred.

Dolly's impending death makes Dutcher confront directly the outbreak of the long anticipated war—he heardly felt it, he thinks, but knows that "we'll feel it later" (*FD*, 160). In bed alone, Dutcher's epiphany continues: "The war was on, and it was on here, too, among these idle, unbombed, frivolous people. I'd stay here in Hollywood, Dutcher thought, if I could bear *Murder at Midnight* and all the Murders at Midnight to come. I don't want to write any more books. An honest book is a criticism. Why should I torture myself into criticizing this poor, corrupt, frantic, tortured, agony-stricken world? Later, let the criticism come later" (*FD*, 160). Instead, Dutcher fantasizes about getting married, buying a farm, and involving himself in the "eternal motion" of the seasons (*FD*, 161). The reader feels that Dutcher will, in fact, do nothing fundamentally different. Earlier in the story Maxine has revealingly read Dutcher's palm: "You're fickle, jealous, selfish. . . . and in the long run, you're not going to be very successful" (*FD*, 158). Maxine's "criticism" is "honest"—Dutcher has submerged himself in the profane for so long that he is incapable of a conversion to the sacred.

"The City Was in Total Darkness" is the bleakest and most pessimistic of Shaw's fictional warnings against fascism. Its Hollywood characters have compromised with the trite and superficial for so long that they are incapable of a meaningful response to the tragedy around them. Shaw is especially effective in juxtaposing linguistic references to petty "murders" with Dutcher's recurring vision of the young German bomber pilot and the heroic Polish cavalryman. Still, despite the bitter pessimism of the story and the brutality of "Sailor off the Bremen," a tone of poignant nostalgia dominates these prewar stories. They depict a world in which moral choices, even if reluctantly made, are clear and obvious.

Anti-Semitism

Not surprisingly, throughout his career Shaw, a Jew, wrote fiction protesting anti-Semitism in America and Europe. He sometimes, but not always, relates oppression of Jews worldwide to the torture and execution of Jews by the Nazis. These stories range in tone from militant anger to thoughtful forgiveness and in setting from Czarist Russia to post–World War II Austria. The most militant of them, "Residents of Other Cities," which seems to advocate violent revenge by victims of anti-Semitism, is set in 1918 in revolution-torn Kiev. The 16-year-old narrator recounts the horrible vulnerability of Kiev's Jewish residents as control of the city switches chaotically from the Bolsheviks to the

Cossacks: *"The city changed hands many times as the war rocked around it, and the full record of those changes could be read in the eyes of the Jewish residents"* (*SS*, 124).

The story establishes a "debate" between Daniel, the secular, artistic narrator, and his otherworldly father about the proper reaction to the atrocities committed by the Cossacks. In the first part of the story, Daniel objects to his father's religiosity, primarily because he perceives it as an unnatural denial of life: "I didn't believe in my father's prayers. My father was always at the side of God and he neglected life. I hated his insane holiness, this neglect of flesh, the denial of the present for eternity" (*SS*, 130). The unbelievability of the father's inhuman forgiveness is, in fact, a central flaw in the story. When the Cossacks first enter Daniel's home, according to Daniel, they threaten to gang-rape his 19-year-old Aunt Sara while "My father, thin and tall, stood looking dreamily at the ceiling, pulling from time to time on his little beard" (*SS*, 127).

At this point in the story, Daniel's political commitment to and identification with his people is incomplete. When the Cossack sergeant asks him if he is a Bolshevik, he maintains a stance of apolitical aestheticism: "'I'm a painter,' I said. I said it proudly, even then" (*SS*, 128). Soon, Daniel becomes involved with his people because their oppressors assault the house 19 times in the course of one day, torturing the inhabitants with the constant threat of death. Twice, they beat Daniel and his father and strip two of the young women completely naked and make them stand "for all to see." Still, the father merely says after the second violation, "God's will be done. They will suffer finally" (*SS*, 131). Daniel, in contrast, does not want to wait for a hypothetical revenge: "Vengeance, I thought, listening to the women of my family cry; feeling the bruises stiffen where I had been beaten, sighing, as I moved and cuts opened and bled into my clotted clothes, vengeance, vengeance" (*SS*, 132). His father cries only when one of the assailants shaves off his beard with a bayonet.

The story reaches its climax when Kirov, a neighbor, offers Daniel and his family sanctuary, and instead, in a cold basement, Kirov and five male members of his family torture and brutalize those whom they have promised to hide. Sara is gang-raped, and her husband, Samuel, is murdered while trying to protect her. At this point Daniel's apolitical stance vanishes completely as he plans an immediate and personal revenge: "I kept alive by planning, with cold reason and ingenuity, torture, mutilation for the men in that room" (*SS*, 135). When the Bolsheviks are again in charge of the town, Daniel has the opportunity he desires—a Bolshevik captain gives him a gun and offers him help in tracking down the Kirovs. Incredibly, the father attempts to protect his victimizers: "It is not our part to punish" (*SS*, 138). Daniel's mother, however, tells her son and the Red soldier accompanying him where the Kirovs are. After finding them, Daniel systematically executes the six Kirovs.

"Residents of Other Cities" is perhaps a prime example of the kind of Shaw story that Chester E. Eisinger finds irresponsible. The logic of its plot advocates an Old Testament code of vengeance, but it is important to note that Daniel's execution of the Kirovs does not provide him the satisfaction he has anticipated: "I felt disappointed and cold and let down. . . . The balances were not even. They had died too easily. They had not suffered enough pain. They had come off best in the bargain, finally" (*SS*, 140). First collected in *Sailor off the Bremen*, "Residents of Other Cities" can perhaps best be approached as a companion work to that volume's title story. Shaw was saying, in the late 1930s, that fascism and anti-Semitism had to be forcefully resisted. Any attempt to ignore these forces or confront them peacefully and intellectually constituted a form of suicide. The story seems written not so much to advocate Daniel's final action as to depict the fallacies of both his initial apolitical stance and his father's abstract religiosity.

Shaw could not, of course, ignore American anti-Semitism, and "Select Clientele" focuses on the growth of prejudice against Jews in America and its implications for the American writer. The story's focal characters are Max and Sam, two American writers staying at a rural New York writers' colony. While out bicycling the two men encounter a group of bullies who call them "a coupla Jews from old lady Spear's free-love colony" and hurl stones at them (*SS*, 547–48).

Max is not Jewish, but he is outraged by the incident: "I left Berlin, I left Vienna, . . . I thought I wouldn't see any more things like that. It must be a terrible thing to be a Jew" (*SS*, 548). Sam is Jewish, and his anger intensifies as he remembers selling stories to magazines that carry ads for resort hotels and specify " 'Distinguished clientele' or 'Exclusive clientele' or 'select clientele' " : "A hotel advertises that its clientele is exclusive . . . if it allows in everybody but six million Jews and fifteen million Negroes" (*SS*, 549).

Max tells Sam that he should write about American anti-Semitism, but his Jewish friend responds with anger that turns into a self-defeating bitterness: "Sam laughed. 'The world stinks. People are terrible and there is only despair. Should I write that? Who gets any good out of it? Why should I tell it?'" (*SS*, 549). His anger is not appeased even after he, Max, and a colony handyman, armed with pitchforks and a baseball bat, confront the four bullies and extract an apology. Sam decides that he is going to Hollywood: "I want to write about things that never happened and people that never happened. I need a vacation" (*SS*, 552).

"Select Clientele" is not a truly successful story because the plot is too forced and arbitrary. Sam is, nevertheless, an interesting study of the Jewish-American Writer so embittered by his country's anti-Semitism that he can no longer produce interesting work. Ironically, Max sees the necessity of the artist's protest against prejudice and discrimination. Sam's assertion that "people are terrible" prefigures his final decision to retreat to the superficiality of Hollywood. In both instances Sam attempts to deny his artistic responsibility to his nation and his people. Irwin Shaw's position, of course, was identical to Max's.

The characterization of Noah Ackerman in *The Young Lions* illustrates that Shaw found in World War II a powerful background for protest fiction, and two of his most famous stories dealing with anti-Semitism occur in the late stages of that conflict. "Retreat," which takes place during a momentary delay in the German retreat from Paris, is essentially a debate between a German major and a Jewish man named Segal. The major is described as an ordinary, unexceptional man: "under the warlike dust his face was tired and quiet and intellectual, not good-looking, but studious and reasonable, the face of a man who read after business hours and occasionally went to concerts without being pushed into it by his wife" (*FD*, 236). The major superficially resembles one of Shaw's "gentle people," yet in his acceptance of German atrocities against the Jews and other residents of occupied France, he has forfeited any claim to decency, the most important characteristic of the "gentle people." Segal, a musician, can be viewed as an adult prototype of the young painter, Daniel (from "Residents of Other Cities"). He is tormented by a need for revenge so strong that he cannot simply dismiss it.

With the German cause on the brink of defeat, the major attempts to excuse his participation in Nazi atrocities. Spotting Segal sitting at an outdoor café, he approaches the Parisian Jew and asks to have a drink with him. Old habits die hard, and the major reminds Segal that

Jews are forbidden to enter French cafés. He tells Segal that he is "very brave" but asks if a drink is worth the risk of deportation. Segal responds, "It isn't for the drink . . . Maybe you won't understand, but I was born in Paris, I've lived all my life in the cafés, on the boulevards" (*FD*, 237).

Dropping the mode of mock intimidation, the major attempts to excuse himself from guilt for the Nazi atrocities to the Jews: "The army knew nothing about it . . . I, myself, have never lifted my hand, or done one bad thing against any Jew in Germany or Poland or here in France. At this point, it is necessary to judge accurately who did what." Segal calmly rejects his excuse: "Why is it necessary?" (*FD*, 238). Segal's unspoken point is that the Germans did not concern themselves with fine, individual distinctions when they sentenced millions of Jews to death. Segal informs the major that the Germans, through their systematic and sustained anti-Semitic propaganda, have, in fact, cultivated a legacy of hate that may last forever: "The Germans have various accomplishments to their credit, and this is another one" (*FD*, 239). Finally, the major admits defeat in the debate: "Yes, we're guilty. Granted, we're guilty. Some of us are more guilty than the rest. What are we to do now? What can I do to wash my hands?" (*FD*, 241). Segal, speaking "for the first Jew brained on a Munich street long ago and the last American brought to earth that afternoon by a sniper's bullet outside Chartres, and for all the years and all the dead and all the agony in between," answers "wearily, . . . 'You can cut your throat . . . and see if the blood will take the stain out'" (*FD*, 241–42).

Chester E. Eisinger sees "Retreat" as proof that Shaw is "a vigorous and implacable hater . . . "[who] writes about the Germans as though he were cutting them to pieces, systematically and joyfully. No reconciliation is possible, in his view, with the German mind" (Eisinger, 109). This assessment seems, among other things, to ignore the logic of fiction. It would be asking a great deal indeed to expect a Parisian Jew in the last stages of World War II to be open to immediate and total "reconciliation . . . with the German mind." Most importantly, "Retreat" is an exploration of the concept of cumulative guilt, a concept that would dominate Black American fiction in the 1960s. The story asks if indirect, even passive, acquiescence in evil does not itself constitute a form of evil, and the story answers in the affirmative. Of course, the major's acquiescence, as shown in his initial mock-threatening stance with Segal, has not been entirely passive. Certainly the Holocaust has made the question of cumulative guilt central to the last half of the twentieth century. It does, in fact, seem too easy to let the major simply "wash his hands" and walk away from responsibility for a world drenched in horror.

Revenge and violence by the victimized against their oppressors are explicitly rejected in "Act of Faith," one of Shaw's best and most frequently anthologized stories. Much like the ending of *The Young Lions*, its conclusion affirms that human decency continues to exist in the world that will be ushered in by the end of the war. In that way, it introduces a new hopefulness into Shaw's protests against anti-Semitism.

The story focuses on the bond between three American soldiers, Welch, Olson, and Norman Seeger, who are in France waiting to be shipped home after the fighting has ended. The story emphasizes the ordinariness of the three. About Olson, Shaw writes: "He had a high, childish voice and a pretty face. He was very good-natured, and had a girl waiting for him at the University of California, where he intended to finish his course at government expense when he got out of the army" (*FD*, 244). Welch is described as a deceptively angry-looking, good-natured young man from a large family. Seeger, "a large, lanky boy," is "cheerful and dependable" and a competent, courageous soldier (*FD*, 244). Seeger's Jewishness is all that potentially separates the three.

When the story opens, Olson and Welch are attempting to convince Seeger to sell a German Luger that he has won in combat so that the three will have enough money to enjoy their leave in Paris. Because the Luger has a special significance for him, Seeger hesitates. He had killed its previous owner, "an enormous SS major" (*FD*, 248), in Coblenz and had intended to take the gun home with him "as a kind of vague, half-understood sign to himself that justice had once been done and he had been its instrument" (*FD*, 253). Seeger's hesitation about parting with the weapon is soon intensified by a long letter from home, which introduces a central concern of the story.

The letter, from Seeger's father, is a bitter, painful account of virulent anti-Semitism in America. Shaw juxtaposes Seeger's reading of the letter with Olson's and Welch's descriptions of the glories of Paris. The letter initially informs Seeger of the paranoia that is destroying his brother, Jacob. Jacob received a medical discharge after being "pretty badly wounded in the leg at Metz." Far worse than his leg wound is a special form of "combat fatigue" from which he now suffers. He crouches behind the living room window looking out for "the new rocket bombs [designed exclusively] for the Jews" (*FD*, 250). Jacob is certain that soon "they are coming for the Jews." His father does not know everything that happened to him in the war but he does know that Jacob "has devoured all the concentration camp reports" and the news of massacres of Jewish refugees in the Middle East (*FD*, 249–50).

After describing his son's psychological destruction, the father gives an account of his own paranoia, induced and accelerated by events in the States. Introducing the account with a reference to Jacob's terror: "The terrible thing is, Norman, that I find myself coming to believe that it is not neurotic for a Jew to behave like this today," he then details the growing American horror: "Wherever you go these days—restaurants, hotels, clubs, trains—you seem to hear talk about the Jews, mean, hateful, murderous talk. . . . The day that Roosevelt died I heard a drunken man yelling outside a bar, 'Finally, they got the Jew out of the White House.' And some of the people who heard him merely laughed and nobody stopped him. And on V-E Day, in celebration, hoodlums in Los Angeles savagely beat a Jewish writer" (*FD*, 251). Moreover, anti-Semitism is having a direct and personal impact. The father tells about an incident at his Thursday night poker game. A friend suddenly proclaimed that "the Jews were getting much out of this war," and when Mr. Seeger demanded an apology, he saw that none of his long-time friends were on his side. "I know the poison was spreading from Germany before the war and during it, but I had not realized it had come so close," he comments (*FD*, 250–51).

Worst of all, Mr. Seeger writes, he is starting to feel self-hatred: "And I hate to see Jewish names on important committees, and hate to read of Jews fighting for the poor, the oppressed, the cheated and hungry. . . . And, most hateful of all, I find myself looking for Jewish names in the casualty lists and secretly being glad when I discover them there, to prove that there at least, among the dead and wounded, we belong" (*FD*, 251). Finally, he writes, he fears that Jews are becoming boring, that "they are making demands upon the rest of the world by being killed, they are disturbing everyone by being hungry and asking for the return of their property" (*FD*, 251–52).

Mr. Seeger's letter is a tour de force because it allows Shaw to describe specific examples of American anti-Semitism and, more importantly, the form of psychic suicide the father is experiencing. A part of

Mr. Seeger wants to prove that he is a good American who, like everyone else apparently, hates Jews. Shaw achieves a powerful ironic effect by juxtaposing the details of Mr. Seeger's letter with Olson's and Welch's intonations of the glories of Paris. After reading the letter, Seeger knows that now he too has to think about what awaits him at home.

Not surprisingly, he is now more reluctant to surrender the Luger than he had been. He abruptly realizes why he has sometimes seemed a heroic figure to the suffering, tortured Jewish inhabitants of Europe. "A large young man in the uniform of the liberator, blood, as they thought, of their blood, but not in hiding, not quivering in fear and helplessness, but striding secure and victorious down the street, armed and capable of inflicting terrible destruction on his enemies" (*FD*, 253). His father's letter makes him remember all the stories he has heard of prejudice in the U.S. Army, as well as his own actual encounters with it. Seeger feels that he can no longer be certain about just who his "enemies" are, and he resolves not to be destroyed like his brother Jacob: "if the mobs were coming down the street toward his house, he was not going to die singing and praying" (*FD*, 253). For a moment, then, Seeger echoes the 16-year-old Daniel from"Residents of Other Cities."

Shaw ends "Act of Faith" on an affirmative note—with an act of faith. Welch and Olson tentatively and sensitively retract their request that Seeger sell the Luger, and the young Jewish-American remembers all that the three have meant to each other in the war. Suddenly, he knows that he will, in fact, sell the gun: "Seeger peered at the faces of his friends. He would have to rely upon them, later on, out of uniform, on their native streets, more than he had ever relied on them on the bullet-swept street and in the dark minefield in France" (*FD*, 256). Seeger chooses to make a commitment to the promise and hope of postwar brotherhood. The story's ending constitutes a moment of conversion to a secular religion based on trust and acceptance. It is a tribute to Shaw's skill in writing fiction that, after the extended passage devoted to recapitulating Mr. Seeger's letter, Norman's conversion is believable. Seeger chooses essentially to make a commitment based on immediate empirical evidence—Olson and Welch have proven themselves, under the most brutal of circumstances, to be good friends and decent men. This experience, the young Jewish-American decides, is more real than the catalog of horrors contained in his father's letter. It is, of course, symbolically important that Norman decides to get rid of the weapon he has acquired by killing the enemy. He willingly surrenders an instrument of war and potential revenge in the name of peace and forgiveness.

Clearly, "Act of Faith" represents a significant shift from Shaw's fictional response to anti-Semitism in "Residents of Other Cities." This evolution is also evident in "The Inhabitants of Venus," another masterful story set in Europe after the war. Brilliantly adapted as a PBS television special in 1979, the story treats the postwar reactions of Robert Rosenthal, an American citizen born in France, to a traumatic prewar experience. The setting is a Swiss ski resort, and the tone is initially light and comic. Rosenthal, a Jew, is vacationing at the ski resort with Mac, a friend. Mac is the source of most of the opening humor and lightheartedness: "Mac was a lieutenant on leave from his outfit in Germany. He had been in Europe nearly three years and to show that he was not just an ordinary tourist, called all pretty Italian girls Contessa" (*FD*, 527). When the story opens, Rosenthal and Mac are on a crowded ski lift waiting to take their turn down the slopes and enjoying the lift's atmosphere of "generalized cordiality" (*FD*, 528). Robert is especially entertained by the conversation of a group of young Americans beside him and begins a flirtatious conversation with one of the young female members of the American party: "She had on a black, fuzzy, lambskin hat, and she looked like a high-school drum majorette pretending to be Anna Karenina" (*FD*, 529).

Abruptly, the story's opening mood is shattered when Rosenthal overhears a German voice making disparaging comments about Americans. Initially, he attempts to ignore the voice and cling to the sense of goodwill and harmony he has been feeling: "he could let it slide, along with many of the other things that Germans had said during his lifetime" (*FD*, 531). But he cannot "let it slide." The hate-filled voice increasingly disturbs him and occasions an extended negative passage about the German people. Robert first reflects on the presence of German tourists in Switzerland: "[German] men and women both pushed more than was necessary in the lift lines, with a kind of impersonal egotism, a racial, unquestioning assumption of precedence. When they skied, they did it grimly, in large groups, as if under military orders" (*FD*, 531). He then remembers that for him V-E Day was "a personal liberation" from the Germans, "a kind of graduation ceremony from a school in which he had been forced to spend long years, trying to solve a single, boring, painful problem" (*FD*, 531–32). Next, he reflects that at resorts the Germans act like "sun gluttons . . . greedily absorbing each precious ray of sunlight. It was as though they came from a country perpetually covered in mist, like the planet Venus, and had to soak up as much brightness and life as possible in the short periods of their holidays to be able to endure the harshness and gloom of their homeland and the conduct of the other inhabitants of Venus for the rest of the year" (*FD*, 532).

Gradually, Robert's focus narrows to the man whose voice introduced the note of discord on the ski lift, and he notices that "the man had on a white cap of the kind that had been worn by the Afrika Corps during the war" (*FD*, 533). When the adopted American looks closely at the man's face, he feels certain that he will have to kill the German.

This feeling occasions a flashback, which constitutes the heart of the story, to "the winter of 1938" when Rosenthal was 14. Then, also at a Swiss resort, Robert, foolishly attempting a dangerous, isolated slope by himself, had fallen and broken a leg. Lying in the snow unable to move, he had realized that he would freeze to death unless help came. Somewhat miraculously, help had come in the form of a lone skier, who had stopped beside the fallen boy: "'You are a stupid little boy,' the man [had] said severely in clipped, educated German. 'And very lucky. I am the last man on the mountain'" (*FD*, 535). Soon, the German's words had taken on a bitter irony for Robert. Hearing that Robert's last name was Rosenthal, "the rescuer" had left the Jewish boy alone to freeze. Robert had crawled slowly and painfully in search of help. Just as he had been ready to surrender to exhaustion, he had been found by a peasant.

Later Robert's father had decided not to try to find the German who had left his son to die. His reason for this decision recalls Mr. Seeger's letter in "Act of Faith": "There's plenty of Nazis in Switzerland, of all nationalities . . . and this will just give them more ammunition, they'll be able to say, 'See, wherever the Jews go they start trouble'" (*FD*, 541). Mr. Rosenthal, like Mr. Seeger, is afraid that the victimized will annoy the world with stories of their victimization.

When the narration shifts back to the postwar present tense, the reader learns that the belligerent German on the ski lift is the man who, years before, had left Robert to freeze in the snow. Robert's need to kill the man now becomes immediate and concrete. It is the direct result of a personal injury, rather than an abstract prejudice. Still, Robert cannot separate his trauma of 1938 from all the horror that has since engulfed the world:

He hated [the German] for the attempted murder of a fourteen-year-old boy in 1938; he hated him for the acts that he must have condoned or collaborated in during the war; . . . he hated him because he was here, bringing the idea of death and shamefully unconsummated vengeance into this silvery holiday bubble climbing the placid air of a kindly, welcoming country. . . . The German deprived him of a sense of normalcy. . . . The German sent him back through the years to an older and truer normality—murder, blood, flight, conspiracy, pillage, and ruins. (*FD*, 542)

He thinks about his need to kill the man as an inescapable obligation: "When the war was over, he had been secretly thankful that he had been spared the necessity of killing. Now he understood—he was not to be spared; his war was not over" (*FD*, 543). But as he waits to trap the German, the anticipated act begins to seem something other than a mere duty: "For the first time in his life he understood the profound, sensual pleasure of destruction" (*FD*, 545).

Seeing the German clearly outside the ski lift, Robert is startled to learn that the man has lost a leg and immediately feels "a bitter sense of loss . . . [b]ecause he knew he was not strong enough to murder a cripple, to punish the already punished" (*FD*, 545). Finally the war is over for Robert, who "knew there was nothing more to be done, nothing more to wait for, except a cold, hopeless, everlasting forgiveness" (*FD*, 545).

"The Inhabitants of Venus" is the story of Robert Rosenthal's belated individual armistice. He realizes however reluctantly, that hate must be abandoned. Seeing the crippled German makes him remember his own helplessness when he lay with a broken leg awaiting a seemingly inevitable death, and he understands that present violence cannot erase the pain of the past. Like "Act of Faith," the story raises the issue of Old Testament vengeance only to reject it. Robert Rosenthal chooses not to do what Daniel of "Residents of Other Cities" does.

The early extended description of German arrogance is an instance of what Eisinger and other critics see as Shaw's "vigorous and implacable" hatred of the Germans. Again, it is necessary to remember fictional logic—the passage reproduces the thought processes of a Jew who has been personally victimized by German anti-Semitism. Such a man might well have a great deal of hatred pent up inside.

The story's title is symbolically important, implying that those who perpetrated the Holocaust are simply incomprehensible in terms of normal human standards; they indeed seem like "inhabitants" of another planet. "The Inhabitants of Venus" is ultimately not as affirmative as "Act of Faith"; it ends not with an expectation of a new world of brotherhood, but with a grudging acceptance of the necessity of "a cold, hopeless, everlasting forgiveness." The oldest "normalities" are "murder, blood, flight, conspiracy, pillage, and ruins."

The War and Its Aftermath

The "murder, blood, flight, conspiracy, pillage, and ruins" of "The Inhabitants of Venus," the "normalities" of the 1940s and 1950s, pervaded Shaw's fiction during those decades and afterward. World War II, the subsequent attempt to establish a Jewish homeland in the Middle East, and postwar McCarthyism in America are the subject matter of some of his most memorable stories from this period. In these stories, human decency is under constant and severe threat, but it is never quite eradicated.

The War Stories

Shaw served in a noncombatant status during World War II. He was present during such major events of the war as the invasion of France and the liberation of Paris, though he saw no actual combat. Not surprisingly, then, his war stories are not combat stories. They focus instead on soldiers waiting between battles and members of the French Resistance. Two of the war stories, "Walking Wounded" and "Gunners' Passage," rank with the best of Shaw's short fiction.

Shaw described "Walking Wounded," which won the 1944 O. Henry Memorial Award First Prize, as "one of the best things I've ever done" (see Giles interview in part 2). The story, set in Cairo, describes the stress and mental exhaustion of Peter, a soldier from Scotland who has been stationed in Egypt for three years. It opens with Peter waking up the morning after a drunken brawl with a British major and two lieutenants. After Mac, a friend and fellow soldier, helps him remember the senseless events of the previous night, he exclaims in bewilderment, "Mac, this is the first time anything like this ever happened to me." Mac calmly replies, "I know" (*FD*, 204). It is becoming obvious to those around Peter that he is close to some kind of breakdown. The relentless tedium of an army desk job, the suffocating atmosphere of Cairo in wartime, and three years away from his wife have stretched his nerves to the breaking point.

Later, trying to work at his desk, he is still assaulted by the pressures of his environment: "The heat of Egypt was like the inside of a balloon . . . and flies, the true owners of Egypt, whirled cleverly and maliciously before his eyes" (*FD*, 204–5). He hears a donkey braying outside, which "sounded like the death of all the animals of Egypt on this hot morning" (*FD*, 205). Away from actual combat, Peter still feels he is drowning in a suffocating atmosphere of death. Seeking solace outside the office by walking the streets and trying to think about his wife, Anne, he merely discovers another cause for despair. He realizes suddenly that he does not clearly remember Anne: "he remembered that he loved her. But her face, the sound of her voice . . . lost" (*FD*, 206). The horror of this realization is intensified by the poverty and ugliness surrounding him: "A horribly dirty woman with a horribly dirty child . . . followed him, whining for half a block," then he is accosted by "a tiny, filthy ten-year-old boy" demanding to know if he "wanna lady?" (*FD*, 206–7). The grotesque voices of the old Egyptian woman and the 10-year-old boy function as a savagely ironic commentary on his attempt to envision the distant woman he loves. Combat-free Cairo is so ugly and sordid that Peter begins to remember how happy he had been fighting in the desert: "There were no women in the desert, no reminders of a civilized and normal life. There was clean, sterile sand, the noise of armor, thousands of grumbling, good-humored men intimate with an equal death, and above all there was the sense of immense and hardy effort and accomplishment, as first they had held the Afrika Corps and then driven it back" (*FD*, 208).

If there were no women in the desert, there is no sense of comradeship and accomplishment in his present desk job. Back in the office, Mac, increasingly aware of his friend's desperation, suggests that Peter try to get a girl in Cairo. Peter considers Mac's suggestion and acknowledges to himself that he had been unfaithful to Anne when he was stationed in France. But now, he knows, things are different: "But when he'd got back to England with the gray-faced remnants of his regiment, after the hideous, bloody days of the break-through, and had taken his wife silently into his arms, all frivolity, all smallness and lack of faith had seemed wanton and irreligious in the face of so much ruin, such agony. Leaving England for Africa, he had felt that behind him he had to leave the best part of his life orderly and decent" (*FD*, 209). It is not simply female companionship, or even simple sexual release, that Peter most needs. He longs for a decent, normal life of love, family, and friendships. He yearns for life before the war, before the world was overwhelmed by blood and agony.

He, in fact, feels no little anger toward women in military zones: "Women . . . have been among the most horrible of the war's casualties. All humility's gone, all normal value, all friendship. They're man-greedy. They're profiteering on the war, like the worst usurer and manufacturer of machine tools, except that their profits are lieutenants and generals, not cash" (*FD*, 209). There are undeniable sexist overtones in this passage—why, after all, should women necessarily embody "humility" and "normal value"? Still, the passage contributes to the reader's understanding that Peter is most shaken by the loss of the familiar, stable world that he could comprehend and in which he could find security.

Peter does, however, let Mac arrange a date for him with a young woman named Joyce. He goes that night with Joyce and Mac and his girl for dinner and dancing at an exclusive Cairo hotel. Joyce, it turns out, confirms all Peter has thought about women in military zones. While they are dancing, she asks Peter to stay near the edge of the dance floor: "'I'd like people to see me.' . . . 'It's amazing,' she said, brightly and loudly, 'how many men I know in Cairo'" (*FD*, 210–11). Still, her mere presence inspires a "confession" from Peter that she cannot comprehend: "After France . . . I felt as though my wife had healed me of a dreadful disease. She healed me of mud and death and friends dying on all sides. She's most beautiful, but I don't remember what she looks like. She's very clean and simple and her voice is low, although I don't remember that, either. I sent her my photograph today" (*FD*, 211). Peter is very sure about one thing—Joyce is not Anne—and is relieved when she deserts him for a colonel.

Shaw briefly lightens the tone of the story when Peter flees the exclusive hotel for a bar where he meets some South African and American fliers who are discussing the advisability of Princess Elizabeth marrying an American. Their conversation provides Shaw with the opportunity to write some amusing drunken dialogue: "Excellent idea . . . Some upstanding representative citizen of the Republic. Post-war planning on all fronts. My nomination for Prince Escort is Maxie Rosenbloom" (*FD*, 214).

More importantly, the American fliers miraculously offer to fly Peter home for a leave. Almost unable to believe in such good fortune, Peter rushes immediately to the residence of his commanding officer, Colonel Foster, to ask for leave. Once there, he is told by a stranger named Colonel Gaines that Foster is gone. Gaines is obviously a decent man, but Peter is too disoriented and too embarrassed at waking the colonel in the middle of the night to ask him for a favor. Peter leaves, and the story ends with him standing sobbing, staring "across the river at the minaret, faithful and lovely in the light of the moon" (*FD*, 217).

"Walking Wounded" is a subtle, delicately constructed story. Shaw does a masterful job of conveying Peter's search for stability and the old order in a new, chaotic world. It is significant that all the other male characters in the story are depicted as kind and decent, but unable to offer Peter any meaningful help. Mac's attempt to distract Peter from his loneliness only produces more bitterness, and the American fliers' miraculous offer of a trip home results in an especially painful moment of disillusionment. Colonel Gaines embodies the crumbling British Empire: "He stood there, red-faced, huge, British, like a living Colonel Blimp, lonely and tired, with [a volume of] Robert Browning in the foreign night" (*FD*, 217). The story's subtext is that the future will be, for Peter, an extended "foreign night"; even if he is finally able to return home to the wife he cannot remember, the old, stable world will no longer be there.

"Gunners' Passage" won the O. Henry Memorial Award second prize in 1945; and Shaw has described it as "probably the *best* story I ever wrote" (see Giles interviews in part 2). Set in North Africa, it is a moving character study of three young American servicemen during a lull in combat. The narrative focus is 19-year-old Sergeant Stais, born in Minnesota of Greek descent; and the story is essentially told through his extended conversations with Whitejack, a North Carolinian whose "speech was Southern, but not the kind of Southern that puts a Northerner's teeth on edge" (*FD*, 221), and Novak, "a farm boy from Oklahoma" who has yet to face combat (*FD*, 224). The three are decent young Americans struggling to survive in the indecent, terrifying world of war. Their conversation focuses, then, on "girls" and other subjects that distract them from the horror surrounding them.

The story opens with Whitejack's reminiscences about Brazil: "In Brazil . . . the problem was girls. American girls" (*FD*, 221). He tells about his involvement with an American girl in Rio who was not physically attractive, but was openly interested in him: "Sometimes . . . a man feels mighty small if he just thinks of himself and turns down an appeal like that" (*FD*, 222). Soon, Whitejack's memory of the girl in Rio leads him to other reassuring memories of America. Specifically, he recalls attending the funeral in Asheville of Thomas Wolfe, his state's most famous writer: "There were a lot of important people from

New York and over to Chapel Hill down for the funeral and it was a hot day, too, and I'd never met the feller, but I felt it was only right to go to his funeral after readin' his book. And the whole town was there, very quiet, although just five years before they were yellin' to lynch him, and it was a sad and impressive sight and I'm glad I went" (*FD*, 223). Whitejack's account of his, and Asheville's, reaction to Wolfe's death emphasizes Shaw's faith in the inherent decency of the American people. Even if belatedly, America's "gentle people" do embrace their own. For Stais, the North Carolinian personifies the goodness of their nation: "Stais liked to listen to Whitejack. Whitejack talked about America, . . . and Whitejack's talk made his native country seem present and pleasantly real to him" (*FD*, 222).

Novak is writing a letter to a girl from "Flushing, Long Island" during the conversation. He tells Stais about the girl from Flushing who had first asked him for a date and then had gone out with him every night for three and a half weeks: "Nothing like that ever happened to me before in my life—a girl who just wanted to see me every night of the week" (*FD*, 229). When Novak had left to go overseas, the girl had given him a box of Schrafft's chocolates; and he writes her regularly even though she has written him that "she has a Technical Sergeant now." Novak seeks assurance from Stais that he is right in continuing his correspondence with her: "I haven't seen her in a year and a half and what's a girl to do? Do you blame her?" When Stais answers that he does not blame the girl, Novak offers a grateful apology: "I hope I haven't bored you" (*FD*, 229).

Paralleling Peter from "Walking Wounded," Novak is an American innocent thrust suddenly into a chaotic world of shifting, uncertain values and standards. Moreover, he attempts deliberately and consciously to preserve his innocence. When Whitejack tries to get him to acknowledge that the girl from Long Island is now the Technical Sergeant's girl, he refuses: "'I prefer it this way,' Novak said with dignity" (*FD*, 225).

Still, talk of girls and home cannot keep away the reality of the present for long. Novak insists that Stais tell him about his recent experience of being shot down in Greece and spending 14 days in the hills before being rescued by Greek farmers. Then, the frightened farm boy asks how it felt to "personally" shoot down German planes. Stais is unable to answer the question: "There was no way of telling these men, no way of remembering in words, himself. 'You'll find out,' he said. 'Soon enough. The sky's full of Germans' " (*FD*, 227). When Novak persists in asking if "guys" are afraid, Stais does have an answer: "You'll be afraid." The young Greek-American is, in fact, suffering, and trying to hide from Novak, the symptoms of battle fatigue: "Stais felt the old waving dizziness starting behind his eyes that the doctor in Cairo had said came from shock or starvation or exposure or all of these things, and lay back, still keeping his eyes open, as it became worse and waved more violently when he closed his eyes" (*FD*, 227).

Stais's experience in Greece is not all that brings the horror of the present home to the three young men. Novak is concerned about a change that seems to have come over the Lieutenant: "I used to think they never came better than the Lieutenant. . . . Now . . . If he does see you, he snaps at you like he was General George Patton" (*FD*, 224). Later, after the farm boy has left, Whitejack explains to Stais that the Lieutenant is faced with being forced to order the grounding of two men ("both good fellers, [but] not fighting men"): "He's twenty-two years old, the Lieutenant. It's a strain, something like that, for a man twenty-two years old" (*FD*, 232). The lieutenant is, like the three central characters, a decent, young man. In a world of violence and death, his gentleness becomes a source of pain and agony.

Whitejack has his own pain: two planes from his squadron had been shot down, 14 men had been killed, including a man named Frank Sloan with whom Whitejack had bitterly quarreled over a girl. The North Carolinian is still tortured by the guilt occasioned by Sloan's death.

Stais, Whitejack, and Novak separate; Stais goes to sleep, only to be shortly awakened by Whitejack. His friend has good news for Stais— because of his battle fatigue, Stais will be sent home that night. In contrast, for Whitejack, there is only more pain and anxiety. His best friend, Johnny Moffat, has not come in with the rest of the squadron. Hearing this, Stais is silent: "he had learned that there was nothing to say. He was only nineteen years old, but he learned that" (*FD*, 230). He simply listens as Whitejack talks about Johnny Moffat, who may marry his sister after the war: "There's nobody in the whole world I'd rather have living on my property than Johnny Moffat. I've known him for twenty years and I've had six fist fights with him and won them all, and been alone with him in the woods for two months at a time, and I still say that" (*FD*, 231).

Later, Stais says goodbye to Whitejack while boarding the plane to go home:

[Stais] "See you . . . in North Carolina."
[Whitejack] "Some October." (*FD*, 234).

In the world they now inhabit, no future can be anticipated with certainty. When Whitejack asks Stais if he thinks he will be sent out to fight again, Stais replies: "I wouldn't be surprised . . . There's nothing really wrong with me. I'm just tired" (*FD*, 231). Still, the story ends affirmatively when Johnny Moffat's plane lands as Stais's plane prepares to take off.

"Gunners' Passage" is an unashamedly sentimental story that avoids excess through Shaw's craft. Its three young central characters maintain and affirm their dignity in the face of the obscenity of death, while Shaw effectively understates the irony of their youth throughout the story. Their constant talk of "girls" cannot hide that, for them, combat represents the truly meaningful loss of innocence. At one point Stais says, "I tried smoking . . . I think I'll wait until I get a little older" (*FD*, 231). Whitejack can understand that the responsibilities of the lieutenant are too much for a 22-year-old, but he does not apply that truth to himself. Early in the story, the fact that Stais, who has been shot down and nearly killed, is more than "tired" is effectively conveyed through some brief dialogue. After Stais tells Novak that he is only 19, Whitejack says, "You look older. " "Yes," Stais agrees. When Whitejack adds, "A lot older," Stais again simply says, "Yes" (*FD*, 226–27). Despite their chronological age, Stais and Whitejack possess a wisdom that should only come with age, if at all. Still, they attempt to preserve some optimism and remain faithful to each other and to their own code of morality—each tries not to "just think of himself." Ultimately, this story is more affirmative than "Walking Wounded." Like "Act of Faith," it conveys hope for a world of selfless brotherhood after the war.

Shaw wrote two memorable stories about the French Resistance movement during the war, "Part in a Play" and "The Priest." The first presents the results of a wrong, if understandable, moral choice by a French actor, Alexis Constantin. Before the war, Constantin had been a successful, if obscure, minor actor on the French stage. He had shared an apartment and a friendship with the famous and brilliant leading man, Philippe Tournebroche. Their apartment had been the social center of Parisian theatrical life: "All in all, it was the sweet, rich, glamorous life it was possible for an artist to live in the 1930s and which we are repeatedly warned will never return to the face of the earth" (*SS*, 640). Constantin is, on the whole, content with this "sweet, rich, glamorous life," even though he is inwardly tortured by the degrading roles in which he has always been cast. His pain is not significantly lessened by Tournebroche's attempts to reassure him: "Alexis Constantin . . . the eternal pillar of the French theater. What would we do without the cuckold?" (*SS*, 640).

After the Germans occupy Paris and take over the theater, Tournebroche convinces Alexis that it would be "treason" to appear in a play (*SS*, 642). Soon, however, Alexis is offered a leading role as a miser in a tragedy, and the part is simply too good for him to turn down. His success as the miser proves even greater than he could have dreamed possible: "Overnight his name became a tradition in the French theater. The comic, aging cuckold was forgotten, and in his place was a tragic actor of historic stature" (*SS*, 645). Tournebroche is unforgiving, however, and repudiates his old friend.

The two do not see each other again until three years later, on the eve of the American liberation of Paris. During this period, Tournebroche has become a leader in the Resistance movement. Seeing him on the street with other members of the Resistance, Constantin begins to give money to the cause of liberation: "You haven't got the right to turn me away. . . . I want to do something to help. . . . Myself, too. . . . Forget the last three years" (*SS*, 646). Tournebroche accepts the money from his old friend but offers no gesture of forgiveness or acceptance.

In the story's painful ending, Alexis is fatally wounded while saving Tournebroche and the others from a German ambush. As he is dying, Alexis looks up at his old friend and knows that "in this last instant . . . he was unforgiven" (*SS*, 651).

Shaw gives the story its force by making what Constantin does so understandable. Alexis is, in all other respects, a decent man; and certainly any actor who had long languished in obscurity would find a career-making part a strong, almost irresistible, temptation. Moreover, it is difficult to see that taking a part in a play would actually hurt anyone, even though the Germans consider Constantin's portrayal of the miser as emblematic of the French people. Shaw further makes Tournebroche, the story's voice of morality, more than a little condescending and patronizing. A leading man in the theater, he quickly becomes a leader in the Resistance. Finally, Alexis dies a heroic death, literally sacrificing himself for the Resistance movement. Still, Shaw's point is that there can be no forgiveness for collaboration with an evil as total as nazism. Thus, Alexis Constantin, as he is dying, cannot forgive himself.

In contrast, "The Priest" is a story of heroism. Its focal character is Solomon, a French Jew in the Resistance movement posing as a Catholic priest. Solomon's disguise presents Shaw with the opportunity to satirize the failure of organized religion to take a stronger stand against the Nazis. When the story opens, Solomon has been called in to Gestapo headquarters to hear the confession of Maurice, another underground member who has been captured, tortured, and condemned to death by the gestapo. In Maurice's cell, Solomon gives voice to some frustration and anger: "If we could really get the holy men of France into the movement, we would have a system of intelligence, better than any telephone network," to which the condemned Maurice responds, "The Church has its own spiritual problems" (*SS*, 655).

Solomon has learned to survive by adopting a mask of nonfeeling for others in the underground, but the sight of Maurice, tortured and soon-to-die, shakes his resolve: "You found yourself loving the good ones better than a wife or a son, and then the trick, of course, did not work" (*SS*, 656). During the "confession," Solomon yearns to give Maurice some reassurance that he will not be forgotten, but the priest can think of nothing. Before being led away to his death, Maurice, ironically, gives Solomon the reassurance that despite the torture, he has "told the Germans nothing, that no plans were invalidated by his death" (*SS*, 660). "The Priest" is a story of two "good ones," two decent, courageous men resisting a pervasive and insidious evil.

Shaw knew, despite the optimism of "Act of Faith" and "Gunners' Passage," that the end of the war did not bring an end to evil. At home and abroad, needless pain, suffering, and death continued. Shaw was especially angered by the brutal prejudice inspired by the Jewish struggle to establish a Middle Eastern sanctuary for refugees from Europe and by the rise of McCarthyism in the United States.

Postwar Stories

Shaw's most memorable treatment of the injustice and suffering occasioned by the resettlement of European Jews in the Middle East is

"Medal from Jerusalem." The story derives its power from Shaw's characterization of Ruth, a tragic, haunted Jewish refugee in Palestine. Its narrative focus is Mitchell Gunnison, a nice, but shallow, young American whose unsuccessful attempt to identify with Ruth's pain gives "Medal from Jerusalem" a note of memorable irony. Shaw introduces the irony through a light, teasing dialogue between Ruth and Mitchell at a restaurant-bar in Tel Aviv:

> [Ruth] "You're as pretty as an English lieutenant. I'm not fond of the English, but they have the prettiest lieutenants of any army."
> [Mitchell] "We send our pretty ones to the Pacific. . . . Guadal-canal. We preserve them for American womanhood." (*FD*, 189)

Guadalcanal, of course, did not preserve anyone; and Mitchell's prettiness images his intellectual and emotional shallowness. He, in fact, will never be ready for a meaningful relationship with a woman like Ruth. Soon, Mitchell and Ruth are joined by a technical adviser to the American army named Carver, who attempts to warn the young lieutenant that he is out of his depth. Carver advises Gunnison not to "become involved with Palestine." When Ruth protests that Mitchell is becoming involved with her and not Palestine, Carver continues his admonition: "Beware Palestine. . . . The human race is doomed in Palestine. For thousands of years. . . . This is no place for an American" (*FD*, 191). Carver's admonition is a variation of an idea that has been central to American fiction at least since Henry James, and one that will dominate Shaw's expatriate fiction: the innocent American can only intensify the Old World's legacy of centuries of injustice and pain by trying to comprehend it.

Shaw's description of Tel Aviv effectively evokes an ageless culture of beauty and grace that has been virtually destroyed: "They walked past the corner where the Italian bombers had killed a hundred and thirty people on a Friday morning the year before, and turned into Ruth's street. . . . Mitchell couldn't help smiling and realizing that one of his strongest memories of Tel Aviv would be the strains of Tchaikovsky and Brahms and Beethoven coming through the opened windows on every street of the town, as the furiously cultured inhabitants practiced runs and cadenzas with never-ending zeal" (*FD*, 195). Once, Europe had exported great music and a graceful culture to Palestine; more recently, its bombers rained down death on Tel Aviv. The city of Tel Aviv and the character of Ruth merge in the story—she too is beautiful, delicate, ageless in her pain, and doomed.

The story's tone is further darkened by Ruth's debate with Taif, an anti-Semitic Arab journalist. After complaining that Palestine has taken in more than its share of Jewish refugees, Taif says, "If the rest of the world really wants to see the Jewish race survive let them take them in. America, Britain, Russia. . . . I do not notice those large countries taking in great masses of Jews" (*FD*, 193). Ruth's answer to this challenge, "There are no great masses. . . . There is only a handful," foreshadows the story that she will soon tell Mitchell about her past. Taif presses on, "the truth may be that the rest of the world really wants to see the Jewish race die out" (*FD*, 193). (This concept, which of course evokes the Holocaust, is also central to Mr. Seeger's letter in "Act of Faith.")

Finally Ruth tells the innocent American about her past as they walk through the streets of Tel Aviv to her house. She tells first of escaping from Europe with seven hundred other refugees on board an old, poorly ventilated Greek ship. Then she recounts the story of how her mother died on board another ship that was blown up in Haifa Harbor. The British would not let the ship dock and had ordered it back to Germany. Someone among the refugees set off a bomb, apparently hoping that the explosion would force the British to allow the ship to dock: "Some people would die, but some would be saved. If the boat went back to Europe, everybody would be killed. Of course, they bungled it somewhat, and they didn't figure on the fire, and they thought the boat would sink more slowly and only a few people would be killed, but even so it was a pretty fair bargain" (*FD*, 200). After telling her story, Ruth gives Mitchell a Saint Christopher medal: "It's for voyages . . . Something like this, something holy, might have a tendency to be more effective if it comes from Jerusalem, don't you think?" (*FD*, 201).

Ruth knows that Mitchell will leave her and that she will be destroyed, but she wants him to understand and remember the holiness of the pain she and the other Jewish refugees have experienced.

Later, Ruth tells Mitchell that she will probably marry Khazen, a Palestinian contractor who supported the Nazis during the war: "I'm not strong any more. . . . Americans can't understand how tired the human race can get" (*FD*, 194). Ruth hopes, while knowing better, that Mitchell will be strong enough to save her. But the story's powerful ending emphasizes what the reader already knows—the young American is too weak in spirit and imagination to give her even that reassurance: "he wanted to tell her that the terror and courage would not be forgotten, but he didn't know how to say it, and besides, being honest with himself, he knew it would be difficult to remember, and finally, back in Vermont, it would blur and cloud over and seem unreal as a story in a child's book, read many years ago and now almost forgotten. He held her tightly, but he said nothing" (*FD*, 202).

The concluding image of "Medal from Jerusalem" is unforgettable—Ruth sees Khazen waiting outside her apartment and says to Mitchell, "I suppose finally he'll kill me . . . Now, Lieutenant, . . . tell me about Vermont" (*FD*, 202). Ruth accepts and even anticipates the inevitability of her destruction, but she wants to hear about the innocent land that has escaped the Holocaust.

Shaw's creation of the courageous and doomed Ruth makes "Medal from Jerusalem" one of his best stories. The sincere, but futile effort of the shallow Mitchell Gunnison to comfort Ruth and give her some assurance that her pain will be remembered provides the story with its pervasive irony. Moreover, a level of healing irony is implicit after all— the reader will not forget Ruth even if Mitchell does.

In other stories, Shaw depicts a postwar America that has lost its Mitchell Gunnison innocence. The suffering and brutality of World War II did affect Americans who, like the rest of the world, saw their old faith in stability and permanence shaken. One of Shaw's best fictional treatments of America's legacy from the war is the story "Widows' Meeting."

The narrative focus of "Widows' Meeting" is an older woman named Emily who remembers a history of tension between her two grown daughters, Peggy and Irene. Now she, along with Peggy, awaits the arrival of Irene on a plane from Germany. Emily remembers that from childhood Irene had been an attractive, independent, and willful child, while Peggy, in contrast, "had been all sliding smiles and oblique glances" (*SS*, 691). Still, Irene and Peggy had maintained a calm and peaceful relationship, until, one evening in the early 1930s, Peggy had brought home a new fiancé, Reinhold Weigen, a German citizen visiting the United States.

Irene had stolen the German's affections from her sister, had married him, and had moved to Germany. On the rebound, Peggy had married a man named Lawrence, "very handsome, so tall, with an angular, long, honest face" (*SS*, 694). While this description of Lawrence evokes Lincoln and thus an American ideal of masculine honesty and integrity, Peggy nevertheless has remained bitter over the loss of Reinhold Weigen.

Peggy's bitterness had intensified when, in 1936, Irene and Reinhold had returned to America for a visit and, at a dinner party hosted by Peggy and Lawrence, had insulted the other guests by reciting Nazi propaganda: "I tell you that if Hitler hadn't come along, we'd have all been destroyed by the Jews and the Communists" (*SS*, 697). In anger, embarrassment, and some triumph as well, Irene had ordered her sister and brother-in-law out of her house. When the war had finally come, all communication between the two sisters had ended. Yet the war's legacy had only intensified Peggy's pain—both she and Irene had suffered the deaths of their husbands and sons: "And Lawrence was dead, and Reinhold was dead, . . . Bud [Peggy's son] was dead, at the Saar River, which he had tried to cross but had not managed; and Irene's two sons were dead in Russia, and what rivers had they failed to cross?" (*SS*, 698).

Now Irene wants to come home and "forget the horrible things that have happened" (*SS*, 699). Peggy initially refuses to consider her sister's request, but Emily finally convinces her to welcome and forgive her sister, "if she's changed" (*SS*, 699). Almost as soon as she is off the plane, it is obvious that Irene has changed only in superficial ways. While she appears "at least sixty, dowdy, poorly dressed" and has "a fat, very wrinkled commanding face," she is still crudely and offensively pro-German and hostile to her native country. Peggy will not go to her, and Emily is left to say "welcome home" to her daughter (*FD*, 701).

The story's concluding irony is especially effective. Irene's loss and suffering have only intensified her intolerance, and she has no real home to welcome her. For Peggy, the loss of her husband and son and the death of Reinhold Weigen have meant the end of forgiveness. The war's dark legacy is deep—too many sons have died in unnamed rivers for genuine peace to come quickly and easily. A profound isolation is the only future awaiting all three of the story's central female characters. The story is especially effective in communicating the ambiguity of Peggy's resentment of Irene. In part, this animosity results from a legitimate abhorrence of Irene's Nazi sympathies and from grief over the deaths of her loved ones in the war. Clearly, though, it is also the expression of a woman who lost her lover to a more attractive, more aggressive sister.

In the United States, the postwar legacy of intolerance and injustice was made manifest in the rise of McCarthyism in the 1950s. Shaw was a victim of McCarthyism—for a time, his books were blacklisted. In the 1980 interview in part 2 he discusses this experience. Because the *New Yorker* paid little, if any, attention to the blacklist, Shaw says, his work was not significantly repressed: "But it *affected* me. I didn't like the fact that there were people going around trying to destroy me. I could see what they were doing. My phone was tapped. And everybody who had to go to Washington was asked about me" (see Giles interview in part 2).

The irrationality of McCarthyism created a climate of paranoia that particularly inhibited and threatened writers, artists, academics, and government employees. In his story "Goldilocks at Graveside" Shaw memorably evokes the national mood of bitter suspicion and despair that McCarthyism created. Except for an introductory and a concluding scene, the narration consists of a story-within-a-story written, but never published, by Victoria Bryant, the widow of a foreign service officer whose life and career were destroyed by blacklisting. "Goldilocks at Graveside" acquires an added dimension of pessimism through Victoria's account of her failed attempt to get "From the Desert," a fictional account of the tragedy of her husband, John, published. Initially, she feels that she cannot fail in writing the story: "Writers of the first class, I have read somewhere, are invariably men or women with an obsession. While I do not deceive myself about my merits or the grandeur of the heights I might ultimately reach, I share that one thing with them. I have an obsession. That obsession is my husband and it is of him that I shall write" (*FD*, 405). An ironic subtext of Shaw's story is that Victoria's obsession is destructive of creativity—as was McCarthyism. Through Victoria's attitude toward her failed story, "Goldilocks at Graveside" indirectly conveys the intellectual and creative sterility of the time: "while I have had no experience in the field of letters I am encouraged by the dismal quality of the writing which is published daily in this country" (*FD*, 405).

Shaw's title conveys the banality of McCarthyism's evil. "Goldilocks" is the sarcastic nickname another Embassy employee gives to a man named Borden. Because of his weakness and fear, Borden had set in motion the destruction of John Bryant. Borden is hardly a classic figure of sinister evil; instead, the very real evil he has caused is inextricably tied to his pettiness and insecurity.

In the introductory scene, Victoria, at John's funeral, sees Borden for the first time since her husband's destruction: "It was a dark, rainy day, and he was sitting alone, in the rear of the church, near the door, but his blond head was unmistakable" (*FD*, 399). After the service, "Goldilocks" approaches her and after proclaiming that Bryant was "an able man," asks what John did "after he retired." Victoria responds coldly, "He read" (*FD*, 400). In fact, as Borden well knows, there was nothing left for Bryant to do after his career was terminated in disgrace. Then Borden makes a "confession": "I did see you that afternoon, Vicki. When you smiled and I turned away. I've always felt foolish about it and guilty and I . . ." (*FD*, 401). Initially, the confession makes no sense to Victoria, and in an attempt to understand it she locates and rereads "From the Desert."

Shaw delays an explanation of the confession while, through the story-within-a-story device, he depicts the spread of fear in the office at which Bryant had worked. In "From the Desert" Victoria does not name the embassy where her husband had worked; she writes instead that "at this moment in our country's history candor is foolhardy, re-prisals devastating" (*FD*, 406). The climate of fear then was so perva-sive that, even after her husband's career had been senselessly and randomly destroyed, she still fears worse can happen. The destructive chain of events at the embassy had begun when John Bryant's superior, Munder, had been forced to resign: "When the time came to offer up a sacrifice to the exasperation and disappointments of the electorate, Munder, because of his earlier distinction, was forced to resign. While they did not understand it at the time, his friends and aides in the Service were also marked for eventual degradation, or, what is almost as bad, stagnation in humiliatingly unimportant posts" (*FD*, 406). Not surprisingly, in this atmosphere of externally induced paranoia, every-one at the embassy had become suspicious and abnormally watchful of each other. That Munder had been sacrificed because of his previous "distinction" emphasizes a subtheme in the story: a side effect of McCarthyism was the survival, and thus the triumph, of mediocrity throughout American society.

John Bryant had contributed to his own destruction. He had had an affair with a diplomat's wife who had then tried to commit suicide. John had believed that he had effectively neutralized the potential harm of the scandal ("Luckily, the people at the hospital were civilized and sympathetic, and my husband managed, with a minimum of brib-

ery, to keep the entire matter out of the newspaper" [*FD*, 407]) and
Victoria had quickly forgiven him ("I had no intention of allowing the
central foundations of my life to be laid in ruins for the fleeting pleasure of recrimination or to satisfy the busy hypocrisy of my friends"
[*FD*, 407]).

But in the charged atmosphere of the embassy, no past indiscretion
could be safely buried. John had soon been warned by a colleague of
the rampant governmental solicitation of anonymous information and
the use of wiretaps and surveillance. The colleague had called "the
senator who was freezing the Foreign Service into a permanent attitude
of terror" Il Blanko and had told John the rumors he had heard about
Il Blanko's European network of spies. John had attempted to make
accommodations to the climate of paranoia. He and Victoria had dras-
tically reduced their social life: "To judge, professionally, the virtue of
colleagues and applicants, is one thing—it is quite another to be
forced, on the most innocent occasions, to speculate on the politics,
the discretion, the potential future disgrace, of dinner companions and
tourists to whom one is introduced, by chance, in a bar" (*FD*, 411).
Most important, when a wealthy colleague named Trent had sought
John's advice about denouncing a former college professor who had
once asked Trent to join the Communist party, John, fearing a trap,
had told Trent to proceed with the denunciation. Part of the artistic
plausibility of "Goldilocks at Graveside" originates in Shaw's decision
to make John Bryant a man with real flaws and weaknesses. His con-
senting to Trent's plan to destroy the professor, even if motivated by
fear and self-interest, represents a moment of complicity with the
forces that would destroy him.

Soon thereafter, Borden had asked Bryant for his resignation; the
alternative was to be called up on a morals charge because of the attempted suicide of the diplomat's wife. Borden, by describing the
extensive surveillance assigned to Bryant, had made clear the impos-
sibility of emerging undamaged from an investigation—he had pro-
phetically told John that "there are no extracurricular affairs any more"
(*FD*, 414).

In disgrace, John and Victoria had left Europe and returned to the
United States to hide in the southern California desert. Victoria had
long suspected that Borden had somehow played a larger role in her
husband's destruction than she had at first suspected: "There was
something I found vaguely unpleasant and false about him" (*FD*, 413).
In the desert, Borden had become, for John and Victoria, a symbol of

the cynical corruption of the times. In Europe, Victoria had bought a pair of hurricane lamps that "under the stormy desert sky" function as symbolic protection against memories of Borden and Europe (*FD*, 415). But when the couple had read that Goldilocks had experienced his own disgrace and had also been forced to resign, John and Victoria had celebrated: "We bought a bottle of Bordeaux that my husband said was of a quality he hadn't expected to find so deep in the heart of America" (*FD*, 417).

Now, looking back, Victoria suddenly understands Borden's confession and knows that she and her husband had been right to blame him. She remembers that once in Europe she had accidentally encountered Borden as he emerged from the apartment of a wealthy homosexual. That occasion, she knows, was the afternoon to which Borden had referred. The superficial young man, frightened that the Bryants might reveal his homosexuality, had discredited John. Still, this vindication does not please Victoria. Instead, she comprehends with regret the full price of her husband's and her own bitterness: "What sort of love could it have been that demanded that price for its survival? In a time of sharks, must all be sharks?" (*FD*, 417). The story ends with Victoria remembering Borden's blond hair first at the funeral and then on that fatal European afternoon: *"The blond hair had been wet that day, too, although Borden was young then and had not yet begun to use dye"* (Shaw's italics, *FD*, 417).

"Goldilocks at Graveside" is a dark, angry story, but it is considerably more than propaganda. By emphasizing, in its conclusion, that Borden is, in the last analysis, simply a superficial, weak, and frightened man, Shaw undercuts any exaltation on Victoria's or the reader's part over his humiliation and disgrace. John Bryant, though a much more honorable man, had also contributed to his own destruction. The only truly strong character in the story is Victoria, and circumstances have reduced her strength to a narrow determination to survive. Still, at the end, while not forgiving Borden, she, at last, repudiates her earlier exaltation over his fall. Vindication through the sufferings of another, she has learned, is not healing or restorative.

The story convincingly depicts the McCarthyism period as "a time of sharks." During such a time, the cultivation of paranoia was essential to survival. Even in the desert, John and Victoria had believed that they were under surveillance; and Victoria writes in "From the Desert" about the effects of living under a constant and anonymous threat: "I have become accustomed to a permanent quiver of uneasiness" (*FD*,

403). Art and creativity, like trust and loyalty, must suffer in such an atmosphere. Victoria's title, "From the Desert," symbolizes the artistic, intellectual, and spiritual sterility that was McCarthyism's legacy. Not surprisingly, the major aesthetic limitation of "Goldilocks at Graveside" is its unrelieved pain and bitterness.

It is, then, a pleasant surprise to discover Shaw treating the virus of McCarthyism with absurdist humor in "The Green Nude." The story is a satiric treatment of all totalitarian political interference with the creative process. In addition, it reaches out to satirize critics, the postwar women's movement, the commercialization of art in America, and Freudian theories of art.

The focal character in "The Green Nude" is Sergei Baranov, a resolutely innocent and nonpolitical Russian painter. As a young man, Baranov had specialized in painting richly colored displays of fruit. He had joined the Russian Revolution because he "did not like to refuse anyone anything, and all his friends were joining" (*FD*, 365). He proved himself to be a most unexceptional soldier, but still received "a modest decoration for an action at which he was not present" (*FD*, 365). Thus, after the revolution, he enjoys the status of a privileged artist. Initially, he still specializes in fruit; and his work is widely praised "since he had the trick of making all his garden products seem marvelously edible" (*FD*, 365). Soon, Baranov begins painting female nudes instead of fruit and enjoys even greater popularity: "as edible as ever, his paintings now combined the most satisfactory features of the orchard and the harem, and examples of his work, rosy, healthy, and very round, were much sought after by even more important officials of the regime" (*FD*, 365–66). It is, of course, impossible to miss Shaw's salaciously playful analogy between Baranov's edible fruit and the equally edible "round," "healthy" female nudes.

Baranov's troubles begin when he marries Anna Kronsky: "one of those sharp-featured and overpoweringly energetic women that the liberation of women from the nursery and kitchen had turned loose on the male world. Angular, voracious, and clever, with a tongue like an iron clapper in a new bell, racked by indigestion and a deep contempt for the male sex, she was the sort of woman who in this country would run a store or report wars for the Luce publications" (*FD*, 366). Throughout the story, Shaw's portrayal of Anna does remind one of Claire Boothe Luce. More importantly, though, she personifies the newly assertive woman who emerged after World War II. This satire of the new and "unfeminine" postwar woman is the least satisfying aspect of Shaw's story, and it detracts from the more important themes.

Anna's effects on Baranov are undeniably disastrous. He no longer shows female nudes, instead he is "confined once more to the vegetable world." Even his painting of fruit communicates "a haunting and melancholy fragrance" as though the subjects come from "trees and vines through whose dying leaves and frozen branches the cruel winds of winter were already moaning" (*FD*, 367). Yet Baranov has not exactly deserted nudes—at a one-man show he unveils a painting of a grotesque green nude that he has secretly produced. The hideous painting, dominated by the nude's "howling" mouth and a "stunted and uprooted" cherry tree in the foreground of the canvas and "like no other nude that Baranov had painted before," gives the impression "of madness, genius, energy, disaster, sorrow, and despair" (*FD*, 368). The green nude is Baranov's statement of his spiritual confinement and artistic castration by the rapacious Anna.

The initial reaction to the painting is highly favorable, and Baranov enjoys brief recognition as the foremost Russian painter. Suvarnin, "the critic for *The Sickle*," applauds the painting as "great" and asks to interview its creator (*FD*, 368). In the interview, the innocent artist tells the critic that the green nude had been inspired by a sequence of nightmares: "The worst dream, and one that I had over and over again, was that I was in a small room and it was crowded with women, only women. All the women could talk, but I couldn't" (*FD*, 370). Unlike everyone else who sees it, Baranov and Anna are blind to the resemblance between the green nude and the painter's wife.

Through the characterization of Suvarnin, Shaw satirizes careless and self-indulgent art criticism. The Russian critic never takes notes before writing an article "since he was of the firm opinion that accuracy in reporting was the foe of creative criticism" (*FD*, 370). He also talks in clichés: "Out of anguish, . . . comes the great art. Out of the depths of despair only can we reach to the skies. Look at Dostoyevsky" (*FD*, 371). But Baranov is stunned when Suvarnin's printed review of the green nude denounces it as "FILTH IN THE GALLERIES . . . a nauseating sample of decadent, bourgeois 'art'" (*FD*, 371).

Later Suvarnin shows the painter the favorable review that the Central Committee forced him to suppress, and Suvarnin's account of the committee's reactions occasions the story's first painted satire of a totalitarian response to art: "That Klopoyev, the president of the committee, the one who had made eighty-four portrait heads of Stalin, he was especially anxious" (*FD*, 372). Baranov is subsequently denounced by the governmental propaganda machine; and Shaw uses a fictional diatribe in *The New Masses* by the same Klopoyev as an in-joke: "[Baranov is] a traitor to the working class of the world, a lecher after Western fleshpots, a Park Avenue sensationalist, a man who would be at home drawing cartoons for *The New Yorker*" (*FD*, 373). The *New Yorker* mention is Shaw's oblique reference to the common criticism by leftist critics that he abandoned his political principles after the success of *The Young Lions*. This play on Irwin Shaw's own associations with New York City and the *New Yorker* magazine also makes clear that the story's satiric attack is aimed at any government repression of the arts, whether it comes from the Right or the Left.

Disgraced, Baranov and Anna retreat to Germany. In their adopted country, the Russian experience repeats itself. Baranov only shows paintings of fruit and soon acquires great popularity, and Anna becomes "a physical-training instructor in one of the new organizations for young women that were springing up at the time" (*FD*, 374). Again, though, the painter's dreams and repressions are too much for him, and he secretly paints a Berlin green nude: "It was heroic, gigantic, god-size. Baranov had plunged to the sub-cellars of despair" (*FD*, 375). In his description of the Berlin green nude, Shaw is again having fun with Freudian theory. The exaggerated size of the green nude is a projection of Baranov's sexual frustration. Inevitably, this second green nude is discovered by the gestapo, and the Baranovs enter their second period of disgrace and exile: Anna is "sent to work as an assistant dietician in a home for unwed mothers near the Polish border," and Baranov is imprisoned, interrogated, tortured, and "twice condemned to death" (*FD*, 376). In addition, the painter is denounced by the Berlin *Tageblatt* as "this barbaric worm of a Baranov, né Goldfarb" (*FD*, 376). Again, Shaw is satirizing the propensity of the totalitarian mind to scapegoat "dangerous art."

Ultimately, the painter is released by the gestapo and, with Anna, flees to the United States. Baranov quickly adjusts to life in New York City—"he patriotically developed a taste for Manhattan cocktails, which he rightly assumed to be the native drink" (*FD*, 378). By this point in the story, the reader expects the cycle of initial success and ultimate disgrace to be repeated. Baranov once again publicly devotes himself to fruit and enjoys a distinctly American popular success: "a large wine company used Baranov grapes on all their labels and advertising and a large Baranov still life of a basket of oranges was bought by a California packing company and blown up into twenty-four sheets and plastered on billboards from one end of the country to another" (*FD*, 378). Here, of course, Shaw is satirizing the commercialization of art in America.

Shaw cements the resemblance between Anna and Claire Boothe Luce by having the painter's wife assume editorial prominence in a popular American news magazine: "By the end of the war the magazine for which she worked had put her in charge of the departments of Political Interpretation, Medicine for Women, Fashion, Books, and, of course, Child Care" (*FD*, 378). That the childless and decidedly unmaternal Anna is repeatedly placed in positions of authority concerning the care of children is a running joke in the story. In addition, the lists of "departments" in Shaw's fictional news magazine represent *Time*'s compartmentalizing of the news. Another implicit joke in the story is that while Anna is given power in Russia and Germany by totalitarian governments, she rises to dominance in America through her association with a popular magazine.

Inevitably, Baranov, more depressed than ever by Anna's new power, paints a New York green nude. Suvarnin, who has also emigrated to New York, sees it and proclaims that "this is the great one" (*FD*, 379). Baranov's American period of critical and popular acclaim is even greater and more schizophrenic than the comparable Russian period: "Picasso was mentioned in the same sentence as Baranov countless times and several writers brought up the name of El Greco. Bonwit Teller had six green nudes in their windows, wearing lizard shoes and draped with mink" (*FD*, 379). In the logic of Shaw's plot, it is also inevitable that the New York green nude will cause its creator to be denounced in an epidemic of McCarthyism.

Shaw's talent for absurdist exaggeration is evident in his account of the delayed hysterical American reaction to Baranov's painting. First, in Congress, a representative denounces the "green nude by a Russian foreigner as sickening twaddle, Communist-inspired, an insult to American womanhood, a blow to White Supremacy, atheistic, psychological, un-American, subversive, Red-Fascistic" (*FD*, 380). Of course, the only woman who ever should have been insulted by the green nude does not even see that it resembles her. The congressman's disparaging use of the word "psychological" will make sense to anyone familiar with the militant anti-intellectualism of the 1950s in America.

The congressman's attack inspires further denunciation of the Russian painter. He is investigated by "several newspaper chains," one of which reports that "a samovar stood in place of honor in the Baranov living room and that the outside of the studio was painted red" (*FD*, 380). Soon the FBI takes up the investigation and discovers that the Baranovs "often spoke Russian in front of the servants" (*FD*, 381). American right-wing political hysteria during the 1950s was strongly linked to a traditional national xenophobia. As the reader anticipates, Anna is forced to resign from the magazine.

The story concludes with a variation on the Mark Twain snapper. Belatedly, Baranov notices that the green nude resembles Anna, only to be assured by Suvarnin that it actually does not. The painter then begins to plan his next exile in the Caribbean or South America. Once again promising to paint only fruit, he wonders, "What sort of fruit . . . do you think a man could find to paint in Costa Rica?" (*FD*, 382).

Much of the success of "The Green Nude" derives from Baranov's determined innocence. His lack of political sophistication is part of what condemns him to continual political repression, whereas his inability to recognize his own inner frustrations and repressions except unconsciously in his art is a sustained joke throughout the story. His brief epiphany that the green nude is a projection of his unacknowledged resentment of Anna completes the joke.

Shaw's satire is perhaps given too loose rein in "The Green Nude." His use of Anna as a means of satirizing the postwar new woman, Claire Boothe Luce, and *Time* magazine inevitably reduces her to a plot device. Similarly, Shaw's ridicule of the inconsistency and subjectivity of critics seems not truly integral to the story. In contrast, the fun he has with Freudian theories of art is infectious. But the most important element in "The Green Nude" is its treatment of the absurdity of any totalitarian repression of art. In this respect, the story's cyclical plot implies a parallel between Stalinism, nazism, and McCarthyism: totalitarian thinking anywhere is an enemy of art and the human spirit. On balance, Shaw is more effective in making this point through the exaggerated absurdist satire of "The Green Nude" than through the unrelieved bitterness of "Goldilocks at Graveside."

Marriage, Adolescence, Academia, and Some Stubborn Individuals

Shaw responded, in his short fiction, to the most dramatic events of three turbulent decades of American history—the Great Depression, World War II, and McCarthyism. In 1951 he moved to Europe, where he lived until 1976. It is not surprising, then, that the short fiction he produced in the last half of his career increasingly emphasized Americans abroad in a manner reminiscent of Henry James and F. Scott Fitzgerald. Before discussing this body of expatriate fiction, let it be said that some of Shaw's most memorable American stories do not emphasize New York City as setting, nor do they significantly reflect historical events.

Several of Shaw's best stories are concerned with universal subjects such as marriage and adolescence, a few focus on the narrow world of academia, and several depict resolutely stubborn individuals defying an impersonal society.

Love and Marriage

The theme of fidelity in marriage recurs throughout Shaw's writing in association with the concepts of loyalty and decency. For more than one of Shaw's fictional males, sexual loyalty is especially difficult, and the story that depicts this most memorably is the early "The Girls in Their Summer Dresses." Shaw has said that he completed both "The Girls in Their Summer Dresses" and "Sailor off the Bremen" in just one week when he was 25; "The Girls in Their Summer Dresses," he recalled, took only one morning (Morris and Matthiessen, 259–60).

The strengths of "The Girls in Their Summer Dresses" are its cohesiveness and ambiguity. It is reminiscent of Ernest Hemingway's "Hills Like White Elephants" in the way that it communicates complex and ambiguous human motivation almost exclusively through deceptively simple dialogue. According to Shaw, the story is "about a man who tells his wife that he's going to be unfaithful to her" (Morris, 259–60).

91

Yet critics have seen the story as considerably more complex than that. In *Understanding Fiction*,[15] Robert Penn Warren and Cleanth Brooks analyze the story as a fictional study of a marriage based on "convenience," wherein the two focal characters, Michael and Frances, have "stumbled on the recognition" that they "really mean nothing to each other": "Each is, as it were, merely a convenience to the other. This is, of course, especially true of Michael's attitude toward Frances. Despite his actual faithfulness, Frances is just another girl, the one he 'happens' to have married" (Brooks and Warren, 89). Moreover, Brooks and Warren argue, Frances can only "bitterly accept" this dehumanizing role—"she hasn't the idealism, after all, to struggle for more" (Brooks and Warren, 89).

Two later critics, Joe L. Baird and Ralph Grajeda, object to the emphasis Brooks and Warren place on Michael's guilt.[16] Baird and Grajeda argue that the story depicts the "common experience of a breakdown in communication between two people—toward which each unwittingly though unerringly contributes" (Baird and Grajeda, 4). They do not excuse Michael, but they emphasize Frances's role in forcing the quarrel that dominates the story. Frances, they argue, "misjudges Michael woefully," seeing his response to other attractive women as being primarily sexual, when it is actually a *"sensuous,"* not a *"sensual,"* appreciation of "the beauty and mystery of beautiful women," akin to Wordsworth's delight in nature (Baird and Grajeda, 3–4). Thus, the story is about "the upsetting of the delicate mechanism of unity, of communication between two people through lack of sympathy or understanding on the part of each" (Baird and Grajeda, 4).

Baird and Grajeda's analysis, in turn, prompted a response from Jacqueline Berke, who agrees that the Brooks and Warren analysis is inadequate but argues that more is involved in the breakdown of communication between Michael and Frances than Baird and Grajada suggest. She views the story as "an exposure of romantic excess, as bleak and relentless in its outlook (and within its narrower scope) as *Madame Bovary* itself.[17] Michael and Frances fail, according to Berke, not so much in understanding each other as in understanding themselves. Each character refuses to acknowledge "extravagant, irrational needs," each is an "incurable romantic" who will never change and confront reality more directly. The girls on the street are to Michael, Berke argues, primarily reminders of his compulsive longing for something unnameable and, thus, unattainable.

The controlled ambiguity of "The Girls in Their Summer Dresses" emerges from Shaw's mastery of fictional technique. In telling the story almost exclusively through dialogue, Shaw chooses to work within the kind of minimalist structure found in much modernist fiction. He denies himself the luxury of explanation through exposition and instead allows the story's fictional logic to develop through shifts in mood. Initially, the mood is one of innocent pleasure as Michael and Frances stroll down Fifth Avenue in New York City: "Fifth Avenue was shining in the sun when they left the Brevoort and started walking toward Washington Square. The sun was warm, even though it was November and everything looked like Sunday morning" (*FD*, 62). In their opening dialogue, the couple plan an idyllic Sunday alone and discuss getting out of a party to which they have been invited.

In this early part of the story Shaw skillfully conveys the couple's discontent. Frances expresses dissatisfaction with the emotionless, public hedonism of their life-style: "You and me. We're always up to our neck in people, drinking their Scotch, or drinking our Scotch, we only see each other in bed . . ." (*FD*, 63). Michael attempts to transform the seriousness of her criticism into a joke: "The Great Meeting Place . . . Stay in bed long enough and everybody you ever knew will show up there" (*FD*, 63). His flippant allusion to infidelity strikes the most disturbing possible note with Frances and intensifies her awareness that he is following his customary practice of deliberately looking at all the pretty girls around him. Shaw's skill is especially apparent in the way he has earlier introduced Michael's undisguised admiration of a woman passing by. The reader indirectly learns that he has looked admiringly at the first woman through Frances's seemingly light-hearted admonition to him: "Look out . . . You'll break your neck" (*FD*, 62). By describing Michael's first admiring glance through Frances's reaction, Shaw raises, precisely to leave it open, the question of how calculated or even conscious Michael's behavior really is. If one accepts Shaw's analysis of his story, it becomes possible to argue that Michael is deliberately admiring the passing women to provoke a confrontation with Frances.

At any rate, Frances's repressed tension is intensified when Michael does not react positively to a kiss on the ear: "Darling, . . . This is Fifth Avenue," he says (*FD*, 63). Still, she attempts to outline a program of sensuous enjoyment for the afternoon. Her recital is soon destroyed by her realization that her husband is staring at another attractive woman. Now, she can no longer repress her anger: " 'That's it,' Frances said flatly. 'That's the program for the day. Or maybe you'd just rather walk up and down Fifth Avenue' " (*FD*, 64). In naming Fifth Avenue, Frances is issuing a challenge to Michael. She understands, and intends to deny, his sense that the street, and indeed the entire city, are his private theater of exotic and erotic stimulation into which she must not transgress. After her challenge, the couple's previously repressed tension is acknowledged and brought to the surface.

"You always look at other women. . . . At every damn woman in the City of New York," she accuses (*FD*, 64). After a failed effort to counter her anger with more kidding, Michael begins an extended confession that dominates the remainder of the story. He argues that he merely employs the senses God gave him—"I casually inspect the universe," he claims (*FD*, 64). Then he assures Frances that he loves her and considers himself happily married. But when Frances will not stop her accusation, he challenges her: "What do you want, a fight?" (*FD*, 65). Abruptly and unexpectedly frightened, Frances attempts to return to the innocent gaiety with which their walk began.

Having begun his confession, though, Michael is now determined to finish it. First, he assures Frances that he has thus far been physically faithful throughout the five years of their marriage. Frances, now on the defensive, attempts a confession of her own—she explains that his admiring other women bothers her because it is so reminiscent of how he first looked at her: "I see that look in your eye and that's the way you looked at me the first time, in Alice Maxwell's house. Standing there in the living room, next to the radio with a green hat on and all those people." Michael responds coldly and matter-of-factly, "I remember the hat" (*FD*, 66). Desperation and fear having now dissipated her anger, Frances announces that she wants a drink, so the couple retreats into a bar.

In this story, the bar functions in a manner familiar to readers of modern existentialist fiction; as in Hemingway's "A Clean, Well-Lighted Place," it is a temporary sanctuary in a world without faith. Inside, Frances, knowing that she cannot stop Michael's confession, presses for the truth that she does not want to hear: "You look at them [the women on the street] as though you want them . . . Every one of them" (*FD*, 66). Agreeing that she is right "in a way," he tries to explain, to her and to himself, the reasons for his "looking." The beautiful women remind him, he says, of when he was a young man in New York City: "When I first came to New York from Ohio that was the first thing I noticed, the million wonderful women, all over the city. I walked around with my heart in my throat" (*FD*, 66). It is important that Michael came to New York City from Ohio—he is a midwestern innocent unable to regain sobriety after becoming intoxicated with eastern cosmopolitanism and sophistication.

Now that he is "getting near middle age, putting on a little fat," he is still attracted to the women, in part because they appear distant and unapproachable (*FD*, 66). Like F. Scott Fitzgerald's Dick Diver in *Tender Is the Night*, Michael is a middle-aged man feeling and fearing the loss of strength and vitality, and nostalgic for his vanishing youth. As with Dick Diver, Michael's admiration for the beautiful young women is largely narcissistic—both characters yearn to discover a lasting, external reflection of their own inevitably fading attractiveness. The remoteness of the women is essential because they function as embodiments of youth and physical attractiveness; they must preserve the illusion that they, and thus Michael, can remain unaffected by time. Their role is, thus, similar to that played by Susanna and "you" in Wallace Stevens's poem "Peter Quince at the Clavier"—their beauty must escape "Death's ironic scraping."[18]

Frances, frightened and desperate, still demands all the truth. She demands that Michael admit first that he "wants" the other women, then that he would "like to be free," and finally that "some day" he will "make a move" (*FD*, 68). Somewhat reluctantly, Michael agrees with her analysis. Yet a central strength of the story is that the reader cannot be certain of the accuracy of Frances's assessment. This ambiguity adds essential depth to the characterization of Michael. Even he does not really know why the young girls so fascinate him. He may, in fact, merely want them in the way that he wants his youth; he may want to be free just as he wants to be young. His inner confusion makes him more complex as a character—and not simply an unthinking sexist. Should he actually "make a move," the results might well destroy the necessary illusion of permanence. One almost feels that Frances forces him, for the first time, to consider seriously a calculated plan of seduction.

The story's ending is a brilliant ironic stroke. Now defeated, Frances leaves the table to make a phone call. Watching her walk away, Michael thinks "what a pretty girl, what nice legs" (*FD*, 68). He has succeeded in transforming her into an "Other," in making her seem distant and remote just like all the anonymous "girls in their summer dresses."

After reading this story, one cannot be certain that the quarrel is not a ritualized substitute for meaningful conversation. Shaw's genius in capturing surfaces is exactly appropriate for his depiction of Michael and Frances—they are afraid to look very deeply beneath the surface of their sustaining beliefs and values, afraid of truly confronting their spiritual emptiness.

Shaw uses a similar narrative technique in "Mixed Doubles," another memorable story about a troubled marriage. In this story, the quarrel is largely silent and one-sided, but Shaw depicts marital tension by combining the wife's interior monologue with the language and action of a tennis game. Jane Collins, the narrative focus, is, at the beginning of the story, seemingly happy in her marriage with Stewart: "[They] had been married six years, but even so, as she watched him stride before her in that curious upright, individual, half-proud, half-comic walk, like a Prussian drill sergeant on his Sunday off, Jane felt the same mixture of amusement and delight in him that had touched her so strongly when they first met" (*FD*, 418). Yet by the end of the story, she feels neither amusement nor delight in her husband.

Jane and Stewart are, in the story's present tense, partners in tennis as well as in marriage. Shaw amusingly and ironically presents the underlying tensions of the Collins marriage through their afternoon opponents. Mr. Croker is a "serious little man" who plays "a steady, dependable game" (*FD*, 418). The word, "Croker," of course, has slang associations with the idea of death; it thus hints at the potential death of Jane and Stewart's marriage. Moreover, Croker, the character, embodies those qualities most noticeably absent in Stewart. The other partner is "soft and attractive" Eleanor Burns (*FD*, 418); and Jane's perception that her husband is beginning to "burn" for the young woman prompts her interior monologue.

Stewart begins his flirtation with Eleanor before the match begins. He promises to go easy on her when play starts: "No mercy for women. The ancient motto of the Collins family" (*FD*, 419). While he is teasingly comparing himself to the archetypal merciless seducer, Jane speculates that there might be some truth in the joke, and her anger grows stronger as the tennis match progresses. She and Stewart start losing after he senselessly gives away a crucial point: "it *was* just like Stewart. It was awful how everything he did was all of a piece. His whole life was crowded with gestures" (Shaw's italics, *FD*, 421). Later, as he plays more aggressively and stupidly, Jane thinks, "That *is* the way he is. Form above everything" (Shaw's italics, *FD*, 423).

Momentarily, she tries to arrest and reverse her thoughts: "Marriage, after all, was an up-and-down affair, in many ways a fragile and devious thing, and was not to be examined too closely" (*FD*, 424). But as he prepares to serve match point, she thinks of all his professional failures: "On the sporting pages, they called it coming through in the clutch. There were some players who did and some players who didn't. . . . If you looked at it coldly, you had to admit that until now Stewart had been one of those who didn't" (*FD*, 424). His tennis, she decides, mirrors his life: "Gifted, graceful, powerful, showy, flawed, erratic . . ." (*FD*, 425). Irrationally, she hopes that his serve will be good and, thus, "a turning point," "a symbol" of change (*FD*, 425). When he double-faults and loses the match, she knows "that she wasn't going to Reno, but . . . that the word would pass through her thoughts again and again, more and more frequently, with growing insistence, as the days went by" (*FD*, 425). Shaw thus makes it clear that Jane has already been considering divorce. Shaw concludes the story with an effective and amusing snapper: Stewart, walking off the course in defeat, typically finds an excuse: "Late in the afternoon, like this. It's impossible to see the service line" (*FD*, 425).

"Mixed Doubles" can be read as an overtly comic companion story to "The Girls in Their Summer Dresses." Shaw masterfully uses the language of tennis—"love" and "fault"—to underscore the more amusing aspects of plot and characterization, especially the manner in which Jane gradually becomes incensed with those aspects of Stewart's personality that were initially so attractive to her. Like Michael, Stewart Collins is a perennial adolescent seeking compensation for the disappointments of his life in sensuous stimuli and youthful games. He is also a boy-man who prefers not to look too closely at himself.

Like Frances in "The Girls in Their Summer Dresses," Jane Collins examines her fragile marriage too closely. In Shaw's stories, marriage is often an uneasy truce, an arrangement of convenience or habit that cannot bear any meaningful scrutiny. Thus, Shaw's married couples not infrequently indulge in ritual quarrels to avoid really looking at the tensions underlying their relationships.

"A Wicked Story" is reminiscent in theme and technique of both "The Girls in Their Summer Dresses" and "Mixed Doubles." Like them, it recounts a marital quarrel over an imagined infidelity between the husband and an actress. The story's setting is familiar Irwin Shaw territory, a New York play and restaurant. Robert and Virginia Harvey, the focal characters, are recognizable Shaw types as well—attractive, well-to-do, slightly jaded New Yorkers.

The couple's quarrel develops in the restaurant as a result of their having attended the play. Virginia believes that her husband had applauded too loudly and vigorously for an actress who had had a minor part in the production they saw. Initially, she baits her husband quite indirectly about his behavior. She complains about the female characters who dominate the contemporary theater, "All the women always are drunks or nymphomaniacs or they drive their sons crazy or they ruin the lives of two or three people an act" (*SS*, 427). With apparent illogic, she then berates the ordinariness of current actresses: "When I was a little girl, actresses used to be so affected you'd *know* you had to pay to see them, because you'd never meet anybody like that in real life in a million years" (Shaw's italics, *FD*, 428).

Eventually, she gets from Robert the confession for which she has been fishing—he had previously met the young actress from the play. In this story Shaw's dialogue works like the character names and largely unspoken "language" in "Mixed Doubles"—it maintains a comic tone and mood. After Robert's key admission, Virginia's attack on the young actress is direct:

> "She looks as though she came from California," Virginia said, making it sound like a criticism.
> "Oakland," Robert said. "It's not exactly the same thing." (*FD*, 428).

The actress, whose name is Miss Byrne, soon enters the restaurant. After a brief conversation with the Harveys, she leaves to join a table of theater people. But seeing her only adds to Virginia's accelerating anger, and she soon accuses Robert of having exchanged "the most intimate confidences" with Miss Byrne (*FD*, 431).

Inevitably, Virginia next reminds Robert of his one actual infidelity two years earlier. Having established that he is undeniably capable of transgression, she accuses him of being a womanizer. The story's comic mood receives particular emphasis in the subsequent dialogue. Robert defends himself reluctantly against her charge: "'It's charming for you to think, even after being married to me for five years, that women just drop at my feet after speaking to me for five minutes, but I have to disillusion you. It has never happened to me. Never,' he said slowly and distinctly and with some disappointment" (*FD*, 433). Virginia is hardly appeased. After berating him for "fake modesty," she traces her husband's alleged womanizing propensities back to the damaging influence of his mother. Understandably, Robert is bewildered by the sudden shifts in her attack: "Good God . . . Now we have my mother, too," to which Victoria responds enigmatically, "She has a lot to answer for, . . . your mother. Don't think she hasn't" (*FD*, 433).

In developing the Harveys' quarrel, Shaw demonstrates his special gift for absurdist exaggeration within the framework of a fiction of manners: Robert applauded too loudly at a play and consequently finds himself in the position of having to deny that he is a compulsive seducer of women and the victim of a dominant mother. Robert thus appears a comic victim in the climax of the story. Shaw, however, has a snapper waiting for the reader.

The story ends with Robert, after Virginia has stormed out of the restaurant in anger, staring at Miss Byrne, who smiles back at him. He then understands that he will attempt to seduce the young actress: "he knew, helplessly, that he was going to call her next day and he knew what her voice was going to sound like on the telephone" (*FD*, 434). This dynamic parallels that of "The Girls in Their Summer Dresses"— an angry wife accuses her husband of harboring thoughts of infidelity, and the husband then considers acting on such thoughts.

As mentioned, Shaw constantly uses marital infidelity as an inherently dramatic violation of the code of personal loyalty central to his concept of decency. Living in a secular world dominated by images of the flesh, his male characters are often tempted to be unfaithful to their wives and, thus, to violate this particular demand of decency. Although Michael, Stewart Collins, and Robert Harvey are not fundamentally indecent, they are weak characters confronting temptation, and one can have no assurance that they will ultimately withstand it.

The husband in Shaw's distinctly unpleasant but powerful story "Dinner in a Good Restaurant" stands in sharp contrast to these three characters. Primarily consisting of dialogue, the story is an interesting variation on the confession story. Mr. Hood is a cruel, cynical man who unashamedly lives off his wife and tortures her with quite public affairs. Mrs. Hood tries without success to induce in her husband some sense of shame. She taunts him with her support for him: "It's a lucky thing for you . . . there are women in this world, women with incomes," to which he simply responds, "You bet" (*SS*, 592). Next she calls him a "pimp," and says, "the work you have to do to support yourself with me, you don't mind doing—too much." Again, Hood refuses to take the challenge: "'It's a privilege,' he said, the smile set on his face" (*SS*, 593).

The story ends with a powerful final irony. After telling her husband that she will no longer endure his infidelities with other women, Mrs. Hood is overcome by sexual desire for him and demands that they rush home immediately. This ending is foreshadowed by one of her remarks early in the story: "When I'm dead . . . people will sit in restaurants and say, 'What a fool!' and they'll be partly right and partly wrong because they don't know the whole story" (*SS*, 592). Ultimately, Mrs. Hood confesses her helpless acquiescence in her own victimization. The masochistic nature of her passion leaves her vulnerable to her husband's sadism. "Dinner in a Good Restaurant" is one of a handful of Shaw stories that treat, if indirectly, the subject of sexual perversion. The hint of sexual perversion underscores Shaw's total characterization of Mr. Hood, who embodies a more pervasive and fundamental kind of perversion, the cynical repudiation of decency. Cruelty and infidelity are not really temptations to him; rather, they are the values by which he lives.

Stories of Adolescence

A subject as universal as love and marriage, male adolescence is the thematic focus of a few of Shaw's stories. In "Pattern of Love" Shaw tells a simple story that revolves around archetypal images of childhood and love. Shaw describes a youthful romantic triangle in a powerful, matter-of-fact style that transcends the familiarity of his subject matter. Its title, in fact, reveals that Shaw intends to create fresh dramatic vitality within a clichéd plot. There are three focal characters in the story: Harold, a shy, bespeckled, violin-playing boy, Katherine, the beautiful young femme fatale, and Charley, the school athletic hero.

The story makes use of a reversal of the standard plot as Harold rejects the advances of Katherine who, in turn, spurns the attention of Charley. The ending, in which a baffled and frustrated Charley demands that Harold fight him, is the key to the effectiveness of the story. Shaw avoids the obvious trick of allowing Harold to miraculously win the fight; instead, the resolutely nonathletic boy stoically endures a brutal beating. Charley, in contrast, briefly "seemed to enjoy the pitiless administration of justice" (*FD*, 667). But when Harold refuses to cry after the fight, Charley breaks down in tears, realizing that he can never make his opponent weep.

Charley thus comes to realize his human limitations. He has had a glimpse of impending adulthood, in which physical strength alone will solve few meaningful problems; and for the first time he has experienced helplessness, understanding that he cannot force Katherine, and future Katherines, to respond to him. Charley is a childhood counterpart to Christian Darling of "The Eighty-Yard Run," an innocent about to enter into an incomprehensibly complex reality.

Despite its brutal and painful ending, "Pattern of Love" contains elements of comedy that result primarily from its ironic parallels to the courtly love tradition. Harold and Charley are young twentieth-century urban knights goaded to combat by the queenly Katherine. In recounting the "courtship" of Harold and Katherine, Shaw makes effective use of broad comedy. When the young femme fatale invites Harold to keep her company on Thursday night, the youthful violinist is overcome by a fit of coughing. After her overtures are repeatedly rejected, Katherine announces that she is "going to retire to a nunnery" (*FD*, 663). Innocently walking behind her, Charley "looked at the spot on her neck where he had kissed her for the first time and felt his soul drop out of his body" (*FD*, 665). Desperation forces Charley to make his own dire threat to Katherine: "I'll tell your mother. . . . You're going around with a Methodist. With a Protestant!" (*FD*, 665). The comedy here is the result of adolescents' ritual imitations of the values and prejudices of their parents. In desperation, Charley tries to intimidate Katherine by echoing his mother's religious bigotry. He appears ridiculous, as adolescent boys in "romantic" situations often do. In this story, Shaw succeeds in capturing the sheer absurdity of adolescent love and passion. These broad comic elements in combination with the story's painful evocation of a vanishing childhood innocence make it a fresh and unusual kind of initiation story.

The theme of endangered innocence is also central to "Strawberry Ice Cream Soda," in which Shaw largely undercuts any potential seriousness in offering a comic account of brotherly devotion. The central character in this story is Eddie Barnes, a 15-year-old New York City native vacationing with his younger brother and his parents in the Adirondacks. Eddie's thoroughly urban sensibility is emphasized early in the story after he captures a butterfly. "Listlessly" addressing his prey, he commands, "Give honey or I'll kill yuh" (*FD*, 42). He is frustrated by the failure of some radish seeds he had planted to take root: "Nothing was happening to them. . . . He was sorry he'd ever gone in for farming" (*FD*, 43).

Homesick for the city, Eddie is somewhat pacified by the knowledge that for the first time in his life he has a date for the evening and 35¢

to spend on it: "Thirty-five cents ought to be enough for any girl" (*FD*, 43). Yet even this security is threatened by his little brother, Lawrence, who begs him for a strawberry ice-cream soda. Hoping to distract Lawrence, Eddie steals a boat and two paddles, and together they row into the middle of the lake. Even there, however, Lawrence continues to demand the soda, and Eddie's troubles are compounded when the boat's owner, a huge, burly farmer, demands that they return his property to shore.

Once ashore, they discover that the farmer is with his son, Nathan, who demands to fight Lawrence. Another version of Harold from "Pattern of Love," the younger brother is a decidedly unathletic boy who is devoted to the piano. Not surprisingly, he initially refuses to fight the farmer's son and looks to Eddie for support. His older brother, however, ridicules him as a coward and virtually forces him to march off into the woods for combat. The key to the story's success is Shaw's choice of not dealing directly with the Lawrence-Nathan fight; instead, he recounts a comic conversation between Eddie and the farmer as they stretch out on the grass to await the outcome of the battle in the woods.

The farmer offers Eddie a cigarette, and the city boy takes it, even though he has never smoked before: "'Thanks,' Eddie said, sitting, pulling daringly at the cigarette, exhaling slowly, with natural talent" (*FD*, 49). Soon, the farmer is praising the glories of the country to a receptive Eddie. Not to be outdone, Eddie brags about Lawrence's prowess as a fighter: "I remember one day, Larry fought three kids all in a row. In a half an hour. He busted all their noses. In a half-hour! He's got a terrific left jab—one, two, bang! like this—and it gets 'em in the nose" (*FD*, 50).

Inevitably, though, Lawrence returns from the woods badly beaten. Yet he has acquitted himself well and, in doing so, he has discovered a proud new self-image: "in the one eye that still could be seen shone a clear light, honorable, indomitable" (*FD*, 50). In turn, Eddie finds in his little brother's heroism an unexpected source of fraternal honor. At the end, the two brothers walk away together experiencing "the silence of equals, strong men communicating in a language more eloquent than words (*FD*, 51). His date apparently forgotten, Eddie suggests that they go get strawberry ice-cream sodas.

As in "Pattern of Love," irony and reversal of traditional plot devices in "Strawberry Ice Cream Soda" allow Shaw to bring a fresh perspective to the traditional initiation story. The "education" of the urban

Eddie by the farmer is an especially unexpected twist. Shaw lightly mocks traditional male bonding throughout "Strawberry Ice Cream Soda"—Eddie derives more enjoyment from his brother's fight than he would from a date, even with 35¢ to spend. Finally, Eddie is, of course, more than a little bit of a rogue—it is his idea to steal the boat, yet he allows Lawrence to suffer for it. "Strawberry Ice Cream Soda" is in the American tradition of Mark Twain and Hemingway: Eddie is a modern, urban version of Huck Finn and Nick Adams.

In "Little Henry Irving" and "Peter Two" Shaw describes boys with more serious problems. The central character in the first of these two stories is also named Eddie and also has a distinctly urban outlook. But he is confronting something much more disturbing than the boredom of a summer or a demanding little brother. By the end of the story he has to acknowledge to himself that his father does not care, and will never care, about him.

Before the story opens, Eddie has been sent to a military academy in Connecticut. He is initially seen shooting craps with the school custodian on Christmas Eve while proudly proclaiming his New York City background. After Eddie wins the crap game, the custodian asks, "how old *are* you, anyway, a million?" Eddie replies, "I am thirteen years old. . . . But I come from New York" (Shaw's italics, *FD*, 315).

In this opening scene Eddie reveals why his father sent him to the academy: "I hit my sister with a lamp. A bridge lamp. . . . I would do it again. Her name's Diana. She's fifteen years old" (*FD*, 315). The father treats the sister as a little goddess—she plans to become an actress, and he lovingly calls her "his little Bernhardt" (*FD*, 315). In contrast, the father refuses Eddie even the slightest gesture of affection.

This rejection has not damaged Eddie's love for, and admiration of, his actor father. Eddie has fallen into the habit of disobeying his father regularly so that he will be whipped and, thus, receive "some attention, some evidence of paternal love" (*FD*, 317). He brags to the custodian that "My Pop can act better than anybody since Sir Henry Irving" (*FD*, 315), and he fantasizes about acting so successfully as the Merchant of Venice that his father will call him "a little Henry Irving" (*FD*, 317–18).

Eddie is spending Christmas alone because no one has notified the school authorities to send him home for the holidays. In desperation, he decides to start a fire in the basement of the academy, reasoning that if the school burned down, he would have to be sent home. After setting the fire, he escapes to New York and rushes to the theater where his father is appearing in *The Merchant of Venice*. Rather than welcoming his son, the actor is outraged by his unexpected presence: "I am paying that money-grubbing Military Academy forty-five dollars extra to keep you there and you tell me you are home for Christmas!" (*FD*, 320). The story thus implies an ironic parallel between the cruel, miserly father and Shakespeare's Shylock.

When Eddie in desperation explains that he had to come home because the school burned down, the father begins slapping him and accuses him of arson: "If the school burned down . . . and you were there, it was your fault" (*FD*, 320). Finally, Eddie is sent away to his aunt in Duluth. Duluth will be, for him, an even worse exile from New York than Connecticut was.

The story's fundamental underlying irony is that, while the father's accusation of arson is accurate, Eddie is not a bad boy; instead he is a lonely child crying out for the acceptance of a cold, adamantly unfeeling parent. Shaw does not need to resolve the outcome of the fire Eddie set—what is important is the boy's future, which appears dark and uncertain.

"Little Henry Irving" is an intense brief study of a deeply troubled and profoundly isolated young boy. Whereas 13-year-old Peter of "Peter Two" also appears alone and vulnerable, this story is closer in tone and mood to "Strawberry Ice Cream Soda" than to "Little Henry Irving." Peter—he is nicknamed "Peter Two" to distinguish him from two friends with the same name—who initially has a media-inspired concept of the hero as violent adventurer and fearless rescuer, learns something about the true nature of heroism.

The boy is first seen alone in his parents' apartment eating grapes while watching a violent television program at 11 P.M. He is luxuriating in the recurrent images of carnage and death flashing across the small screen: "It was Saturday night and people were killing each other by the hour on the small screen" (*FD*, 444). This vicarious violence causes Peter to remember a recent school fight in which he had defended the physically weaker of his two friends (who is ironically nicknamed Peter the Great) against a bully. The bully had broken his arm by hitting Peter Two on the head, so the gallant rescuer now feels ready for more serious challenges: "'Let them come,' he muttered obscurely, munching grape seeds and watching the television set through narrowed eyes, 'just let them come'" (*FD*, 445).

What does come is not something Peter has anticipated. At midnight he hears someone beating on the front door. No longer fearless, Peter goes to the door and overhears a quarrel between Mr. and Mrs. Chalmers, the neighbors, in which the husband seems to be threatening to kill his wife. Finally opening the door, he sees Mrs. Chalmers on her knees in the vestibule with her husband standing over her holding "a big, heavy pistol" (*FD*, 448). Peter, despite the pleas of Mrs. Chalmers, fails to fulfill his heroic destiny and immediately slams the door shut.

The next day, the failed rescuer is mystified to see the Chalmers calmly walking down the street as if nothing had happened the night before. Now frightened by the essential incomprehensibility of adult reality, he rushes home to the protection of the television set. For a moment he watches a spy program, but he abruptly switches it off: "after the night in which he had faced the incomprehensible, shameless, weaponed grownup world and had failed to disarm it, ah, they can have that, that's for kids" (*FD*, 450). The quality of heroism, Peter has learned, is much more complex than what is described in the mass media.

Shaw's direct experience with the radio equivalents of Peter's television programs informs this story, and Peter can be seen as an unsuspecting victim of the kind of scripts written by Andrew in "Main Currents of American Thought." Shaw wrote scripts for "Dick Tracy," just as Andrew does for "Dusty Blades" and "Ronnie Cook and His Friends." Like Charley in "Pattern of Love," Peter catches a disturbing glimpse of the sheer irrationality of adulthood; and like the young arsonist in "Little Henry Irving," he is forced into an awareness of how alone and vulnerable a child truly is. Yet "Peter Two" is ultimately a light, amusing story. The adult reader, unlike Peter, is amused by the ridiculous behavior of Mr. and Mrs. Chalmers; and Shaw signals his tongue-in-cheek approach to the narrative by referring to the least imposing of the trio of Peters as Peter the Great.

In Shaw's stories childhood and adolescence are periods of confusion and emotional intensity and pain, as well as times of excitement and fresh experience. Even though his boys are usually militant New Yorkers, they are fundamentally no different than their young counterparts in the fiction of Twain, Hemingway, and Sherwood Anderson; they are innocents as well as rogues, and their essential decency remains intact.

Although not a story of adolescence, "Where All Things Wise and Fair Descend" is nevertheless Shaw's most memorable study of youthful devotion and pain. One of his late stories, it was collected in *God*

Was Here but He Left Early. In 1980 Shaw discussed "Where All Things Wise and Fair Descend" with obvious and justified pride: "That's an elegy. Toward friendship and brotherhood. It's a sad elegy. About how unjust a family has to be" (see Giles interview in part 2). In its textual richness and subtle explorations of the interrelated themes of love and rivalry between brothers, friendship and loyalty, and secret, irrational guilt, it is the work of a masterful storyteller at the peak of his form.

The story's focal character initially seems to be a youthful version of a familiar Shaw type. Steven Dennicott is a privileged southern California college student, an essentially decent young man whose character is, at the first of the story, superficial and unformed:

> He woke up feeling good. There was no reason for him to wake up feeling anything else. . . .
> . . . He got A's in English and history and had memorized most of Shakespeare's sonnets and read Roethke and Eliot and Ginsburg. He had tried marijuana. He was invited to all the parties. . . .
> Nobody he had ever cared for had as yet died and everybody in his family had come home safe from all the wars.
> The world saluted him.
> He maintained his cool. (*FD*, 708–9)

While the southern California setting is, of course, somewhat unusual for a Shaw story, Steven Dennicott, with his young male arrogance and sense of invulnerability, recalls Christian Darling, Michael of "The Girls in Their Summer Dresses," and Stewart Collins of "Mixed Doubles," among other Shaw characters. Throughout much of the narrative the perennially warm and sunny California climate serves as a metaphor for Steve's inexperience and largely unchallenged self-confidence. Yet by the end of the story Steve shows promise of attaining a real and sustaining maturity.

The inspiration for his growth comes from an unlikely source. Crane, a fellow student, on the surface, appears to be Steve's opposite: "He didn't seem to have any friends and he never was seen with girls and the time he didn't spend in class he seemed to spend in the library" (*FD*, 711). Crane's mere appearance is "a discredit to the golden Coastal legend" (*FD*, 713); his pale, awkward, thin form is clearly out of place among the strong, golden bodies around him.

Not surprisingly, Steve's involvement with Crane is sudden and unexpected. Steve arrives at his English class early one Tuesday morning to find Crane writing Shelley's elegy "On the Death of Keats" on the blackboard. Like the rest of the class, Steve silently observes the grief-stricken young man as he continues his furious, barely controlled performance. He knows that, on the previous Saturday, Crane's brother, a football player, had been killed in an automobile accident. Yet like the rest of the campus he has, until this moment, rarely thought of Crane as the dead athlete's brother: "the fact that the huge, graceful athlete and the scarecrow bookworm were members of the same family seemed like a freak of eugenics to the students who knew them both" (*FD*, 711). On this occasion, however, something prompts Steve to stay behind after class to talk to Crane as the other students wordlessly file by.

The grieving young man is not really surprised by Steve's approach to him. He "absently" comments that "of the whole class," Steve would, of course, be the one to express concern. Crane apparently detects a still masked capacity for sensitivity and growth in Dennicott, who responds by agreeing to accompany Crane to the site of his brother's fatal accident. They drive together to where a huge tree, one side of which has been ripped open, leans over the bend of the highway.

Here Crane makes a prolonged confession of guilt. Underlying his admission of guilt is a strong undercurrent of as yet unacknowledged anger:

> If I had been a true brother . . . I would have come here Saturday morning and cut this tree down. My brother would be alive today. . . . You'd think . . . that if you loved a brother enough you'd have sense enough to come and cut a tree down, wouldn't you? . . .
> My brother and I were the only children [my parents] had, and they look at me and they can't help feeling, If it had to be one of them, why couldn't it have been *him*? . . . [A]nd they know I agree with them and they feel guilty and I can't help them. (*FD*, 714)

One can understand the parents' reaction—the son who had been the obvious inheritor of "the golden Coastal legend" had died, whereas the son who is an unattractive misfit still lives. Crane understands only too well his parents' feelings and is even struggling to agree with them. But he can never fully agree and, as a result, experiences an almost crippling grief. It is this element of the story that Shaw had in mind when he said the story is about "how unjust a family has to be."

After his confession, Crane begins to praise his brother's "sense of purity." Although not in the way the grieving brother intends, Crane's admiring description of his brother's code constitutes Steve's introduction to the necessity of decency in human behavior. The dead brother's code, as it is enunciated, emerges as a monstrous demand for inhuman perfection. Crane initially equates it with "having a private set of standards and never compromising them. . . . Even when it hurts, even when it's just a tiny, formal gesture, that ninety-nine people out of a hundred would make without thinking about it" (*FD*, 716). Then he relates two examples of his brother's demand for perfection.

First, he proudly recounts the story of the brother's failure to be elected captain of the football team because he had judged the outgoing captain a coward and consequently had refused to shake hands with him. Upon hearing this, Steve is alarmed: "For the first time, it occurred to Steve that it was perhaps just as well that he had never known Crane's brother, never been measured against that Cromwellian certitude of conduct" (*FD*, 717).

Crane's next example of his brother's demand for perfection is even more disturbing. The athlete had once ended his relationship with a girl after seeing her silhouette sitting up in bed and realizing that "she had a fat, loose belly . . . because it wasn't perfect, and he wouldn't settle for less" (*FD*, 717). Dennicott starts to laugh at the absurdity of this story but checks himself: "He was amused, but he couldn't help thinking that it was possible that Crane had loved his brother for all the wrong reasons. And he couldn't help feeling sorry for the unknown girl, deserted, without knowing it, in the dark room, by the implacable athlete who had just made love to her" (*FD*, 717).

Shaw's subtlety is especially evident in this scene, for the reader can only guess about whether Crane understands that his brother's demand for perfection had been cruel and even monstrous. The so obviously imperfect brother's praise of this demand constitutes an intensely ironic moment in the story. Crane has, for whatever reasons, become a disciple of his brother's uncompromising code, and he next asks Steve, "Have you ever done anything in your whole life that was unprofitable, damaging, maybe even ruinous, because it was the pure thing to do?" (*FD*, 717–18). Significantly, Dennicott can only remember one time when he had behaved in such a way—he had let himself get beaten up to avoid embarrassing a "physical-culture idiot, with muscles like basketballs" whom he had pointlessly insulted (*FD*, 718). There is a central difference between Steve's "pure" moment and the dead young man's code of perfection: in the former, Steve, but no one else, got hurt. Thus, Dennicott, though slightly arrogant in his sheltered existence, possesses a potential for truly ethical behavior. He already senses that avoiding cruelty is essential to decency—this inherent gentlessness prompted him to speak to Crane in the first place.

Subsequent dialogue between the two young men indicates that it is probably too late to reverse the psychological damage Crane has suffered before and since the death of his Adonis-like brother. He tells Dennicott that he plans to join the forestry service: "I expect to get a lot of reading done. I'm not so enthusiastic about my fellow man, anyway, I prefer trees" (*FD*, 719). Here, Crane's repressed, but inevitable, anger is obvious—it was a tree, after all, that killed the perfect, adored brother whom he has never been able to emulate. When Steve asks if he will not desire a wife someday, the damaged young man answers "harshly," "What sort of woman would choose me? . . . I look like something left over after a New Year's party on skid row. And I would only take the best, the most beautiful, the most intelligent, the most loving. I'm not going to settle for some poor, drab Saturday-night castaway" (*FD*, 719). Clearly, Crane pretends to adopt his brother's code of perfection in order to deny the inevitability of rejection. In addition to anger, his role as the unattractive, undesirable brother has cost him no little pain.

But if it is too late for Crane to attain maturity and an essential decency, it is not too late for Steve Dennicott. From the first, the subtle emphasis underlying "Where All Things Wise and Fair Descend" is Steve's initiation. His safe, uncomplicated existence is significantly disturbed for the time by his unexpected association with the embittered Crane. Waving goodbye to the grieving brother, Dennicott is surprised to feel not just pity, but also envy for Crane: "Crane had the capacity for sorrow and now, after the day Steven had spent with the bereaved boy, he understood that the capacity for sorrow was also the capacity for living" (*FD*, 720). In the fiction of Irwin Shaw, the "capacity for living" implies the capacity for decency and kindness.

The story's ending effectively underscores Shaw's thematic concerns. After abruptly seeing his girlfriend, Adele, with Crane's eyes and thus realizing the full extent of her intellectual and moral shallowness, Steve almost turns his back on his girlfriend. But remembering Crane's story of his brother's cruel rejection of the girl with the "loose belly," he goes up to her smiling, instead: "Crane had taught him a good deal that afternoon, but perhaps not the things Crane had thought he was teaching" (*FD*, 721). Dennicott will make no monstrous demands for perfection on anyone. He is developing a human code of ethical behavior; and, as the story's last line makes clear, that growth will inevitably destroy the sheltered existence he has previously lived: "he wasn't going to wake up, automatically feeling good, ever again" (*FD*, 721).

Shaw was correct in describing "Where All Things Wise and Fair Descend" as an "elegy toward friendship and brotherhood" and a story about the understandable cruelty of a family. More than that, though, it is an elegy to innocence, a study of the loss of youthful serenity and arrogance and the consequent attainment of maturity. In its association of a rigid, unreasonable demand for perfection with cruelty, it is a subtle tribute to the inevitable pain, but unavoidable necessity, of being human.

A Climate of Insomnia

A few of Shaw's apolitical American stories exhibit a degree of sensitivity toward and comprehension of academia that are perhaps surprising in a writer so apparently removed from that uniquely artificial environment. Certainly, Irwin Shaw never supplemented his income by teaching at a university, and his friends were mainly from the creative world, not from schools. Nevertheless, Shaw was keenly interested in the academic life—who was teaching which of his works, how academic politics (both in individual schools and throughout academia) were currently working, how professors and teachers were being paid and recognized, the tremendous influence of education in his life and its potential impact on all life.

Shaw's most ambitious academic story, "The Climate of Insomnia," is a masterfully crafted example of the kind of modern story in which suspense derives from a pervasive uncertainty about what might be happening, rather than from anything that does happen. This plot uncertainty is closely related to thematic concerns—the story's central character is a representative modern man suffering from an anxiety that can be attributed to no single cause. "The Climate of Insomnia" was first collected in *Mixed Company* (1950); and, to a degree, the anxiety of the main character, Cahill, is the result of living in immediate post–World War II America. The sense that World War II ushered human society into a new universe of vulnerability dominates much of American literature since 1945.

The narrative opens with Cahill, a 40-year-old philosophy professor, returning home late one evening to find a message from the maid that a colleague named Reeves had called and left an urgent message: "He must talk to you. Very important, he says" (*FD*, 383). It is too late to return Reeves's call, and Cahill spends a troubled night trying to guess which particular disaster lies in wait for him.

Not surprisingly, considering he is a philosophy professor, Cahill is an introspective man with a fertile imagination. Introspection and imagination prove, on this night, to be refined instruments of mental torture. The imminent disasters he imagines range from personal and professional problems to sweeping social and political concerns. He tries to go to sleep and forget Reeves' message until morning, but after dozing off for a moment, he is awakened by a siren outside. Inevitably, the siren triggers memories of the war: "somehow he was back in London, in the cold billet, and the planes were overhead and the guns were going off, and he had the old feeling that neighbors were dying by chance in burning buildings on the street outside his window" (*FD*, 384–85).

A member of what has come to be known as the Valium Generation, Cahill tries to induce sleep with pills. Still, he lies awake: "Sleep, he thought, the first great natural resource to be exhausted by modern man. The erosion of the nerves, not to be halted by any reclamation project, private or public" (*FD*, 385). Cahill's insomnia recalls Hemingway's classic depiction, in "A Clean, Well-Lighted Place," of the twentieth-century intellectual paralyzed by the collapse of traditional values and the pervasive threat of *nada*. History since World War II has only intensified this Lost Generation vision.

Cahill is not innocent and begins to speculate that Reeves called to demand an accounting for a personal slight. The two men have been colleagues and friends for years, but in recent years Cahill has been jealous of Reeves's greater success. Two weeks earlier, at a public gathering, the insomniac had ridiculed his old friend's method of teaching, and now he is certain that Reeves has heard about his comments, "as was almost inevitable in the narrow companionship of a college town" (*FD*, 386). Shaw does a fine job in this story of portraying the petty jealousies and senseless quarrels for which academia is noted.

Cahill's imagination quickly transforms him from villain to victim— he is suddenly certain that his wife is having an affair with Reeves. She, after all, laughs at his colleague's jokes and rarely at his: "Well, the truth was he wasn't terribly witty, and a woman might be expected to catch on in eighteen years of marriage" (*FD*, 388). Cahill's speculation about his wife's infidelity, not surprisingly, makes him recall his own prolonged flirtation with a beautiful 19-year-old student. Ultimately, nothing sexual had happened with the young woman, but Cahill is nevertheless certain that he has been belatedly discovered: "Grotesque, he thought, for a few hours of gentle conversation, for an illusory, ephemeral buttressing of the vanity, for the titillating suggestion of sin without the sin itself, to risk so much!" (*FD*, 389).

Through the next sequence of possibilities the philosophy professor considers, Shaw captures the unique uncertainties of academic life. He then gives these uncertainties a broader social relevance. Momentarily, Cahill considers that the hidden message might not be of disaster, after all—perhaps, he thinks, he is about to be promoted: "Twelve, fifteen hundred a year. No more Philosophy 53A, the dullest course in the curriculum. No eight-o'clock classes" (*FD*, 390). But again his sense of himself as victim overwhelms this pleasant speculation, and he feels certain that he is about to be fired:

> He was far from being the most popular instructor on the campus. . . . Ever since he'd come back from the war, the job had bored him. Not that there was anything else he particularly wanted to do. Just sit, perhaps, and stare into an open fire. . . . The last time he had seen the president at a faculty meeting, the president had been . . . frosty. That was the word—frosty. Purge by frost. Execution, university style. The polite death among the library shelves. (*FD*, 390)

Thus, the unpredictable nature of university politics threatens Cahill, and as a postwar man he is particularly vulnerable to any vague, indirect, unseen threat. Like most academics and also like most Americans, Cahill lives on the edge of economic survival; and it is a psychologically exhausting struggle to get through each month with something left in his checkbook: "He supposed that nine-tenths of the people in the country walked, as he did, on the thin edge of disaster all their lives, smiling, dissembling, not sleeping some nights, hoping their nerve would hold out as they saw the edge crumbling, crumbling" (*FD*, 391).

Cahill's anxiety focuses also on his children. He remembers that his daughter, 17-year-old Elizabeth, has been dating Reeves's nephew and fears that the worst has happened: "How could any father know what obscure, shameful invitations of the flesh his daughter was accepting and succumbing to" (*FD*, 391). If Elizabeth is not in trouble, then Cahill's 15-year-old son, Charlie, must be: "At what moment did the high-spirited schoolboy turn into the juvenile delinquent? . . . Consider your son objectively. What did you see? The insolence of the radio-and-comic-book age" (*FD*, 392). (There was, after the war, a concern in America that violent comic books were inducing violent behavior in America's children.)

Cahill begins reading *Time* magazine as a distraction from his anxiety and is initially reassured by the magazine's neat compartmentalizing of events: "Everything in its neat, crisp department. Two minutes with each and you're ready with enough facts and opinions to carry you until the next publication date" (*FD*, 393). Inevitably, though, the magazine simply redirects Cahill's uncertainty by shifting its focus to current history. After he reads a story about the atomic bomb, a pervasive unacknowledged dread comes to the forefront of his consciousness, and he wonders how anyone sleeps "this year" (*FD*, 394). Anxiety and even panic over the bomb were pervasive in America in the late 1940s and throughout the 1950s. To a degree at least, the other national anxieties of the time were submerged in the new threat of nuclear annihilation. In much American writing of that period and since, nuclear holocaust functions as a quite specific and quite terrifying manifestation of Hemingway's "*nada*."

The professor considers too a less universal, but more immediate, external threat: McCarthyism is beginning to flourish in America, and a committee of state senators has been sent to investigate communism on the campus. A chemistry instructor has been the committee's first victim, and Cahill had contributed fifty dollars "secretly, in cash" to the man's defense fund (*FD*, 395). Here, as in "Goldilocks at Graveside," Shaw points to McCarthy's insidious power to transform acts of generosity into acts of shame.

Finally, Cahill mentally backs away from contemporary historical events and, at last, confronts the primary source of his anxiety. He has recently suffered from a slight heart irregularity and, despite the assurances of his doctor, fears that death is near. (In Shaw's secular, accident-dominated world, death is every man's unsleeping foe.) Shaw uses the diagnosis of the professor's doctor—the professor is only suffering from nerves—as a means of encapsulating most of the story's major concerns. A common nineteenth-century diagnosis, especially for troubled women, the "disease" from which Cahill suffers is nonetheless uniquely contemporary: "Nerves, the modern equivalent for

Fate, the substitute for the medieval Devil, which attacked mankind in the form of obscure, and often mortal, ills" (*FD*, 396). Cahill, like most residents of Shaw's "bawdy," uncertain, flesh-obsessed planet, suffers from a pervasive nervousness that is the legacy of the war, the Holocaust, and the bomb. He is the contemporary, painfully vulnerable human being.

The ending of the story is appropriate to the rest of the story. In desperation Cahill calls Reeves only to discover that his colleague is gone for the weekend, leaving behind no further message. The resolution of "The Climate of Insomnia" is no resolution. The professor has no choice but to wait: "Wildly, he contemplated the thought of living until Monday" (*FD*, 398). The story emphasizes that Cahill as a postwar man can have no certainty of living until Monday, but like all the others suffering from "nerves," he has no recourse but to wait for further uncertainty. Nothing happens in the story because nothing needs to happen—the philosopher has the freedom to imagine a limitless range of disasters. Clearly a product of the period in which it was written, "The Climate of Insomnia" is an unusual Shaw story, because Shaw does not typically feature passive, frightened intellectuals as characters.

The Integrity of "The Gentle People"

Some of Shaw's American stories cannot truly be classified except as portraits of embattled "gentle people" stubbornly clinging to their integrity and dreams in the face of considerable odds. "The Monument" is one of these stories. Set in 1938, this story tells of William McMahon, "one of the five finest bartenders in the City of New York" (*FD*, 79), who makes a successful stand for principle. The story is set in McMahon's bar and uses some of the same narrative techniques found in "Borough of Cemeteries" and "Night, Birth and Opinion." Primarily comic in mood, the story still communicates, through the dialogue of a chorus of waiters, a sense of the depression and the impending war. The bartender's opponent in the story is Mr. Grimmet, the manager of the restaurant in which the bar is located. Both names have symbolic overtones: McMahon proves, in his defiance of the manager, to be a man; whereas Grimmet grimly pushes his foe to the limit.

The conflict between the two men is already in progress when the narrative begins. Grimmet has told McMahon that, to save money, he intends to buy an inferior stock of whiskey. For the bartender, the issue is quality, not economy, and he proudly tells the manager, "In my bar, good drinks are served" (*FD*, 78). When Grimmet insists on ordering the inferior whiskey, McMahon gets himself momentarily fired by insulting the food in the restaurant. Defiantly, he then picks up a plaque that reads "William McMahon, *In Charge*" (*FD*, 79). Before leaving he tells the manager that he is "not as fundamentally interested in making money as [he is] fundamentally interested in other things" (*FD*, 80).

Fundamentally, McMahon is interested, as are Shaw's other "gentle people," in such abstracts as quality, reputation, and integrity. Sensing this trait, the manager still tries to deny it and challenges the bartender: "You are not so different from the rest of the world" (*FD*, 80). In a way, of course, the bartender is not an externally remarkable man. As with Shaw's other "gentle people," his very ordinariness is the underlying source of hope for the survival of America's democracy.

Finally, McMahon makes a speech Grimmet has to hear: "When I die people can say, 'William McMahon left a monument, the bar at Grimmet's Restaurant. He never served a bad drink in his whole life'. . . . A monument" (*FD*, 80). He concludes this statement of principle by defiantly calling the manager "a dumb bastard" (*FD*, 80). Clearly, McMahon has left little room for compromise; nevertheless, Grimmet attempts to salvage his pride with the stipulation that the two men never talk to each other again. McMahon agrees, "Yes, sir," and puts his plaque back in its proper place above the bar (*FD*, 80–81).

Like Shaw's play *The Gentle People*, "The Monument" is a fantasy in which integrity and devotion triumph over greed. It is, of course, easier to defy a restaurant manager than to withstand the anxieties of "the Atomic Age." Yet Shaw believed that such defiance is, if anything, more desperately needed than ever before. One can endorse this belief while still viewing "The Monument" as an amusing, well-crafted fable of a simpler age.

An even more unlikely figure successfully defies the odds in "Triumph of Justice," one of Shaw's funniest stories. The determined hero is Mike Pilato, an Italian-American farmer who uses unusual methods to win a lawsuit. In the first half of the story, Shaw stacks the odds against the eventual triumph of Pilato, a determined innocent. Before the story opens, the farmer had agreed to rent a portion of his land to Victor Fraschi, who has opened a truck stop. Fraschi has connections with the mob and never intends to pay Pilato rent. The innocent farmer is baffled by such deceit; early in the story, he pleads with Fraschi, "You were an Italian, I trusted you" (*FD*, 99). Backed by the threat of mob retaliation, the "tenant" merely laughs at Pilato. Walking home in momentary defeat, Pilato thinks, "Farming was better than being a landlord. You put seed into the earth and you knew what was coming out. Corn grew from corn, and the duplicating of Nature was expected and natural. Also no documents were signed in the compact with Nature, no leases and agreements necessary, a man was not at a disadvantage if he couldn't read or write" (*FD*, 99–100). The innocent farmer had not secured any written assurances from Fraschi, but he decides to sue for the back rent and to handle the case himself. Hearing this decision, Pilato's wife, Dolores, is dismayed: "This is in English. They conduct the court in English." Pilato is nevertheless persistent: "I am right. Justice is on my side" (*FD*, 102). The illiterate farmer then prepares to take on the legal system, not to mention organized crime, with only "justice" on his side.

His innocence is further emphasized at the trial. When Fraschi shamelessly lies on the witness stand, Pilato is amazed: "He stared incredulously into the perjurer's eyes, as a man might stare at a son who has just admitted he has killed his mother, beyond pity, beyond knowledge, outside all the known usage of human life" (*FD*, 104). This further evidence of Fraschi's dishonesty transforms the innocent farmer. He grabs a chair and threatens to smash it over his tenant's head: "He stood, the figure of Justice, armed with the chair" (*FD*, 104). Threatened by physical injury, Fraschi abruptly confesses.

The Judge is bewildered by such an irregular cross-examination: " 'Pilato,' screamed the Judge, 'this is not evidence!' " (*FD*, 104). More absurdist comedy dominates the scene's climax. Infuriated by losing control of his courtroom, the Judge shouts at the attending policeman, "Are you going to stand there and let this go on? Why don't you do something?" The policeman is, however, as baffled as everyone else about how to proceed and responds, "I can shoot him. . . . Do you want me to shoot the plaintiff?" "Shut up," answers the Judge (*FD*, 105). Finally, Pilato is persuaded to put down the chair, and the Judge, seething over such an absurd loss of control and authority, prepares to dismiss Fraschi's confession and sentence the farmer to thirty days in jail. "In a mixture of fear, repentance, religion, joy at delivery from death," Fraschi, however, inexplicably resumes his confession and the innocent farmer wins his case (*FD*, 105). The triumphant Pilato then issues a reprimand to Fraschi's young lawyer: "You knew he didn't pay me. A boy with an education. You should be ashamed of yourself"

(*FD*, 106) before leaving the courtroom with Dolores at his side to the applause of the spectators.

This climactic scene employs stock figures from traditional farce: a frustrated authority figure (the Judge), a triumphant innocent (Pilato), a miraculously vanquished villain (Fraschi), and a responsive chorus (the courtroom spectators). Such scenes of wrong suddenly and illogically righted are central to comedy from the classic plays of Shakespeare and Molière to the absurd exploits of the Marx brothers. Shaw also adds an amusing final zinger to the story; instead of congratulating Pilato, Dolores scolds her husband as they exit the courtroom: "Acting like that in a court of law! . . . What are you, a red Indian?" (*FD*, 106). The stereotype of the female as upholder of social conventions is, of course, also a familiar ingredient in comedy. Shaw's "gentle people" are not uncommonly males who have learned to look for sympathy from each other first.

Not all of Shaw's gentle innocents are as ultimately successful as McMahon and Pilato in their stubborn stands for principle. In "The Dry Rock" Leopold Tarloff, a small, 50-year-old cabdriver with a heavy Russian accent, is defeated by the arrogance and indifference of others. As the story opens, Tarloff's cab is being run into by an arrogant young man named Rusk. When the cabdriver demands that restitution be made, Rusk knocks him down. Tarloff then decides "wearily" that he has to take a stand for principle; he tells his assailant, "You have committed a crime . . . and there is a punishment for it" (*FD*, 286).

The passengers in the cab at the time of the accident are the Fitzsimmonses, a couple on the way to a party. Mr. Fitzsimmons is a well-meaning but ineffectual representative of the upper middle class, and his wife, Helen, is self-centered and superficial. Despite his wife's objections, Fitzsimmons initially tries to help Tarloff by agreeing to accompany the cabdriver to the police station to fill out a complaint against Rusk. No longer quite so arrogant, the young Rusk attempts to bribe Tarloff to forget the whole thing, but the little man is indignant at such a suggestion and says that his "dignity" will not allow him to take money from his assailant. Besides, he proclaims, an issue of principle is at stake: "I'm a Russian . . . But I'm in the country twenty-five years now, I know what the rights of an individual are" (*FD*, 287–88).

To the consternation of Rusk and Helen Fitzsimmons, the little man with the thick Russian accent has been transformed into an uncompromising defender of American democratic ideals. The selfish Helen responds angrily to this transformation: "I had to go to Bergdorf Goodman . . . to get a gown to spend the evening in a police station" (*FD*, 291). At the station, the lieutenant in charge tells the idealistic immigrant that he should avoid further trouble by accepting Rusk's offer of a $10 settlement. Initially, Tarloff is indignant at such a suggestion: "There is a principle. The dignity of the human body. Justice. For a bad act a man suffers. It's an important thing" (*FD*, 293).

Sensing Fitzsimmons's growing impatience with the entire episode, the cabdriver ultimately has no choice but to surrender: "Tarloff drooped inside his old coat, shook his head wearily, shrugged, deserted once and for all before the lieutenant's desk, on the dry rock of principle" (*FD*, 293). He nevertheless retains his dignity by refusing Rusk's $10. As Tarloff prepares to leave the station, a guilty Fitzsimmons apologizes for not offering him stronger support. The little man of principle is resigned to, instead of bitter about, his passenger's retreat from conviction: "I understand. . . . There is no time. Principle. . . . Today there is no time for anything" (*FD*, 293).

The story's central irony is that the immigrant cabdriver can find time for "principle" whereas the well-to-do Mr. and Mrs. Fitzsimmons and the police lieutenant cannot. Justice, human dignity, and the sanctity of the individual are abstractly important concepts, but, in this story, only Tarloff is prepared to defend these ideals when such defense becomes inconvenient.

Like *The Gentle People*, "Triumph of Justice" is a "fable" or fairy tale in which democratic principles impossibly subdue arrogant power and unfeeling bureaucracy. "The Dry Rock," in contrast, realistically depicts the virtually certain defeat of these principles when they collide with greater odds. In effect, then, "The Dry Rock" is Shaw's acknowledgment that, in reality, "the gentle people" rarely prevail. Shaw understood the vulnerability of the socially insignificant and economically powerless individual in twentieth-century America, and yet "The Dry Rock" is not a completely pessimistic story: Tarloff does, after all, retain his dignity. Fitzsimmons, moreover, recalls such Shaw characters as Michael Whitacre of *The Young Lions;* weak and somewhat superficial, he still instinctively wants to do the right thing. In their unwavering faith in democratic justice, Pilato and Tarloff embody the deep, and often naïve, faith in American idealism so often held by the recent immigrant. Shaw chose to have the same faith, even though he knew it would often be violated.

In "The Deputy Sheriff" Shaw dramatizes the dreams and frustrations of another obscure, powerless man. The third deputy sheriff of Gatlin, New Mexico, a dry, boring town far from any center of excitement, Macomber feels trapped by his stale, passionless marriage. To escape the dull reality of his existence, Macomber fantasizes about Hollywood and glamorous movie actresses.

The story opens with the deputy learning that a minor criminal named Brisbane, who had previously escaped from captivity in New Mexico, has been apprehended in Los Angeles. While Brisbane is a hobo whose only crime is "committing entry into a boxcar," Macomber convinces himself that the escaped man is a ruthless criminal who must be returned to jail in New Mexico and that only he can be trusted with such a dangerous mission. In actuality, of course, the deputy wants to go to Los Angeles, the home of his fantasies: "He could see himself stepping out of a barber shop in Hollywood, . . . Greta Garbo walked the streets there, and Carole Lombard, and Alice Faye" (*FD*, 118–19).

Macomber's fantasy is doomed to remain unfulfilled because he is unable to convince either the sheriff or the district attorney to give him expense money for the trip. Infuriated, he tries unsuccessfully to convince the editor of the *Gatlin Herald* to write a denunciation of the lax and corrupt county law enforcement authorities. Shaw is especially effective in depicting Macomber's willful delusion that Brisbane is a real threat to public safety. Brisbane's ruthlessness becomes a secondary fantasy for the deputy.

In an interesting essay, Michael Moorhead compares Shaw's story to Hemingway's "The Short Happy Life of Francis Macomber."[19] Both the third deputy and Francis Macomber are, he says, "losers" seeking escape from boring, pointless lives and destructive marriages. He argues, moreover, that while Hemingway's hero does have "a moment or two of joy and complete aliveness" before dying, "Shaw's is the bigger loser because he continues to live with his empty, dreary life and his dull wife" (Moorhead, 43). Moorhead concludes with the assertion that "The Deputy Sheriff" is a successful story "undeserving of its total obscurity in the canon of Shaw's work," as well as "an excellent example of the literary practice of 'influence,'" the echoing of themes, characterization, or settings from the works of other writers (Moorhead, 43).

Shaw echoes Hemingway's serious story to create his comic portrait of a bad marriage. His Macomber is one of "the gentle people," an obscure, powerless individual surviving a bleak existence in the best way he can.

The Expatriate Stories

After his move to Paris in 1951 Shaw not surprisingly produced a number of stories about American expatriates. Although the Americans in these stories predominantly represent a more affluent class than the "gentle people" back home, they hardly escape moral complexity or ethical challenge. The best of these stories fall into a distinct tradition of American fiction most memorably realized in the "international theme" of Henry James. In Shaw's expatriate stories, American innocents confront, in Europe, not only a sophistication originating in a rich past but also a brutal corruption resulting from the horror and destruction of World War II. The Shaw story that most clearly echoes James is "A Year to Learn the Language." Its central character, Roberta James, is as distinctly an "American girl" as is Daisy Miller. Roberta has been sent by her wealthy father to study painting in Europe for a year. Not surprisingly, she does not become an artist during that time, but she does begin her maturation as a woman.

The story opens on a satiric note. Louise, Roberta's roommate, is overheard pontificating about the unreliable nature of French men: "[She] . . . had already had two affairs, with Frenchmen, that had come out, according to her, disastrously, and she was in an acid and sophisticated period" (*FD*, 329). Shaw uses the character of Louise primarily to gently ridicule American cultural provincialism: "Louise was studying French literature at the Sorbonne for a year, but at the moment was reading *Huckleberry Finn*, in a French translation. . . . She came from St. Louis and at parties she had been heard to say that the Mississippi was the 'Mother-Water of her life'" (*FD*, 328). Louise corresponds to James's Randolph Miller, who is unable to find in Europe anything as good as what he had in Schenectady, New York.

Roberta listens to Louise's pronouncements because she is aware of, and insecure about, her naïveté and inexperience: she worries that she looks "too young, too blue-eyed, too innocent, too American, too shy, too everlastingly, hopelessly *unready*" (*FD*, 330). She is a virgin, and her concern about her inexperience is intensified by her involvement with Guy, a young Frenchman. Announcing that he is "past all that cheap, adolescent promiscuity," Guy has not pressured Roberta to have sex with him; and she adores him for his patience, "sensing that she was getting the best values of Chicago and Paris in the one package" (*FD*, 332).

Roberta's maturation process begins when Guy takes her on his Vespa to an art gallery at which she hopes her paintings can be exhibited. Shaw keeps to a satiric tone in his description of the reaction of the gallery owner, Patrini, to the young American's work: "He still looked as though he was being mildly haunted by a too-rich sauce or a fish that had been too long in Normandy" (*FD*, 334). Patrini's attitude changes when a man in a homburg, identified as "the Baron," appears and praises Roberta's paintings. The Baron says he cannot decide which of her paintings he wishes to purchase, and Patrini suggests that he take two home to study and decide at his leisure. Shaw ironically foreshadows the climax of the story when Patrini informs Roberta, after her admirer leaves, that "the Baron has a famous collection, as you know, of course" (*FD*, 335). Roberta does not know anything about the Baron, but she nevertheless leaves the gallery assured that she is on the way to fame.

When she returns to Guy, she wonders if she is not on the verge of having outgrown him. As inexperienced with alcohol as with sex, she is nevertheless, bothered by the young man's militant refusal to drink: "she couldn't help feeling a little cheated at being connected with the one man in France who ordered Coca-Cola or lemonade each time the *sommelier* came up to them in a restaurant and offered the wine card. It was uncomfortably like Chicago" (*FD*, 337). Guy's abstinence from alcohol is a clue, which Roberta misses, that the Frenchman is not what he appears to be. That evening, she informs the young man that she is now ready to take charge of her life. She does not intend to "grope," she says, "I want to get out of the fog of youth. I want to be *precise*. I don't want anything to be an accident" (*FD*, 337).

Guy is understandably threatened by the changes his American girl is undergoing. After they see a "needlessly bare and explicit" film, he announces that the time has finally arrived for them to have sex. Roberta rejects his proposal: "When the fate of the paintings was known, she would consider Guy's invitation. Not before. Tonight was out of the question for another reason too. However it was fated finally to happen, of one thing she was sure—she was not going to enter the first love affair of her life in blue jeans" (*FD*, 338–39). In the face of rejection, Guy tries to salvage as much masculine pride as he can: "'I warn you,' he said with dignity, 'the next time it will have to be you who will have to make the advances'" (*FD*, 339).

Two days later, Roberta receives, through Patrini, an invitation for dinner at the Baron's and decides to stand up Guy in order to accept it: "For a moment, she hesitated. Then she thought, Artists must be ruthless, or they are not artists. Remember Gauguin. Remember Baudelaire" (*FD*, 341). At the Baron's she initially feels that she is in heaven. Her host shows her her two paintings hung between works by Matisse and Soutine and pays her 250 francs for them. He adds that she can come and see them whenever she wishes. After drinking the first two martinis of her life, Roberta luxuriates even more in her surroundings: "I am in French Society. Like Proust" (*FD*, 345).

She is ignored throughout dinner, however, and begins to sense some ridicule directed toward her by the other guests. Abruptly, she understands what, besides paintings, the Baron "collects": "I know what *he's* after, she muttered to herself, into the wineglass, and he's not going to get it" (*FD*, 347). She quickly leaves the table to call Guy and, while waiting for him to answer, notices her paintings again: "They looked pallid and ordinary and influenced by everybody" (*FD*, 348).

When Guy arrives on his Vespa to rescue her, she tells the Frenchman that it is indeed time for them to sleep together. On the way to a hotel with Guy her insecurity over her inexperience resurfaces: "She wondered if there were going to be mirrors on the ceiling, and Watteau-like paintings of nymphs. She hadn't heard about much in Paris, but she had heard about *that*" (Shaw's italics, *FD*, 351).

Shaw gives the story's dominant irony a last turn in the hotel room scene. The room is bare and extremely cold. Roberta further discovers that this is not, as Guy had said, one of his special hotels but simply one he can afford. Moreover, Guy is as nervous as she is while they are undressing. The two carefully do not look at each other until they are safely beneath the covers. In bed, Guy's last remaining pretenses dissolve—he is not 21, but only 16, and is, like Roberta, a virgin: "'If only it had not been so cold,' Guy wept, 'if only I had more than seven hundred francs, you would never have known'" (*FD*, 353). Roberta then holds him until he falls asleep in her arms.

In the morning, she awakens him: "You'd better get up. It's time for you to go to school." This time, however, she "candidly" watches him dress. Shaw's ending is an effective bit of understatement. Roberta returns to her apartment still a virgin, but no longer a naïve inno-

777777777777

cent: "She made a firm resolve. Never, NEVER would she tell Louise that Guy was only sixteen years old. She chuckled, turned the key and went in" (*FD*, 354).

"A Year to Learn the Language" is a masterful initiation story. Roberta begins to grow up through experiencing the pitfalls of illusions— the Baron, who appears the essence of Parisian sophistication, is in truth a cynical man interested only in seducing a young American girl; and Guy, the proclaimed jaded seducer, is actually a gentle, frightened 16-year-old boy. Roberta's nudity in bed with Guy is as innocent as Eve's before the Fall, but in the morning she enjoys his nudity with unashamed sensuality.

Constance of "Voyage Out, Voyage Home" is another unfinished American girl who enters maturity in Europe. Unlike Roberta, Constance is directly affected by World War II's legacy of death and suffering. When the story opens, 20-year-old Constance is being sent by her father to Europe for three months so that she will forget about marrying 40-year-old Mark. She is reluctant to go: "I am approaching a continent to which I have no connection" (*FD*, 481).

At a ski resort in Switzerland, she meets an attractive 30-year-old Englishman named Pritchard. Pritchard appears to be a robustly healthy, dashing young man. He is also quite charming. At their first meeting he says to her, "Oh, I know you. . . . You're the grave young American," to which she responds, "And you, . . . you're the gay young Englishman" (*FD*, 481). She remembers hearing one of the ski instructors remarking about Pritchard, "He is too reckless. He thinks he is better than he actually is. He does not have the technique for so much speed" (*FD*, 481). Shaw provides an early hint that the young Englishman may not be all that gay when Pritchard tells Constance that his mother is dead: "I must be careful, Constance thought, avoiding looking at the man beside her, not to ask people in Europe about their relatives. So many of them turn out to be dead" (*FD*, 482).

The idea of death and disease lurking just beneath the surface of health and vitality is intensified when the Englishman asks Constance if she is "one of the delicate ones" and then informs her that the sanatorium that Thomas Mann describes in *The Magic Mountain* is nearby. He adds that the resort experienced a "boom" right after World War II when it became a refuge for "all the people who hadn't eaten enough or had been living underground or in prison and who had been frightened so long" (*FD*, 483). When Constance asks where these people are now, he replies, "Dead, discharged, or destitute," and then asks,

"Is it true that people refuse to die in America?" (*FD*, 482–83). This exchange of dialogue emphasizes a contrast between Europe, a region ravaged by war and brutality throughout the twentieth century, and America, a sanctuary apparently untouched by death and suffering. This contrast, central to Shaw's story, is embodied in the characterizations of Pritchard and Constance.

The bulk of the story describes Pritchard's gentle courtship of the young American woman. He encourages her skiing: "You must always do things that are a little too much for you. . . . On skis. Otherwise, where's the fun?" (*FD*, 483). Constance remembers the stories about his recklessness, but he makes no serious attempt to seduce her; instead, he tells her about World War II. Hearing shots being fired in the mountains to start an avalanche, the Englishman says, "Like old times. . . . Like the good old war" (*FD*, 486). He then tells Constance that he was in the RAF during the war; he was a "night fighter" who flew missions over France by radar. His war stories seem like tales of a distant age to Constance: "It was like hearing about the graduating class two generations before you're in school" (*FD*, 486). In quite another way, Pritchard considers his experience anachronistic and irrelevant: he says, "I speak all the dead languages of Europe . . . German, French, Italian, and English. I was carefully educated for a world of interchangeable currency" (*FD*, 487).

Ultimately, the two become more intimate and personal in conversation. Constance tells Pritchard at one point that she knows what she wants to become: "I want to be responsible and I don't want to be a child and I don't want to be cruel—and I want to move in a good direction" (*FD*, 490). Later, he describes to her, in a self-deprecating manner, his poetry: "Lyric, elegiac, and athletic. . . . In praise of youth, death, and anarchy. Very good for tearing" (*FD*, 491).

When Pritchard prepares to leave the village, Constance, having forgotten Mark, asks the Englishman to marry her. Sadly, he tells her that he has a seemingly incurable case of tuberculosis: "Go home . . . I'm not for you. I'm oppressed. And you're not oppressed. It is the final miscegenation" (*FD*, 497). Sick, dying Europe cannot, he believes, marry young, vibrant America. After his confession, Constance understands, for the first time, his risk taking, his preoccupation with death. Still, after she insists, they do sleep together for the first time. The next morning Pritchard goes off to ski in the mountains, and Constance writes Mark that all is over between them. Then she abruptly learns from an instructor that Pritchard has been killed in an accident: "He was a jolly fine fellow . . . but he went too fast. He did not have the technique to handle the speed" (*FD*, 499). Shaw thus hints that the Englishman's death was a suicide. At the end of the story, Constance returns to America, matured by pain and suffering.

In "The Man Who Married a French Wife," the American who initially misjudges reality is a male, Beauchurch, who is visiting Paris with his French wife, Ginette. The couple's 13-year marriage has survived only because Beauchurch has learned at no little cost to control his potentially violent temper. He has trained himself "to present to the world the image of a calm, balanced, judicious man . . . [while] at his core, he still knew himself to be violent, sudden, ready for explosion, fatally ready to destroy himself for the satisfaction of a moment's anger, a moment's desire" (*FD*, 465).

As the story opens, Beauchurch sees Ginette walking with a strange man. Immediately, he considers the possibility that she will, at some point, leave him. At their hotel, Ginette introduces her husband to the stranger—he is a French journalist named Claude Mestre. The three sit down for a drink, and Mestre talks about the crisis in France over Algeria. When Beauchurch asks who will win if a civil war does come, the journalist replies, "The worst elements. . . . It will not be pleasant" (*FD*, 467–68). Mestre then reveals that because of his articles about Algeria, he is receiving death threats, his mail is being confiscated, and his phone is being tapped. Remembering the 1950s, Beauchurch comments, "We've had times like that in America, too . . . And not so long ago, either" (*FD*, 469).

Eventually, Mestre asks the American a favor that he has already discussed with Ginette: he wants Beauchurch to smuggle approximately $8,000 out of France to an account in Switzerland for him. The journalist anticipates having to leave France soon and wants to provide for his family in that eventuality. He is asking Beauchurch, he explains, because Beauchurch is an American: "Any Frenchman is likely to be searched upon trying to leave the country. He is likely to be questioned. In the times that I see ahead of us, the questioning that will be taking place here in France is likely to be strict" (*FD*, 471).

When Beauchurch is alone with Ginette in their room, his wife informs him that the $8,000 represents Mestre's life savings, and she issues an ultimatum: "If you won't take it through for him . . . I will" (*FD*, 472). Ginette does not try to make the decision easy for her husband. When Beauchurch says that he does not like Mestre because "he's self-important and impressed with his own intelligence, and he has a condescending attitude toward Americans," she laughs and agrees, "That's exactly what he's like. He's the perfect model of the French intellectual" (*FD*, 473). Even worse, when pressed, she confesses that the journalist was her first lover during the war. She then explains that she had wanted to see Mestre again out of "curiosity, nostalgia, guilt—the feeling that middle age was rushing up on me and I wanted to be reminded of a time when I was young—a feeling that maybe I wouldn't see Paris again for a long time and I wanted to straighten out certain memories" (*FD*, 474). After commenting that "a marriage needs a certain amount of confession and we've skimped each other" (*FD*, 475), Ginette then tells the rest of the story. Mestre was badly wounded in the war. She had promised to marry him before going to America, and he still wants to leave his family and marry her. Moreover, she confesses that she saw Mestre three years ago and, though "nothing happened . . . I think I would have had an affair with him, if he had asked me . . ." (*FD*, 477). Still, she has no intention of leaving Beauchurch at this point.

Immediately after this frank discussion, the American's rage almost explodes. After all, he is being asked to take a genuine risk for an arrogant, but nevertheless heroic man with whom his wife is still somewhat in love. But, after exercising his old control and discipline, he forces himself to realize that Mestre had in fact been wronged—Ginette, after all, had left the journalist to marry *him*. Not fully reconciled with what he is promising, he, at last, says, "Of course I'll help the bastard," and then he maintains his pride by insisting, "I don't want to talk to him though . . . You make all the arrangements' (*FD*, 478). Later, as Ginette relaxes in the bathtub, he sits beside her, sipping a drink and realizing that "the holiday was repaired. More than the holiday. And more than repaired" (*FD*, 478).

Beauchurch's marriage has been significantly strengthened by Ginette's confession and his reluctant generosity. He realizes that he is truly fortunate to have her for a wife and that he must prove himself worthy of her. He will take a real risk for Mestre not because he likes the Frenchman, but because it is the decent, brave thing to do. Ironically, Ginette has taught Beauchurch a lesson in fidelity—the importance of being faithful to one's best, most decent self.

One of Shaw's best expatriate stories—indeed, one of his best stories—is "Then We Were Three." A long story, it recounts the changing relationship of three young Americans travelling in Europe. The story opens with the focal character, Munnie Brooks, a responsive, sentimental young man with "the gift of instantaneous nostalgia," staring down from his European hotel window at a hunter and his dog, thinking that "when he was older he would look back upon the summer and think, Ah, it was wonderful when I was young" (*FD*, 560). The summer in Europe, a graduation present from his parents, is drawing to an end, and Munnie feels that it will be "the last real holiday of his life" because it represents "the last days of . . . youth" (*FD*, 560). But Munnie's holiday and his youthful innocence will be destroyed before he ever returns home.

Vacationing with two friends, Bert and Martha, he has a premonition that the three will never again be as close as they have been during this summer. There is foreshadowing early in the story that the trio's relationship is not as idyllic as Munnie wants to believe. After watching the hunter, Munnie awakens the sleeping Bert, calling his friend "Mister": "The rule was that whoever lost in tennis between them had to call the other Mister for twenty-four hours" (*FD*, 561). Later the two go to awaken Martha and stand watching the sleeping girl for a moment, "each of them convinced that the other did not know what he was thinking" (*FD*, 563).

In a flashback, Shaw narrates the initial meeting of the two young men with Martha in the Uffizi art gallery in Florence. From the first, Munnie had been enchanted by her: "Maybe it was because they had first seen her . . . among the Botticellis that gave Munnie the idea, but he thought, privately, that, aside from the fact that her hair was short and dark and irregularly cut, she looked like the Primavera, tall, slender, and girlish, with a long, narrow nose and deep, brooding, dangerous eyes" (*FD*, 563–64). Martha, it turns out, has been travelling in Europe for nearly two years, pretending to study: "I tell my mother . . . that I'm taking courses at the Sorbonne, and it's almost true, at least in the wintertime" (*FD*, 564). Munnie's innocence and attraction to the girl blind him to the warning signs of her "dangerous eyes" and undisguised capacity for deception.

After their initial meeting, the three agree to travel together, with "Rule Number One," as prescribed by Bert, being "no entanglements" (*FD*, 565). There is, however, a time limitation on Bert's rule: "Until the boat sails . . . we treat each other like brother and sister, and that's all" (*FD*, 565). As stated, the rule of innocence is meant to last only until the end of the summer.

Martha is apparently comfortable with the arrangement: "she greeted the events of each day with a strange and almost dreamlike placidity" (*FD*, 566). She says, "For the moment, I'm on a policy of float. . . . I'm waiting for a revelation to send me in a permanent direction. I'm in no hurry to commit myself, no hurry at all . . ." (*FD*, 566–67). Her lack of direction increases her attractiveness to Munnie, who convinces himself that "Martha hadn't settled for anything yet . . . because nothing good enough had come up. . . . When she finally did commit herself it would be for something huge, original and glorious" (*FD*, 567).

Munnie cannot hide from himself that he is in love with the girl. The story returns to the present tense and Munnie watches Martha dress on the beach after he and Bert have awakened her: "[he] felt that never in his life would he see again anything so gay and obscurely touching as Martha Holm, dressed in a sailor's striped shirt, on a sunny beach, shaking the sea water out of her short, dark hair" (*FD*, 568). He is, nevertheless, determined to observe the rules of the arrangement.

On the beach, danger signals begin to emerge. Bert, who is given to cynical teasing, asks rhetorically, "Are we friends and brothers, or will we betray each other by sunset? Search the lady for daggers" (*FD*, 570). Shielded by his innocence, Munnie simply enjoys the rhetoric of Bert's cynicism. He remembers fondly the time that summer when his companion's cutting irony provoked a senseless brawl with some Germans in a bar. He even misses the implications of a long speech on the nature of "gifts" that Bert delivers. The cynical young man first proclaims that "the important thing is to recognize your gift and then use it. And the best way to use it is to keep you from the insufferable boredom of work" (*FD*, 572). He then analyzes the special "gifts" possessed by each one of the trio. Martha's gift, he says, is "beauty . . . That's easy. You use it on a man and the sky's the limit." He says he possesses a double gift: "I have charm . . . and I don't give a damn." Finally, he proclaims, "As for Munnie . . . His gift is virtue. Poor sod. What can he do with that?" (*FD*, 572–73).

Munnie only becomes uncomfortable when Bert instigates openly sexual teasing with Martha: "They had laughed together at a lot of things since Florence, and they had covered all the subjects, but Munnie didn't want to hear Martha laughing now at this" (*FD*, 573). He realizes suddenly that he feels a great deal of sorrow and pain that could only be healed by Martha spontaneously coming to sit beside him. The young man's sorrow does not yet destroy his innocence. He decides that once he is on the boat home and the arrangement is over, he will write the girl and ask her to marry him.

Later, the three drift off to sleep for a while. Munnie is awakened by a cry from a small boat that has capsized. After Bert awakens, he nudges Martha, "Wake up . . . and watch the shipwreck" (*FD*, 575). The "shipwreck" scene illustrates the essential immorality of Bert's cynicism and Martha's passivity. Soon two people are detected struggling in the water. Bert and Martha simply watch them with no inclination to help. As the man in the boat struggles to swim to shore, Munnie realizes the man is in danger: "I don't think he's going to make it." Bert responds, "Well . . . that'll be too bad"; Martha says nothing (*FD*, 577).

Sensing that he can wait no longer, Munnie strips naked and enters the water to help. He is very much aware that Martha is seeing him nude; he thinks, "She's never seen me naked, I wonder what she thinks" (*FD*, 578). The Adam and Eve overtones of this scene are nicely understated—Munnie's consciousness of his nakedness symbolizes a destruction of innocence, that the Fall is imminent. That night, Munnie wakes up to hear Bert going up to Martha's room. Only he, he realizes, has observed the rules of the arrangement. Munnie leaves the next morning, blaming himself for the loss of Eden: "It's my fault. I let the summer go on one day too long" (*FD*, 582).

"Then We Were Three" is a memorable initiation story. Idealistic, responsible Munnie is forced by his companions into an awareness of the world's carelessness and selfishness. At the end, while he is still fighting against the implications of what he has learned, the summer and his youth, have indeed come to an end. A related theme is the story's focus on Shaw's concept of decency. The naked and vulnerable Munnie is contrasted with Bert and Martha and is fully revealed as a decent, caring individual.

In the delightful "Love on a Dark Street," Shaw treats the motif of American innocence in Europe in the mode of absurdist farce. The story's focal character is Nicholas Tibbell, an American in Paris desperately homesick for his native country. Somewhat of a Puritan, Tibbell is intimidated by the open sensuality of Europe. He has rented his Parisian apartment from a German photographer and is uncomfortable with the wall decorations—"blown-up photographs of emaciated nude women whom the German had posed in what Tibbell considered rather extreme positions" (*FD*, 601). "Shy with girls and clumsy with men," the American had discovered "that a solitary man was as likely to find himself alone and unremarked in Paris as in New York" (*FD*, 601–2).

When the story opens, it is night and, even more than usual, Tibbell is intensely aware of the sensuality of France and Paris. Initially, he tries to read *Madame Bovary* "to improve his French," but puts the book down to peer out the window at two lovers in a doorway across the street. Watching them, he thinks, "What a thing it was to be French . . . and experience no shame in the face of desire and be able to display it so honestly, on a public thoroughfare. If only he had gone to Paris during his formative years instead of to Exeter!" (*FD*, 602). The lovers make Tibbell aware that since he is almost 30, he should make a move soon if he is ever to get married. He thus decides to call Betty, his girlfriend in the States, because: "tonight he wanted to make powerful and naked statements to her that until now he had been too timid to voice" (*FD*, 603).

Before the call can be completed, however, he is again drawn to the window by excited voices outside. Looking out, he sees a man of about 60 in a heated argument with a young man and a young woman. It seems that the young man, Raoul, is about to desert Moumou, the young woman with whom he has lived for a year. The girl is pregnant, but Raoul is planning to marry someone else the next day. The older man is Moumou's father, Monsieur Banary-Cointal.

In dramatizing the trio's prolonged argument, Shaw makes use of traditional elements of absurdist farce—exaggeration, irrelevance, action inappropriate to events, and the non sequitur. At one point, M. Banary-Cointal dramatically warns Raoul, "I hold you personally responsible if she throws herself in the river. I, her father, am saying this. Solemnly" (*FD*, 606). Laughing, the young man responds, "Call me when it happens. I will personally accompany her. Anyway, she swims like a fish" (*FD*, 606). Outraged, Moumou then begins beating Raoul with her handbag: "Whacking him ferociously with the huge leather bag, holding it by the handle, swinging it again and again like an Olympic hammer-thrower" (*FD*, 606). In desperation and pain, the young man pleads, "Moumou, Moumou, you're losing control of yourself" (*FD*, 606). Tibbell briefly considers rushing out to help the wronged girl, but decides that his assistance is not needed: "by any system of scoring, the woman was clearly winning by a wide margin, delivering all the blows, gaining many points for what is approvingly called aggressiveness in the prize ring and only suffering such incidental damage as came her way when Raoul's head bumped her forehead as she tried to bite him" (*FD*, 607).

Still, someone does come to Moumou's rescue. The man who has been kissing the woman in the doorway across the street rushes over to separate the embattled lovers. For his trouble, he is condemned by M. Banary-Cointal: "It is the same all over this poor country. . . . Privacy is a thing of the past. No wonder we are on the verge of anarchy. They were on the point of agreement when you destroyed everything" (*FD*, 608). The indignant father is ignoring the fact that a quarrel on a public street is an unusual way to seek privacy and that Raoul and Moumou have already passed the point of anarchy. The father then warns the woman still lingering in the darkened doorway, "You see what's ahead of you? The same thing will happen to you as happened to my daughter. Mark my words, you'll find yourself pregnant and that one [pointing to the new chagrined rescuer] . . . that one will disappear like a hare in a cornfield" (*FD*, 608).

Tibbell then overhears two old concierges commenting on the entire incident:

> [Madame Harrahs] "Young girls these days . . . They deserve what they get."
> [The other concierge] "The one I feel sorry for is the old man . . . the father."
> [Madame Harrahs] "It's probably all his fault. He is obviously lacking in authority. . . . I wouldn't be surprised if he didn't have a little thing on the side himself, a little *poupette* in the Sixteenth, . . . I know the type."
> [Persuaded by this logic, the other concierge agrees.] "Ah, the dirty old man." (*FD*, 609–10)

Shaw employs the two old women as a Greek chorus in the story, their irrelevant and acid judgments intensifying the story's central absurdity.

Believing the scene has ended, Tibbell is on the verge of retreating from his window when he hears Moumou and her father returning. The girl is crying: "I love him, I love him . . . I'm going to kill him" (*FD*, 610). Once again, her grief soon gives way to rage and she assaults the headlight of Raoul's parked Vespa with her shoe. She cuts her hand and yells, "You wanted my blood, take it! I hope it brings you good luck!" and then proclaims a program of revenge and martyrdom: "He will come back for the Vespa. Then I will kill him! And after that I will kill myself" (*FD*, 611).

Abruptly, the street becomes even more crowded with the appearance of a woman in a green dress pursued by a man in a dark suit. The man catches the woman, slaps her, and demands that she return 300 francs to him. Tibbell is outraged at the man's behavior: "[He] had never hit a woman in his life and could not imagine ever doing so, and certainly never for three hundred francs which was, after all, worth just about sixty cents" (*FD*, 613–14). He continues to listen to the argument between the new couple. It turns out that the 300 francs represent the man's investment in flowers for the woman who, he says, led him to expect something in return when she excited his "emotions by kissing [him] on the lips" (*FD*, 614).

The man in the dark suit explains to M. Banary-Cointal, "It is not a question of three hundred francs . . . It is a question of principle. I have been led on, I have been inflamed" (*FD*, 615). To emphasize the depravity of the woman in the green dress, he then points out that she is wearing a wedding ring. Forever gallant, M. Banary-Cointal sides with the woman and contemptuously tosses 300 francs at the man, who instantly throws them back. The old man then threatens to give the dark stranger "a punch in the nose." The man in the dark suit instantly assumes a boxing stance, whereupon the defender of women announces; "I am sixty-three years old, with a faulty heart, and besides, I wear glasses, as you can see. The police will be inclined to ask you some very searching questions in the event of an accident" (*FD*, 616).

Tibbell's observations are interrupted by the overseas operator informing him that his call to Betty is at last ready to be put through. After all he has just seen, the shy American is relieved when no one answers—he no longer wants any romantic involvement.

In this story Shaw uses a narrative motif perfected by Henry James: an initially detached American narrator becomes increasingly involved in a diverse panorama of European events—Winterbourne in *Daisy Miller* and Lambert Strether in *The Ambassadors* are such characters. Shaw's considerably less than serious intentions, especially in comparison to James's European fiction, are made manifest in Tibbell's concluding resolution to remain as sheltered and innocent as he possibly can. "Love on a Dark Street" is, after all, simply an entertaining, skillfully told absurd farce.

"Tip on a Dead Jockey," which Shaw valued enough to make the title work of his fifth published collection, is a very different kind of story. Despite Shaw's apparent fondness for the story, it has bothered some critics. Hubert Saal attacked the story, as well as the entire 1957 collection, as evidence of the appearance of a new, disturbingly cynical Shaw; and, while skillfully told, it is a cynical, ultimately unsatisfying work of fiction.

To a degree, "Tip on a Dead Jockey" is another study of American innocence confronting sophisticated, and in this case clearly corrupt, Europe. Lloyd Barber, the story's focal character, seems to be descended from a Hemingway hero such as Harry Morgan of *To Have and Have Not* and the motion picture persona of Humphrey Bogart. Disillusioned by his experiences in World War II, Barber lives on the fringe of lawlessness in Europe. A contrasting character is Jimmy Richardson, a naïve American who is irrationally loyal to Barber. Shaw conveys Barber's alienation through his reaction to Richardson's loyalty: "Somehow, Barber was always being presented with the devotion of people whose devotion he didn't want" (*FD*, 504).

As the story opens, Barber learns from Maureen, Richardson's wife, that his naïve follower has disappeared. The distraught woman tells him, "I knew we shouldn't have come to Europe. It's different for you. You're not married and you were always kind of wild anyway, not like Jimmy—" (*FD*, 502). Barber is mystified and disturbed by Richardson's disappearance. It causes him to pay particular attention to some comments in a letter he has just received from a war companion who has since become a successful novelist: "Our generation is in danger . . . the danger of diminution. We have had our adventures too early. Our love has turned to affection, our hate to distaste, our despair to melancholy, our passion to preference" (*FD*, 503). To a degree, "Tip on a Dead Jockey" does seem to be a fictional illustration of the danger of "diminution." No one in it, including Barber, is ultimately capable of making a meaningful commitment to anyone or anything.

The story's remaining major character, Bert Smith, seems a personification of diminution. Smith has "an import-export face." Hinting at no specific nationality, "it was a face that was at the same time bland, cynical, self-assured, sensual, hopeless, and daring. . . . It was a face, you felt somehow, that was occasionally of interest to the police" (*FD*, 506).

In a flashback, Shaw tells how Barber first became involved with Smith. Barber had met him at a racetrack, where Smith had held tickets on a losing horse. Undisturbed, Smith had pulled out of his pocket other tickets on the winner and had advised Barber, "One must always think of the insurance" (*FD*, 507). Later, the American had joined Smith for a drink at the track bar. There, Smith had asked Barber about the war: "I suppose you are one of the young men who were nearly killed a dozen times" (*FD*, 508). After this supposition had been confirmed, Smith had said, "I prefer that in Americans . . . It makes them more like Europeans" (*FD*, 508). Later in the conversation Smith had issued a pronouncement: "While it is on, a war is absolutely boring. But then when it is over, you discover peace is even more boring. It is the worst result of wars" (*FD*, 509). Certainly, the idea that boredom is the worst aftermath of a war represents a severely diminished response to massive human suffering.

Two weeks later, Smith had abruptly contacted Barber again with a proposition: he would pay the American $25,000 to fly to Egypt to pick up a box containing English pounds in an amount approximating one and one-half million American dollars. The American's reaction to this offer is what most disturbs Saal about the story: "What is astonishing for Shaw is the amorality of the story. Not for a moment does Barber decline the opportunity because it's dishonest" (Saal, 12). Instead the American flier had been attracted by the illegality of what Smith had proposed: "You don't think about it, but then, suddenly, when it enters your life, you realize that subconsciously you have been accepting the idea of crime as an almost normal accompaniment to everyday life" (*FD*, 517). Of course, American films and popular culture contain numerous examples of the criminal-as-hero, for example, the gangsters portrayed by Bogart, James Cagney, and Edward G. Robinson, as well as Jesse and Frank James (especially as portrayed by Tyrone Power and Henry Fonda), and Butch Cassidy and the Sundance Kid. But there is a crucial difference between these outlaws and Lloyd Barber. Shaw does not envision his character as heroic; instead, Barber is primarily bored and jaded. His responsiveness to Smith's offer thus seems essentially cynical.

The story's title derives from a second racetrack scene. While still considering Smith's proposition, Barber had gone back to the track with Jimmy Richardson and, inevitably, had encountered Smith again. The enigmatic gambler had given the two Americans a tip on a race that he had gotten directly from a jockey. During the race, there had been an accident, and the jockey-tipster had been killed. Smith's reaction to this tragedy had been in keeping with his character: about the dead man, he had said, without any feeling, "he was getting too old, . . . he kept at it too long" (*FD*, 520). The accident had helped

Barber come to a resolution about Smith's proposal—he had decided against it because the risk was too great: "I'm getting too old. I don't want to keep at it too long" (*FD*, 521).

Throughout the day at the track, Smith had questioned Richardson about his experience as a flier during the war. Barber had understood that the gambler was seeking insurance in case his offer of $25,000 was rejected. Still, Barber had been convinced that Smith would find Richardson too stupid and too unimaginative for such a dangerous mission: "For all that he had been through—war and marriage and being a father and living in a foreign country—it had never occurred to Jimmy that people might not like him or might try to do him harm. When you were enjoying Jimmy, you called it trustfulness. When he was boring you, you called it stupidity" (*FD*, 523).

Shaw returns to the present tense for the story's ending. Richardson reappears as suddenly as he disappeared; he is safe and happy as well as quite rich. Barber belatedly understands that Jimmy's naïveté and lack of imagination constitute the "insurance" that Smith is never without. The story ends with a chastened Barber deciding to leave Europe: "I better get out of here . . . This continent is not for me" (*FD*, 526).

Shaw's abandonment of his theme of decency is the most puzzling aspect of this story. Everyone in it, except Jimmy Richardson, seems too jaded and bored for ethical action, and Richardson lacks the intellect to comprehend moral issues. Still, this story did not, as Saal believed, herald the emergence of a cynical, bored Irwin Shaw; its cynicism is as unrepresentative of Shaw's best expatriate stories as it is of his other fiction.

In terms of craft and technique, there are things to admire in "Tip on a Dead Jockey." Smith's ability to project virtually any European nationality without finally claiming any makes him an unforgettably sinister figure. He has diminished to the point that there is no sustaining identity left for him. Lloyd Barber is himself not far from the same fate.

The Death of Decency

Perhaps Shaw's darkest story is "God Was Here but He Left Early."
Its central character has stepped outside the limits of Shaw's decency
even more clearly than has Lloyd Barber. Still, while cynicism is one
of its central concerns, "God Was Here," unlike "Tip on a Dead
Jockey," is not a cynical story. It is rather a grim, despairing fictional
investigation of the moral drifting and aimlessness of the 1960s.

The title story of Shaw's last published collection, *God Was Here but
He Left Early*, is an expatriate story that nevertheless focuses on the
central American social and political crisis of the 1960s—Vietnam. To
a degree, the story exemplifies the evolution of Shaw's short fiction,
for although the story has a European setting, it echoes the social protest of the early proletarian stories. Shaw's familiar emphasis on the
necessity of decency in human relationships is central to "God Was
Here," but the story's tone is despairing because only one character
seems committed to such an old-fashioned ideal. More powerfully than
any other Shaw story, it illustrates the twentieth century's many and
diverse temptations and perversions.

The story opens in Geneva with the focal character, an American
woman named Rosemary, seeking a referral from a psychiatrist for an
abortion. Bert, a homosexual English friend, has recommended this
course of action, and he further advises Rosemary about how to conduct herself with the psychiatrist: "Be lugubrious, Love, . . . They
dote on sorrow. Suggest suicide. Just the merest hint, Love. Name me
if you want. . . . I'm sure it'll be all right. Three of my friends have
been and have lived happily ever after" (*FD*, 583). Rosemary feels
only contempt for herself for being trapped in so trite and ludicrous a
situation. She is pregnant as a result of a weekend affair at a ski resort
with a Frenchman named Jean-Jacques, which she considers "a senseless weekend in the mountains with a man you never had met before
in your life and finally didn't like and whom you never really wanted
to see again. . . . The vulgarity was inescapable. . . . Jean-Jacques! If
an American woman had to take a French lover, the name didn't have
to be *that* French. The hyphen. It was so banal" (Shaw's italics, *FD*,

584–85). Love affairs have for some time seemed banal and boring to her. Just before coming to Europe, she had ended a three-year affair: "When the man had said he could get his divorce now and they could marry, she had realized he bored her" (*FD*, 586). When the Swiss psychiatrist refuses her the abortion referral, Rosemary returns to Paris to seek assistance from Jean-Jacques. The Frenchman promises to help her after he returns from a weekend trip to Switzerland. While waiting, she receives a phone call from Eldred Harrison, an English friend of Bert's, who asks her to dinner. Hoping the dinner will be a diversion while she awaits Jean-Jacques's return, she accepts. The dinner party, certainly among the most unpleasant in American literature, is the heart of Shaw's story.

Harrison appears at the restaurant with Anna, a Polish girl desperately searching for an American to marry. Initially, the conversation focuses on Bert's dangerous lifestyle. Harrison comments, "I fear for him . . . He is always being beaten up. He likes rough trade. One day, I'm sure they'll find him floating in the harbor of Piraeus, some harbor. A peculiar taste" (*FD*, 591). Rosemary remembers the brutal death of an American interior decorator she had once known: "He was beaten to death by three sailors in a bar in Livorno. Nobody ever could figure out what he was doing in Livorno" (*FD*, 591). The conversation shifts somewhat to another illustration of physical and psychological brutality when Anna describes her imprisonment in Poland at the age of 16. She had been locked in a cell with two prostitutes who had made an imitation penis out of cloth: "They use it on each other . . . They want to use it on me. I scream and the guard comes and they laugh. They say in three months I'll be screaming for them to lend it to me" (*FD*, 592).

The story then shifts from a preoccupation with sexual horror to more general protest. Shaw describes the hors d'oeuvres for which the ornate restaurant is famous: "There were two large carts loaded with plates of tuna, sardines, little radishes, céleri rémoulade, eggs with mayonnaise, raw mushrooms in oil, ratatouille, a dozen different kinds of sausage and pâté. The armies of the poor could be fed indefinitely on these tidbits of Paris" (*FD*, 593). Soon Rosemary, Harrison, and Anna are joined by Carroll, an American news photographer who has just left Vietnam, and a young Englishman. Carroll passes around the table a photograph he had taken in that tragic country: "It was the sort of photograph you were used to seeing these days. A woman who looked about eighty years old, in black, [is] squatting against a wall, her hand held out, begging, . . . with a small, starved, almost naked child . . . A slender Eurasian girl, heavily made up, with a bouffant hairdo and a long slit in her silk dress showing a marvelous leg [is] walking past the old woman without a glance at her. On the wall that fill[s] the background of the picture somebody ha[s] scrawled in large chalk letters, God was here, but He left early" (*FD*, 593–94).

The social protest implicit in the photograph is striking. In Vietnam only the young woman, probably a prostitute—whose hairdo symbolizes the grotesque effects of American culture on Vietnam—seems likely to survive. Because sex has been reduced to a commodity here, those who can barter for it keep the right to exist. Even God has abandoned the Vietnamese.

Apparently inspired by Carroll's photograph, Harrison begins telling atrocity stories of his captivity by the Japanese during World War II. Sickened by Harrison's stories, Rosemary leaves the table to go to the women's room. When she prepares to return to her party, she finds Rodney, the young Englishman, waiting for her. He wants to explain why Harrison persists in telling such horrible stories: "It's because you're Americans. You and the photographer. He's obsessed with what you're doing in Vietnam, his rooms're cluttered with the most dreadful photographs, he collects them . . . he's too polite to argue with you openly, he's very fond of Americans, so he keeps on about all those other horrors he went through. It's his way of saying, Please stop, no more horror, please" (*FD*, 595–96). Harrison is the voice of conscience and decency in the story. He wants the horror to stop, but his own experience and his desperation at other people's seeming indifference to brutality have transformed him into an obsessed man. Shock effect, he feels, is the only way to force others to confront injustice. Rosemary's response to Rodney indicates that Harrison may be right; "I'm not doing anything in Vietnam," she says (*FD*, 596).

When she and the young Englishman return to their table, Harrison is telling the story of Brother Three-Iron, a sadistic Japanese prison guard who had enjoyed beating Harrison with a golf club. "I lost count of the number of times he beat me senseless. . . . But if the war had lasted another month I doubt I would have lasted" (*FD*, 596–97). After the prison camp had been liberated, Ellsworth, a British officer, had encouraged Harrison to beat Brother Three-Iron with his own golf club, but Harrison had refused the opportunity: "I got out of Ellsworth's sight. Never saw him again either. Luckily for me. His contempt was unendurable" (*FD*, 598). The obsessed man ends his story by looking at his watch and saying, "It *is* getting late" (Shaw's italics, *FD*, 598). The point of the Brother Three-Iron story is clear: Harrison, even with an enormous amount of provocation, chose in that instance to end the horror. Surely, he hopes, the Americans—with comparatively little real provocation, considering Vietnam, after all, had never aggressively assaulted the United States—can make a similar choice. His hope is growing dim, however; it *is* getting late.

In the story's conclusion, Shaw ties the major strands of the narrative together. Rosemary leaves the restaurant accompanied by Rodney. Walking along the Champs-Élysées, she is assaulted by images of interrelated sex and violence: "People were coming out of a movie theater. On a giant poster above the entrance, a gigantic girl in a nightgown pointed a pistol the size of a cannon at a thirty-foot man in a dinner jacket. Whores cruised slowly in pairs in sports cars, searching trade" (*FD*, 599). These grotesque, mammoth images merge in her mind with her awareness of her pregnancy and her search for an abortion: "The various uses and manifestations of the flesh. To caress, to mangle, to behead, to kill with a karate stroke on a city street, to prepare out of cloth a derisive simulacrum of the instruction of sex in a Polish prison. To cherish and despise. To protect and destroy. To clamor in the womb to become flesh. . . . Violence, costumed, pursues us" (*FD*, 599–600).

Throughout the twentieth century and especially in the 1960s, Shaw seems to be saying, a chief manifestation of creativity has been the obsessive imagining of ways to assault the human body—to transform it into something less than human, into the Other. The famous sexual freedom of the sixties, the story implies, was actually a form of sexual self-loathing—the human body had to be abused and brutalized.

The story's last scene conveys this point. When Rodney asks to go to her room with her, she consents, hoping simply for some relief from the ugly violence that has surrounded her: "Even if she hadn't remembered his name it would have been all right" (*FD*, 600). But when they are in bed, Rodney only wants to spank her, not make love to her, and she consents: "She allowed him to do whatever he wanted to do. Who was she to be spared?" (*FD*, 600). After he leaves, she looks at herself in the mirror and "[begins] to laugh, coarse, unstoppable laughter" (*FD*, 600). In the world of this story, American innocence has long since been lost. Through obsessive violations of the body, the American of the 1960s has forfeited the soul.

To a large degree, "God Was Here but He Left Early" is such a despairing and bitter story because it encapsulates Shaw's response to the 1960s and early 1970s. He saw America's involvement in the Vietnam War and the subsequent emergence of a youthful counterculture devoted to unrestrained experimentation with sex and drugs as a collapse of traditional American values. He feared that the ethical chaos of the sixties would constitute as great a threat to the survival of American decency as had World War II and McCarthyism. In his biography of Shaw, Michael Shnayerson quotes Donald Fine, Shaw's longtime editor: "I don't think Irwin liked the sixties, . . . It was alien territory to him."[20]

In 1980 Shaw talked about what he thought "God Was Here but He Left Early" is really about: "That's social criticism about Vietnam, about the abortion laws, about sex and people's attitudes toward sex. . . . That people take sex too lightly, that they indulge in it without knowing what the consequences are going to be. That [emotionless sexual experimentation] is cruel, and the perversity lurks everywhere. The criticism of the war in Vietnam is very strong in that story." (See Giles interview in part 2.)

Shaw's response to the unfolding tragedy in Vietnam was ambivalent. Initially he was reluctant, primarily because of his loyalty to the Democratic party, to criticize U. S. involvement in Vietnam, and he severely castigated liberal writers and intellectuals who saw the North Vietnamese as heroic victims of American imperialism (Shnayerson, 301–2). Soon, though, Shaw was, like most other Americans, forced to acknowledge the tragic futility and senseless bloodshed of the war; the criticism of the war in "God Was Here" is clear and obvious. The story's implicit comments about abortion and homosexuality are, however, less clear and more troubling. The story could work successfully without the opening sequence, in which Rosemary seeks the abortion—it is not particularly relevant to the crucial restaurant scene that follows. Moreover, it is difficult to see whether the story criticizes any specific abortion laws. What truly matters in the story is the characterization of Rosemary as a selfish and superficial woman.

Shaw seems to use Rosemary as a personification of the new, 1960s American who "takes sex too lightly," who "indulges in it" without thinking or caring what the consequences will be. To the degree that he also may have intended her desire for an abortion, or for that matter abortion itself, to represent the moral disintegration of the decade, the story inevitably becomes problematic for readers empathetic with women's reproductive rights. Shaw's treatment of "the perversity" that "lurks everywhere" results in another troubling ambiguity. This perversity obviously includes the references to sex with violence that dominate the story. But it is impossible to escape the feeling that Shaw, much like F. Scott Fitzgerald in *Tender Is the Night*, is guilty of more than a little homophobia in "God Was Here but He Left Early." Along with the Vietnam War, sexual freedom without responsibility, abortion, and sadomasochism, homosexuality seems to be emblematic in the story of the moral chaos and degeneracy of the age.

From the early protest stories to the late expatriate stories, Irwin Shaw's short fiction is distinguished by a mastery of craft and a concern with the importance, and the difficulty, of observing decency in human relationships in a flesh-obsessed world without God. Cumulatively, his fiction reveals a recurrent pattern in which each decade presents threats to the survival of the innate decency of the American. The depression of the 1930s forced "the gentle people" to concentrate, to a large degree, on individual survival rather than generosity to others. The family in "Second Mortgage" finally locks Mrs. Shapiro out. In the late thirties and the forties Hitler and European fascism and American anti-Semitism threatened the survival of democratic institutions in the United States. Wisconsin's Senator Joseph McCarthy exploited the national hysteria and paranoia of the 1950s and severely damaged, or even destroyed, the lives and careers of a vast number of American writers, artists, and intellectuals. The freedom of expression and open exchange of ideas essential to art were in great danger. We seemed to be moving toward our own form of totalitarianism. For many of the young people of the 1960s, the repression of the previous decade inspired an obsession with sexual experimentation and the removal of all restraints to sensual indulgence. Then, Shaw belatedly had to admit that we, as a nation, were pursuing a bloody war that had become militarily, politically, and morally indefensible.

Still, the totality of Shaw's fiction emphasizes that American decency somehow survived all these threats to its survival. Our unique capacity for fairness, Shaw believed, could withstand the frequent bad moral choices of individuals and momentary national capitulations to dishonor. Like other modern American writers, he believed that one obligation of the artist is to perform the role of secular priest—to condemn the recurrent threats to decency and to celebrate its survival.

Shaw did not, as some of his critics have claimed, abandon his commitment to creating a moral, but not didactic, American fiction when he moved to Europe. He simply approached his work from another

141

angle. His characters were no longer the impoverished children of the Great Depression; instead he focused on their relatively affluent children who were in the process of discovering that material prosperity is not necessarily a protection against ethical conflict and confusion.

The best of Shaw's stories rank with the best modernist American short fiction. If he invented little that was new in fictional technique, he utilized the legacy of Crane, Twain, Anderson, Hemingway, and Fitzgerald to create a unique artistic vision of his country and his age. That this vision found, and continues to find, a response is evident in the frequency with which his stories have been reprinted and anthologized. As a writer, Shaw will be most remembered for his five decades of finely crafted, intensely engaging short stories.

Notes to Part 1

1. James R. Giles, summer 1980 interviews with Irwin Shaw; forthcoming in *Resources for American Literary Study*; included in part 2 of this book.

2. Chester E. Eisinger, *Fiction of the Forties* (Chicago: University of Chicago Press, 1963), 107; hereafter cited in the text.

3. Leslie A. Fiedler, "Irwin Shaw: Adultery, the Last Politics," *Commentary* 22 (1956): 73; hereafter cited in the text.

4. *Lucy Crown* (New York: Random House, 1956), 157; hereafter cited in the text as *LC*.

5. *Two Weeks in Another Town* (New York: Random House, 1960), 316; hereafter cited in the text as *TW*.

6. *Short Stories: Five Decades* (New York: Delacorte Press, 1978), 599; hereafter cited in the text as *FD*.

7. Lionel Trilling, "Some Are Gentle, Some Are Not," *Saturday Review*, June 1951, 8.

8. Hubert Saal, "Disenchanted Men," *Saturday Review*, August 1957, 12.

9. *God Was Here but He Left Early* (New York: Anchor Books/Doubleday, 1973), 12; hereafter cited in the text as *GWH*.

10. Willie Morris and Lucas Matthiessen, "The Art of Fiction IV: Irwin Shaw," *Paris Review* 21 (Spring 1979): 258; hereafter cited in the text.

11. *Short Stories of Irwin Shaw* (New York: Random House, 1966), 62–63; hereafter cited in the text as *SS*.

12. F. Scott Fitzgerald, *The Great Gatsby* (New York: Scribner's, 1925), 7.

13. Leonard Kriegel and Abraham H. Lass, *Stories of the American Experience* (New York: New American Library, 1973).

14. *Love on a Dark Street* (New York: Delacorte Press, 1965), 201; hereafter cited in the text as *LDS*.

15. Cleanth Brooks and Robert Penn Warren, *Understanding Fiction* (New York: Appleton-Century-Crofts, 1959), 89–90; hereafter cited in the text.

16. Joe L. Baird and Ralph Grajeda, "A Shaw Story and Brooks and Warren," *CEA Critic* 28 (February 1966): 1, 3–4; hereafter cited in the text.

17. Jacqueline Berke, "Further Observations on 'A Shaw Story and Brooks and Warren,'" *CEA Critic* 33 (November 1970): 28; hereafter cited in the text.

18. Wallace Stevens, "Peter Quince at the Clavier," in *The Collected Poems of Wallace Stevens* (New York: Knopf, 1964), 89–92.

19. Michael Moorhead, "Hemingway's 'The Short Happy Life of Francis Macomber' and Shaw's 'The Deputy Sheriff'," *Explicator* 44 (1986): 42–43.

20. Michael Shnayerson, *Irwin Shaw: A Biography* (New York: G. P. Putnam's Sons, 1989), 302.

THE WRITER

Interview, 1981

Irwin Shaw was interviewed by the Paris Review *in its infancy over twenty-five years ago. A resident expatriate author, he was a friend to the editors of the magazine in its early years in Paris, and has remained so since. It seemed appropriate to ask for an update to that interview. What follows will be incorporated with the original interview in the fifth volume of* Writers at Work, *to be published by the Viking Press and due out this autumn.*

Interviewer: You have lived in Europe for most of the years since the war, and since the first interview the magazine did with you. Are there advantages in being an expatriate writer?

Shaw: Those years did me a lot of good. First of all I had a great time. Secondly, the charge that I've become less American is ridiculous because I went back and forth all the time. I think I gained a whole lot of insight by living in Europe, and my books reflect it: *Lucy Crown,* for example, *Two Weeks in Another Town, Evening in Byzantium, Rich Man, Poor Man, Nightwork, Beggar Man, Thief,* would never have been written if it hadn't been for that European experience. Plus short stories like, "Tip on a Dead Jockey," "The Man Who Married a French Wife." All those came about because I was living in Europe. Besides, my life in New York was always more provincial than it ever was in Europe because I met only writers, editors, publishers, movie actors and directors, while in Europe I met a whole gamut of people: a writer is much more accepted socially in Europe. I met the Prime Minister of France, and he invited me for lunch. I met many ambassadors, though rarely any of our own. Also, living in a ski resort—as I do—you meet a wide variety of people because everybody somehow comes around to ski: paratroop captains from our army in Germany, Texas oil men, run-down Italian counts, hustlers, hot-shot athletes, politicians, racing-stable owners, all sorts of women from all over. You learn every

"The Art of Fiction IV: Irwin Shaw," by Willie Morris and Lucas Matthiessen, from *Writers at Work: The Paris Review Interviews, Fifth Series,* ed. George Plimpton (Middlesex, England, and New York: Penguin, 1981). © 1981 by the Paris Review, Inc. Reprinted by permission of Viking Penguin, a division of Penguin Books USA, Inc.

147

language, hear every accent, and everything's all marvelously mixed up, which is a very useful thing for a writer to observe. And then, as you can hear from the way I speak, despite my years abroad, the precious sound of Brooklyn is still there in my voice. I can't stop being American. As for being an expatriate, you must remember that anybody with $300 in his pocket can come back to the United States whenever he wants.

Interviewer: The first interview is especially acid about critics. Have your views changed over the years?

Shaw: My views naturally have mellowed. Most of the critics have been more or less kind to me, and the public has been most kind, and I reach my readers regardless of what the critics have written. So that, when I get a bad review now, it doesn't bother me as much as it once did.

Interviewer: Do you read the reviews of your books?

Shaw: Not much anymore, no. Not often. I sometimes glance at them, but I know that all writers are the same way. They forget a thousand good reviews and remember one bad one. Therefore, an excessive amount of spleen is vented on the one critic. You have to expect the raps, when you have achieved popularity as a writer, which in high literary circles is regarded as proof of venality and deliberate debasement of artistic standards. The popularity that I've enjoyed in the last few years has tended to soften the effect of critical blows. There was one critic I was very angry with, who came up to the party for Jim Jones' *Whistle*—after Jim had died—and I was in the receiving line. I put out my hand. He said, "You really want to shake my hand?" I said, "Sure. Forget it." But there are a couple of critics I won't forget from the so-called New York literary establishment, who have their own pets and standards, which I don't understand, and who have a tendency to either snub me or downgrade me. Naturally, I have some sharp things to say about them in the privacy of my own home. But I'd rather not say anything about them here, because the real juicy throat-cutting stories I'm saving for my memoirs.

Interviewer: Do you think writers have it easier today then when you started out?

Shaw: In some ways they do, and then again they don't. When I started out, in the early 1930's, there were a great many magazines that published short stories. And writers of fiction, when they begin, are more likely to try the short form. At that time there was a great market for them, greater interest in the short story, and the young writer had a chance to practice his craft, to get criticism and meet with editors. Since that time, unfortunately, the short story market has dwindled to almost nothing, and that form of expression has become almost obsolete for all writers in America except those who are willing to publish in small magazines or those writers who have enough of a reputation so that they can use the limited space in two or three magazines throughout the country. However, from the point of view of finances, getting started as a writer has become more feasible. Although the number of newspapers has dwindled—and that used to be a field where a lot of beginning writers could serve their apprenticeship—there are many other forms that are lucrative. The chief one is television, which devours huge amounts of the written word, as do advertising and industry. The demand for quality in the writing in magazines like *Time, Newsweek*, etc., is attractive to bright young people of talent and the proliferation of special interest magazines offers a multitude of opportunities for financial security. However, those are dangerous places for writers to start in with because the money is good and the writing quickly falls into a routine and people who had started out as serious are very likely to find themselves in a financial as well as an artistic bind, since working in those mediums is an all-day, all-week job. And they are liable to find themselves artistically exhausted when they want to work on something of their own. On the other hand, in my experience I've found that if you're young enough, *any* kind of writing you do for a short period of time, up to two years, perhaps, is a marvelous apprenticeship. I told my son, who wanted to be a writer, that his newspaper experience—he was lucky enough to get four years of newspaper experience under demanding editors on the U.P.I. and the *Washington Post*—could only help him. But you must avoid giving hostages to fortune, like getting an expensive wife, an expensive house and a style of living that never lets you afford the time to take the chance to write what you wish. So that, while writers in general can make a living much more easily than when I first started in the 1930's, the serious writer who doesn't want to compromise at all, finds it much more difficult. Still, we're fortunate enough. The other day I got a contract from a magazine in Budapest. To reprint a short story of mine they agreed to pay me $50, out of which there would be deducted a 30% tax, a 10% agent's fee, and furthermore I was required to send at my own expense two books to some bureaucratic organization of the

Hungarian government. You can imagine how well writers are doing in Budapest.

Interviewer: How have you changed as writer since this interview in the *Paris Review* with you twenty-five years ago? Habits, energies, attitudes?

Shaw: My habits have remained more or less the same ever since I stopped writing for the theater. Writing for the theater, when you live among actors, you find yourself leading a nocturnal life. You're staying up until 4 or 5 o'clock in the morning, and you work at night more than you do in the day. Now that I'm away from the theater, I find I get up very early in the morning and for the most part, work four or five hours, then go out. I used to ski or play tennis, then come back about four or five o'clock and go over what I'd done. My attitudes have been changed, I imagine, but somebody would have to read all my books to find out how they have. I imagine that my characters have become much more complicated than when I first began, which would be normal. I've become more gentle in my irony. I'm liable to do more with failure and death. My attitude toward women is much less romantic than it was, which is also normal. I'm not as hopeful as I was when I was young. And I can see through trickery and cheating a lot better than I did back then, since I've been exposed to quite a bit of it and some lessons have seeped in. I've also become—naturally, since I have had a family now for a long time—much more involved in the relations between members of a family. In fact the book I'm doing now is just about that.

Interviewer: Have your views changed since that first interview about the writer in America?

Shaw: Yes, they have, because times have changed. First of all, when I gave that interview it was at the height of the McCarthy period when writers *were* being hounded. After that, remember, we had Kennedy, and Kennedy was a man who liked writers and even *I* got invited to the White House. Also, Ernest Hemingway did a great deal toward making the writer an acceptable public figure; obviously he was no sissy. He was a he-man. He made money by his trade, his art. He knew everybody. He moved in very aristocratic and socially acceptable circles. So that helped a great deal. Also, today there are so many more writers. Everybody knows somebody who is writing for television or for the movies. They get much more publicity. People write about them as human beings much more than they used to, and so that has changed. Of course, it hasn't changed completely. A couple of years ago in Switzerland, a gentleman in the insurance business, an American, came to me and he said, "You live here?" I said, "Yes." He said, "Well, what do you *do?*" I said, "I'm a writer." He said, "Yes, I know. But what do you do for a *living?*" But that attitude has changed somewhat. I don't think that the writer anymore is regarded as a freak by Americans. What I said then was accurate, but now no longer is.

Interviewer: If a writer's powers do diminish over a period of time, in what areas does this seem to occur?

Shaw: Since, by all rights, my powers should be in full flood of diminishment, that's a hard question for me to answer honestly. I think that for myself I write with the same enthusiasm—if not with the same speed. I find myself re-doing things much more than I did then. But, remember, that is a particularly American question, because in Europe a writer is supposed to improve up until he's about seventy-five. Europeans seem to have a career curve that's much more regular than that of Americans . . . there are very few flash-in-the-pans in Europe, especially among writers. In America we have the feeling of the doomed young artist. Fitzgerald was the great example of that, who started losing his power at the age of twenty-nine, according to the critics. The fact that he didn't was only found out posthumously. But unless a man becomes an alcoholic or is tormented by life in a terrible way, he shouldn't lose his powers as he grows older. For example, Isaac Singer is 75 years old and although he was born in Poland and doesn't write in English, still he's an American, and he's going as strong as ever. He should be a model for us all. People who light up like Roman candles come down in the dark very quickly. Curiously, the United States is just full of writers who have one big work in their life, and that's all. Tom Haggen killed himself after *Mr. Roberts.* So did Ross Lockridge after *Raintree County.*

Interviewer: Could it be that some writers really only have one book in them . . . and writer's block is simply an excuse?

Shaw: I don't think so. The great writers—Dostoyevsky, Tolstoy, Dickens, Meredith, Thackeray—just kept bringing them out. They didn't care if they repeated themselves. It didn't bother them that they wrote echoes. We seem to go by a different timing mechanism than these writers. The only man who wrote a great deal in our time was

John O'Hara, because he went on the wagon and had nothing else to do. I've gone on the wagon, but my body doesn't believe it. It's waiting for that whiskey to get in there . . . to get me going. I never drink while I'm working, but after a few glasses, I get ideas that would never have occurred to me dead sober. And some of the ideas turn out to be valuable the next day. Some not.

Interviewer: How important to a writer are the adjutants to the profession: editor, publisher, agent?

Shaw: That depends very largely upon the writer. I know writers, very good ones, who lean upon their editors very heavily. There's no onus attached to that, but they want constant reassurance. They are doubtful about their own directions, and they often go to their editors while writing a book for help. I, on the other hand, never show anything to anybody until I've finished it. The only exception I've made to that is my son, because he represents a whole new generation; when I write about young people I want to see whether I'm getting it straight or not. Editors can be very useful. I had a great editor, Saxe Commins at Random House, who helped me cut more than 100,000 words out of *The Young Lions*. If I had kept it in it might have been a terrible flop. The editors I had at the *New Yorker* quietly helped me in peculiar, small ways. One thing they taught me was the value of cutting out the last paragraph of stories, something I pass down as a tip to all writers. The last paragraph in which you tell what the story is about is almost always best left out. The editors I have now are valuable in other ways, occasionally pointing out something they think is a weakness and in getting things straight. In the novel it's hard to keep track of everybody. They also help keep a hold on reality. They say, "That street didn't run that way." For example, in "The Sailor off the Bremen" I described a walk down into Greenwich Village in which a beating took place near the women's YMCA. My poor editor at the *New Yorker* took the time to walk down and time it and come back and tell me I had done it correctly. Also I wrote a story about North Africa during the war—this was *before* I got to North Africa—and I described it as hot, with everybody suffering from the heat. The editors found out just before publication that in the early days of the invasion it had been cold and blustery and everybody was freezing. An editor for prose isn't as important as an editor, say, for film, where the whole thing can be changed by an editor. But the most brilliant example of that in our time, I think, was Ezra Pound's editing of "The Wasteland," which

made the poem infinitely better. Well, there are very few people like
Pound around and very few people like T.S. Eliot who'll listen. So I
don't hope for that.

The writer works in a lonely way, and these people who work around
him are supportive and useful in a general way. Publishers. Agents. I
had a very nice agent, a long time ago, who approved of my stuff and
sold my short stories. But once she said, "I don't think this short story
you sent in to me is right. I think you should do this and that to it."
So I said, "My dear young lady, you have one job, which is selling my
stories, and I have another job, which is writing them. Let's you stick
to your job, and I'll stick to mine." My present agent, Irving P. Lazar,
does a very good job of selling my work, but I get no criticism from
him, which is a happy combination for both of us. Irving is famous,
you know, not only as an agent but for his fear of germs. He'll ask the
hotel concierge for twenty towels to put between his bed and his bath-
room so that after a shower he can walk back into the bedroom on a
path of towels. At the Hotel Chantaco, in St. Jean de Luz, he used up
so many towels that the concierge called him on the phone and asked
him to leave, which got Swifty so angry he took all the towels and
threw them over the balcony. Once, he and Howard Hughes, who was
also nuts about germs, found themselves in the men's room of a casino
in Las Vegas, and it became a question of which one was going to risk
opening the door for the other; in normal circumstances either would
push the door with his *shoulder* rather than risk contamination by using
his hands. Both tried to outwait the other. They'd be in there to this
day if someone had not pushed the door to come in, and both men
were able to slip out without touching anything at all.

Interviewer: Could we ask: what are the writer's responsibilities
to his talent compared to his responsibilities to his state of well-being,
his family?

Shaw: Well, a writer is a human being. He has to live with a sense
of honor. If when I got out of college I had abandoned my family to
starvation, which is just about where we were, I think I'd have been a
much worse writer. I know that the romantic idea is that everybody
around a writer must suffer for his talent. But I think that a writer is a
citizen (which is one of the reasons I went into the war), that he's a
part of humanity, part of his nation, part of his family. He may have to
make some compromises.

Interviewer: Why did you eventually stop writing for the *New Yorker?*

Shaw: Because my friends on it, my editors, died, and I didn't like the policy of the new people who came in. It's a very good magazine, but I felt that I had either outgrown it or fallen behind it. I think there would be differences of opinion there. They've tried to get me to write for them again, since 1952, when I quit, but I just didn't feel that I belonged there anymore, although I like many of their short stories. My favorite short story writer is John Cheever, who writes for them all the time. But it's not within my field anymore. I found that I could publish the stories I wanted to write other places. The *New Yorker* has been very hospitable to me. I had great editors there, starting with Woolcott Gibbs, William Maxwell, Gus Lobrano and above all—Harold Ross.

Interviewer: What constitutes a good editor?

Shaw: A good editor is a man who understands what you're talking and writing about and doesn't meddle too much. A good editor can put his finger on a weakness or on a *longueur* or on a failure in development, without trying to tell you how to repair it. That was the one thing the *New Yorker* never tried to do with me. They never tried to rewrite me. There were times when they said, "Well, we don't like the story this way, but if you change it in a certain way we'll take it." Occasionally their ideas were acceptable, and at other times I'd say, "Nothing doing," and I'd publish the story someplace else. For example, "The Eighty Yard Run" was first submitted to the *New Yorker,* and they turned it down. Another story that became quite famous, "Night Birth and Opinion," which got the best reviews in the book of short stories in which it was included, was turned down. Editors are not infallible. Also, sometimes the prejudices of the group of editors might militate against a certain kind of story. The *New Yorker* editors are the least athletic group of people I've ever seen, and also they were against violence, although they did publish "The Sailor off the Bremen," which is the first long story they ever published and the first politically serious story they'd ever accepted.

Interviewer: Didn't that particular story have something to do with a change in their policy toward short stories?

Shaw: It did indeed. That was the first really serious story they published, and the first time they published a story that long. Now they publish stories 20,000 words long. I was very grateful to them for doing "Sailor off the Bremen," especially since I'd already sent it off to *Esquire*, and had told the *New Yorker* the story wasn't for them. But the editors wormed it out of me, and both *Esquire* and the *New Yorker* chose it the same day, which put me in an ethical predicament, since to submit a manuscript to more than one publisher at a time in those days was considered immoral on the part of the writer. But I preferred at that moment to have it in the *New Yorker*, and that's what I did.

Interviewer: It's true, isn't it, that you wrote "Sailor off the Bremen" and "The Girls in Their Summer Dresses," perhaps your most famous short stories, in one week? You were twenty-five. You wrote "The Girls in Their Summer Dresses" on one afternoon, I think you told me.

Shaw: Morning.

Interviewer: Morning. You left it on the kitchen table, and your wife, Marian, tossed it out the window.

Shaw: Well, that's not quite how it happened. We had one room up on the twenty-eighth floor of this hotel on 8th Avenue, both busted. We were waiting for the rehearsals of *The Gentle People* to start. I wrote "The Girls in Their Summer Dresses" one morning while Marian was lying in bed and reading. And I knew I had something good there, but I didn't want her to read it, knowing that the reaction would be violent, to say the least, because it's about a man who tells his wife that he's going to be unfaithful to her. So I turned it face down, and I said, "Don't read this yet. It's not ready." It was the only copy I had. Then I went out and took a walk, had a drink, and came back. She was raging around the room. She said, "It's a lucky thing you came back just now, because I was going to open the window and throw it out." Since then she's become reconciled to it, and I think she reads it with pleasure, too.

Interviewer: Could you tell us something about Harold Ross of the *New Yorker?*

Shaw: Ross pretended that he was a ruffian and an ignoramus, and he would send back my copy with all sorts of queries saying, "What does this mean? I can't find this word in the dictionary." But he only did it in the interest of clarity—he liked lucid prose—and I'd go in with Lobrano, the editor, mostly, and we'd fight it out. Sometimes

Ross would say, "Well, I don't understand this story at all, but if you guys like it so much, it's gonna be in."

He was a wonderful fellow and a very good friend and marvelous to be with, and I missed him enormously when he died. He could learn to change, which is why the *New Yorker* is still going strong after its dilletantish beginnings. When you think its first cover was the fop with the monocle looking at a butterfly, and they wound up publishing *In Cold Blood* by Truman Capote and *Hiroshima* by John Hersey, you can see the ability to grow that made Ross and made the magazine.

Interviewer: Do you see any change or progression in your own approach to fiction these days? What does one learn regarding technique, say, as one becomes older and more experienced? Does one stick to a formula that apparently works?

Shaw: Well, as you can see from the variety of things I've written, I haven't stuck upon any formula. In a previous interview I said that when I was young, I tried to write each story, each play, each novel in the style suitable to the material and not in a style that could be recognized just as mine. However, that's a very hard purpose to fulfil. In most great writing in America and elsewhere, writers stick to the same style, like William Faulkner and Ernest Hemingway. But I wanted to be more various. That may have come about because of my training in the theatre, where characters have to cut the umbilical cord from the writer and talk in their own voices. Of course, the master of that was James Joyce. He could sound like anybody, and did. But we're not all Joyces.

Interviewer: Do you have any general opinion about young writers starting off?

Shaw: So many young writers I've met are uneducated. They don't read. They don't read what started things . . . produced the trends. They don't know the classics. If they become enthusiastic, it's about someone like Kurt Vonnegut, who is uncopyable. If they try to copy him, they're in for disaster.

Interviewer: What words of advice would you offer them?

Shaw: Keep going. Writing is finally play, and there's no reason why you should get paid for playing. If you're a real writer, you write no matter what. No writer need feel sorry for himself if he writes, and enjoys the writing, even if he doesn't get paid for it.

Interviewer: Why do writers protest so much that writing is no fun at all; they complain about the agonies of creation?

Shaw: I don't believe them. What do they do it for, then? Writing is like a contact sport, like football. Why do kids play football? They can get hurt on any play, can't they? Yet they can't wait until Saturday comes around so they can play on the high school team, or the college team, and get smashed around. Writing is like that. You can get hurt, but you enjoy it.

Interviews, 1980

In the summer of 1980, while writing a study of Irwin Shaw (Twayne Publishers, 1983), I wrote the novelist to suggest an interview. He quickly agreed—we had met two years earlier and had discovered common interests and sympathies—and stipulated only that I submit some questions in advance; he felt that this plan might give the interview a more clearly defined focus. The questions I mailed to Shaw covered a wide range of subjects—his attitude toward his commercial success, the relationship of his work to the tradition of literary realism, the degree of influence Ernest Hemingway and other major figures of the Lost Generation had on his fiction, and the unifying vision of his art.

The interview became a series of interviews. Though pushing himself to finish *Bread upon the Waters*, Shaw set aside two hours an afternoon for five days in July 1980 to talk with me. During the scheduled interviews, which usually took place in his study at home in Southampton, New York, he had no reservations about my using a tape recorder and freely discussed everything I asked about except the nature and degree of Hemingway's influence on his work: "If you don't mind, that's too painful. I knew him, I even introduced him to his wife. I was a kind of protégé of his. And he turned on me . . . as he turned on everyone."

Shaw expressed great admiration for F. Scott Fitzgerald, especially *Tender Is the Night* ("The best thing he ever wrote. A beautiful book. And it failed and that killed him"). Still, he said that he had been most consciously influenced by the English romantic poets. When I expressed surprise, he said, "Look at my stories again. You'll see echoes of Keats and Byron in most of what I've written. I fell in love with those poets in college. Fitzgerald was influenced by them too."

I used my interviews as reference material in my Twayne study, especially Shaw's definition of himself as a "romantic realist." While agreeing that his technique certainly fell within the James / Flaubert tradition, he emphasized that his informing vision was an affirmative,

This interview will also appear in *Resources for American Literary Study* and is published here by permission.

"romantic" one, originating in an abiding faith in the "decency and strength of the American common man." In addition, I emphasized his concept of "accidents" as the controlling force in human affairs.

Irwin Shaw died 16 May 1984. He had survived a series of major illnesses, iatrogenically induced or intensified, and he had fought his way through the financial disasters accompanying this bad luck. He had continued to write. When he felt unwell in Klosters, Switzerland, and went into the hospital this time, no one seemed alarmed. He died unexpectedly, the victim of an accident, he might have said. Hearing my tapes some months later, I realized that, in the Twayne study, I had not used his account of several important biographical matters— his years on the McCarthy blacklist, his Hollywood experience, his service in World War II. I had omitted his comments about two of his plays, *The Assassin* and *Children from Their Games,* and I had laid aside his frank discussion of the phenomenon of commercial popularity.

As a public figure, Shaw had often been interviewed, twice by the *Paris Review.* Yet, prior to 1980, he had not engaged in an extensive discussion of his work with anyone from the academic community. He understood that most scholars were not certain of his importance as a writer and, thus, saw the value of a full and open exchange with me.

I would like to stress that Irwin Shaw was the most generous of men. After the interviews were concluded and I had left Southampton, he sent me his unpublished prologue to *The Young Lions,* which I then published in *Resources for American Literary Study* (Spring 1981).

The last time I saw Irwin tells much about the man. I was in a restaurant with Gloria Jones, the widow of James Jones, and the novelist John Knowles when Irwin appeared with his wife and son and joined our table. He was outraged: "We went to that movie. *The Big Red One.* And it's a lie. [Director Samuel] Fuller makes World War II look like a great, romantic adventure. And it wasn't. It was a brutal, ugly waste of a generation of young men. And Fuller was in it. He was *there.* And he still lied. That's what's unforgivable. If he hadn't seen it, hadn't known, that would be one thing. But he was there and he lied."

I

Giles: I wrote you about a long-range project I have in mind on contemporary realism. So I'd first ask if you consider yourself a realist.

Shaw: Sometimes. I'm a romantic realist, I think. I also have written a lot of fantasy and sort of hyperbolic satire. For some reason the critics don't realize this whole side to me, even though my first play [*Bury the Dead*] is a fantasy. Another play that they are going to revive in New York—I wrote it in 1938, *The Gentle People*—is a fairy tale.

Giles: That's a beautiful play. Why do you consider it a fantasy?

Shaw: Well, it is. I called it "A Brooklyn Fable." I wanted to have a curtain designed, before the play, with a big painting of the Brooklyn Bridge on it and the river; and I wanted to write across it "Once Upon a Time." To tell the audience—this is not . . . reality. And in the program note and as a foreword to the book, I'd say this is a fairy tale in which the meek and humble emerge victorious.

Giles: Is that why it's a fairy tale? Because they don't in real life?

Shaw: Yeah (laughs). And I said the author does not pretend this happens in real life. You see? It's a fairy tale with a moral. The moral is that if somebody uses violence against you, finally you have to use violence in return. And remember that this takes place right before the war [when] Hitler was overrunning everybody, and I saw the war had to come and we had to fight it. And that's what I was saying, but in fairy-tale terms. And the weak and the meek are victorious at the end of the play and escape all punishment. Then in novellas like "The Mannichon Solution" or "Whispers in Bedlam," there's a kind of realism heightened toward ridiculousness. Ludicrousness, see? But the best fantasy is, to my mind, a fantasy that seems real at the moment that you're writing it or reading it or watching it on the stage. And a novel like *Nightwork* is pure fantasy . . . it's comic fantasy. I don't believe that stuff like that is a daily occurrence or that I'm describing ordinary life. So it's partly for my own amusement and entertainment that I write that way. And partly to use satire to show things that I think are ridiculous in the modern world. And that's different from Dreiser, who just wanted to show you exactly how things are. . . . [After mentioning several of his works that *are* realistic:] I think that's one of the things that has hurt me with the critics. They're not quite easy with me. They don't know just where to put me.

Giles: I think one problem with the criticism of your work is that you got labelled early as a social protest writer.

Shaw: Yes. And they feel that somehow I've betrayed *something* and in reality I haven't. . . . *Nightwork* is, despite its fantasy, social protest.

Giles: There's a lot of protest against Nixon.

Shaw: Against Nixon and against the idea that money rules and that people'll do anything for money. It's all so excessive . . . the weird way that people make money and the fact that money is supposed to be a medium of exchange for services rendered. It's not like that any more. It's power. *Rich Man, Poor Man* is a protest against the cruelty of the way the world treats the underdog.

Giles: How would you compare yourself, if this isn't too painful a question, to [James] Jones as a realist? I know you were both close.

Shaw: I think when you deal just in terms of realism, he was much more in the Dreiser tradition than I am. And he didn't vary. I can write like that, but I don't like to do it all the time. Except that he . . . wrote a detective novel that was hardly real. *A Touch of Danger,* a thriller. That's not the real world at all.

Giles: I had a feeling that he didn't really take that too seriously.

Shaw: No. He did it as a lark. . . . The critics think of a man as a serious writer only based on their own terms. They refuse to take a lark from his hands. But that's all besides the point because I'm lucky in that I seem to have found a wide reading public. . . . I'm sixty-seven years old now, and the kids are reading me. And they feel they have found a new writer. . . . My books have gone out of print, and now they're back in print. And also they're everywhere. So kids hanging around the house are bound to pick up one of my books in almost any house in America, and I have [received] letters about that.

Giles: I have an idea that . . . academic critics tend not to be fond of *very* popular writers.

Shaw: That's absolutely true. And they'd tell you there's corruption somehow.

Giles: Yeah. Well, I think I understand, being an academic. I don't sympathize with it, but I understand. (Both laugh.) We're always broke.

Shaw: Yeah. Well, I've been broke a good part of my life. But I don't make a big point of getting down and screaming about it or being angry at other writers because they make money and I don't. But I had to save myself [during] the first twenty-five years of my career—more than that—by going to Hollywood from time to time, . . . just to eat. Remember, I had about ten flops in the theater. And each one would take at least a year to write and produce. I was penniless. I would rush out to Hollywood, do a picture, come back, write another play that would flop, then I'd run out to Hollywood again. See? And remember, I grew up in the depression, and I had a family to support, and I had started out writing radio scripts. Serials, you know, soap operas. I didn't feel there was anything degrading about it. I knew I wasn't going to do it for the rest of my life, and as soon as I could, I quit. [That was] as soon as I had written *Bury the Dead*, and had a little reputation. But even then I had to go to Hollywood because I had a father who hadn't worked since 1928, a mother, a brother who was underage and had to be put through law school and then supported after that. Then I sold something to the movies just before I went to the army. I couldn't even enlist when I wanted to, which was the day the war began, because I had to support these people throughout the war. When I got out of the army, and I was married by this time and [still had my parents and my brother] to take care of, . . . my total financial position on October 13, 1945, was that I *owed* $300. See. And that's how rich *I* am. But I just don't go around wailing about it.

Giles: And that was after *The Gentle People*.

Shaw: After *The Gentle People*. That was after a whole lot of stories in the *New Yorker*, and that was the bread of penury, writing for the *New Yorker* in those days. You know what I got for my first story in the *New Yorker*? $75. . . . You know what I got for "The Girls in Their Summer Dresses"? Two hundred bucks. Go live on that. So even if you'd get ten stories in a year, you'd make $2,000. And to get ten stories in the *New Yorker*, you just have to sweat your balls off.

Giles: What was the first one in the *New Yorker*?

Shaw: It was something called "No Jury Would Convict." A baseball story. And the second was "Borough of Cemeteries." And I got two hundred bucks—no, I think I got $175 for that. Then they raised me to two hundred.

Giles: You had two collections by that time, didn't you? *Sailor off the Bremen* and *Welcome to the City* . . .

Shaw: Two. And that's another thing. The critics don't pay any attention to the war stories for some reason. Even though one won the O. Henry Prize and one won the O. Henry Second Prize, and I had the *Best Short Stories* dedicated to me twice. In the reviews of *Five Decades* nobody mentioned the war stories. . . . "Walking Wounded" is one of the best things I've ever done. . . . "Gunner's Passage" is probably the *best* story I ever wrote.

Giles: The story of yours that I like the best is "Main Currents of American Thought."

Shaw: Well, that's because it's closer to the academic world. (Both laugh.) Do they study "Act of Faith" and "The Girls in Their Summer Dresses" in the classes?

Giles: Oh, yeah.

Shaw: So I don't feel too badly, you know. So you get rapped.

Giles: Do you pay much attention to reviews?

Shaw: No. Well, I imagine you'd rather have a good review than a bad review. But it doesn't make that much difference to me. The critics pick up on my style of living. They feel nobody who lives that well can write well. They read my name in the papers, and they know that I live in Switzerland, I ski, and I play tennis, and they see that I've gone out with pretty girls and I go to big parties. What they don't know is that I get up at seven o'clock every morning and sit there till twelve or one o'clock every day, just writing. And there's no partying going on; I'm not doing anything except work.

Giles: Jones suffered from that criticism too, don't you think?

Shaw: Because he lived in Europe. And he was having a good time in Europe. And the parties, you know . . . naturally, you get to know a lot of famous people. I think they feel an inverse snobbery. . . . Your letter asked whether I think I've gone commercial. No, I haven't. There's been luck lately, but I've been writing the same way, I feel, and with the same intensity, with the same aims as I have [had] all my life. . . . It's just the luck of the draw [if] a writer suddenly becomes popular. Remember, I've been writing commercially, for money, professionally, since I was 20 years old. So aside from getting soldier's pay—private's pay, $20, $21 a month for a while—I have never ever earned money in anything else. . . . I'm a highly professional writer. . . . And I deserve to get paid well for it. [Laughter.] I work hard and honestly and I please a lot of people.

Giles: Yeah. And you've been doing that for, what—45 years?

Shaw: Well, I started out as a kind of cult figure, you know, with *Bury the Dead* and *The Gentle People* and then with the stories in the *New Yorker*. At that time the critics were saying the stories were formless.

The Writer

Now they're saying they're too well formed.

Giles: Yeah, I've read that, the "too well formed" criticism. I don't even understand what that means.

Shaw: It means I do it too well. I follow the rules of logic and literature.

Giles: I think several of your stories are almost perfectly formed . . . "The Eighty-Yard Run" and "The Girls in Their Summer Dresses." "God Was Here but He Left Early" is almost a perfectly formed story too.

Shaw: Yeah. [Laughs.] That's social criticism about Vietnam, about the abortion laws, about sex and people's attitudes toward sex.

Giles: What is your exact criticism of people's attitudes toward sex?

Shaw: In that story? That people take sex too lightly, that they indulge in it without knowing what the consequences are going to be. That [such emotionless sexual experimentation is] cruel, and that the perversity lurks everywhere. The criticism of the war in Vietnam is very strong in that story. Another story in that book, "Where All Things Wise and Fair Descend," is an elegy to friendship and brotherhood. It's a sad elegy about how unjust a family has to be. That is, every time the boy's mother and father look at him he knows that they wish that *he* was the one who was killed [in the car accident].

Giles: Isn't there some satire of southern California in that story?

Shaw: A little bit, yeah. A little bit. I used to think that nobody could think with all that sunshine.

Giles: You didn't like writing for the movies, did you?

Shaw: No, I didn't like writing for those studios. But I *like* the movie *form*. If it weren't such big business, I would write more [movies]. The one time I enjoyed writing for movies, really, all through, was when I produced the picture [*In the French Style*] myself. It came from two stories of my own ["In the French Style" and "A Year to Learn the Language"]. But it took too long to do the whole thing and also I was cheated . . . of some money by the studio. I wasn't writing an epic there. I was writing something very light and charming, and with a look at another culture, and about Americans in Europe. Well, it took a *year, more* than a year, between the time I wrote the original screenplay, worked on the casting, the production, and the cutting as well as the business end and the advertising. It became too much business for me. I thought I was wasting valuable time. You know, you're not immortal. You have a certain number of writing hours in your life. . . . The only way you can protect your work, and even then you can't, is if you direct it yourself. Although I've been offered chances to direct, I've always turned them down because I hate being around sets. And all that wasted slow time, you know, while they're lighting the set and doing women's hair and doing things over and over again. And I don't think I'd be a good director, besides. . . . I'm not that easy with people. You have to be a blarney artist to be a director, and I'm not. Oh, and for the same reason, I have no desire to direct my stuff on the stage. I don't like rehearsals. I'm always slipping out to the bar when it's the most important moment.

Giles: If you were going to define literary realism, as you practice it, would it be the recording of important events in the world?

Shaw: Realism is a term that's absolutely misused when it comes to a work of art, because it's the author's talent that rearranges events and characters. . . . I have a phrase I've [used] when I have taught classes: The truth is what the author invents. And why is that realism? [Because the truth is] seen through a prism, through the author's eyes. So would you say that *War and Peace* is realistic? It isn't. And *An American Tragedy*, which came from a newspaper account of a trial, is shaped by Dreiser. The story doesn't tell what they actually did, or what they may have actually felt. So realism is a catchword that has no real meaning. Some people comment, "Oh, that dialogue is so real," but people don't really talk like I write. The dialogue that you write has to be compressed, has to have a rhythm that real speech very often doesn't have. It has to be much more interesting and amusing and carry forward the plot and evoke the character. A lot of people talk without any character. If you put somebody like that in a book and, well, the dialogue is absolutely flat, that character doesn't help you at all. And also, you write to help what you're trying to say. So you're channeling events, and you're channeling characters. You're making characters to fit. . . . Sure, I draw on many people for the characterizations, but I've never used a single person as a model for a single character. They're all mixed up.

Giles: Are there some autobiographical elements in "Main Currents"?

Shaw: Yes. There are indeed. First of all, the character writes for the radio. And I include a long paragraph in which he dictate[s] something very much like what I used to dictate. He lives in Brooklyn, and he lives on the street where I lived with my mother, my father, and my brother. I played baseball and football in the field opposite. I was in love with a girl like that one—and I didn't want to marry because I knew I'd end up supporting another family, and then I'd be committed to writing just for money all my life. So all those things are very auto-biographical, except [by the time I wrote the story] I'd really broken loose from writing for the radio. I was already a literary success by that time, and the character in the story is not.

Giles: You may not remember, but the last time I talked to you [1978] you said you thought that the story works because of the last line, when the kids call him *Mister.*

Shaw: Yeah. Mister. Which they wouldn't have done even the year before, when he was 25.

Giles: When he was 24, right?

Shaw: Or 24. And I *wrote* that story when I was twenty-four!

Giles: I will stress in my study that you're a very moral writer.

Shaw: Yeah, I am.

Giles: My working title for the chapter on the stories is . . . "The Craft of Moral Fiction." I think in terms of the short stories, nearly everybody acknowledges the craft, but not enough people see the morality.

Shaw: You know why? Because I write indirectly. But it's certainly there. But people don't read carefully . . . and they miss humor; they miss humor and satire. Well, let's say it's foreign to them unless it's *marked*, with great, big, capital letters.

Giles: I say that you're a moral but certainly not a didactic writer.

Shaw: No, not *that.*

Giles: I think there's a different *kind* of morality working in the European stories than in the American ones. In the American stories there's virtually always some degree of veiled social protest.

Shaw: Well, in "Act of Faith," not in "The Girls in Their Summer Dresses," of course. But in some. Something like "Preach on the Dusty Roads."

Giles: A very angry story.

Shaw: It *is* an angry story about how big business used young men and was just interested in reaping profits in the middle of the war.

Giles: What made you the angriest about the war then? That we were not seeing that it had to be and were trying to? . .

Shaw: Before the war? I didn't refuse to *warn* people, but I refused to join with the others who were saying, "Let's go to war now; open up the second front." A lot of those people never heard a shot fired . . . When it was early, I knew there was a way out for me. *I* didn't have to join the army; I was offered jobs in Hollywood. They said, "You're essential to the war effort. Stay here and write." I could have gotten a job as a correspondent. We had a war, and a lot of guys had no way out. So I didn't feel it was right for me to exhort them to go to the war, even though I was willing to go. Naturally, after you *see* a war, it all seems senseless.

Giles: Though I guess if there ever was a war that had to be, it was that one.

Shaw: It need not have happened if we'd been smarter earlier.

Giles: How could we have stopped Hitler?

Shaw: We could have stopped Hitler without a war if we had known that eventually we were going to have a fight. Roosevelt knew this, but not enough people in this country believed him. And if we'd gotten together with England and France and got *them* to move, we could've unseated Hitler without losing a man. Early on. But the Europeans gave into him again and again. They hoped that he was on their side in saving capitalism from bolshevism. But what happened? They made bolshevism ten, a thousand times, stronger than it was before, let it move up into the middle of Europe, lost Asia. That's how they stopped the Marxists!

Giles: Do you think we could've gotten England and France ready?

Shaw: No! They were a dead, dead wind. And they, of course, remembered, much more than we did, the horrors of World War I, when the best part of their population was destroyed, the flower of their youth [cut down] in a senseless slaughter. And *that* war *was* really senseless, like most wars. The history of the world's a history of looting, piracy. What are wars? . . . Bismarck is held up as a great, great German, you know? To say nothing of our Indian fighters and the way the Texans tore Texas away from Mexico. We fought the Mexicans ourselves and got all of California away from them, and Florida—we bought Florida from the Spaniards. And we kicked the Spaniards out of Cuba, for our own interests, and out of the Philippines, for our own interests. Well, we're trying to make amends for it now, but we're also suffering because of it. So my idea about the fundamental nature of war has certainly been heightened by having been in a war myself. It's a dirty business, just about from start to finish. But that was one war that we had to fight because we let matters slide too far.

Giles: What combat did you see in the war?

Shaw: Well, I got to North Africa only when the war was ending there, so I just saw some air raids there. And I was in heavy air raids in London. But then I went to Normandy. . . . I was on the beach, but not on D day. I was in on the battle of St.-Lô, for example, and I was with the Allied troops as they liberated town after town in France. I didn't actually do any fighting myself because I was in the camera crew. But I was *in* the fighting. . . . I could easily have been killed, but I didn't get the chance to shoot anybody. I carried a gun, and it was loaded, and it was ready. It was a long-range war, in a funny way, [because of the] artillery battles. The infantry had the dirty job—getting machine-gun fire. I was machine-gunned, but more or less by accident because I was in a place that was under a lot of artillery bombardment and bombs.

Giles: Were you ever wounded?

Shaw: No. A bullet went between me, right behind my neck, and under the chin of the guy sitting in the jeep behind me. Well, let's see. I was sniped at the first day in Paris. That's in my book, *Paris! Paris!* Have you read that?

Giles: Yeah. As I remember, the first day you came in there were some Germans in the chamber of deputies, is that right?

Shaw: Yeah, some German soldiers were holding out inside the chamber of deputies. I was in on the capture and the resistance. There was some fire and a tank and some soldiers from the Second Army division. And while I was up on top of the Comédie Française—we were trying to get a panorama shot of the fighting in the city—I was sniped at there, from a window.

Giles: In *Paris! Paris!* you say that going to Paris was a sort of accident.

Shaw: Accidents, if you notice, are a major cause in my work, in my books. That's actually my philosophy of life—our lives [are] guided by accident.

Giles: I'm organizing the chapter I'm writing now, which is on the group of novels just after *The Young Lions*, around the theme of accidents.

Shaw: The first one after *The Young Lions* was *The Troubled Air*, and that was centered on cause and effect. I was working in the radio industry. The industry was going through this red-baiting period, and everything is connected to that. Then another one that's cause and effect is the one novel I've written that wasn't a success with the public and certainly not with the critics, but is a novel I like very much— *Voices of a Summer Day.*

Giles: I love that!

Shaw: It's a charming book, but it got ferocious reviews.

Giles: I think it's one of your best books.

Shaw: Yeah. I think so too. It's quiet. But that idiot Stanley Kauffmann called me a prostitute because of it. . . . In *print.*

Giles: Well, it's different from your other books. The tone is very different. . . . almost nostalgic.

Shaw: Accident is not a chief cause in that one, but the book I'm finishing now [*Bread upon the Waters*] starts with an accident.

Giles: Well, the passage I'm using to organize my chapter is from *Two Weeks in Another Town.* It's the passage where Jack Andrus and his ex-wife are in the Sistine chapel and it begins, "He could believe in Michelangelo but not in God."

Shaw: And he didn't think *Michelangelo* believed in God.

Giles: It seems to me that the passage is saying that man has to believe in man.

Shaw: Believe in man, and take the accidents as they come.

Giles: And then there's a line that goes something like, at the last judgment the seating plan is what the waiter lays out at the last minute?

Shaw: Yeah? Somehow I'd forgotten that.

Giles: It seems to me that in *all* those books, the view is that the world *is* a place of chance.

Shaw: Chance. Sheer chance. And that's what I have against the theory that art must show cause and effect. It doesn't work, you know. Art is chaos because the world is chaos. And if you organize chaos, you organize as much as you can to show that it's chaos. It's the way *I* do it. To pretend that it's not chaotic is a lie.

Giles: In that one major way you're a realist. You are reflecting the chaos of reality.

Shaw: That's it. Even my living in Europe [for] so long—it's pure accident. I went there after the war [in 1949], for the first time *since* the war, to spend the summer on the Côte d'Azur, Antibes. And we had planned to stay a few months at least. But my wife discovered she was pregnant, and she'd had a lot of troubles before. So we came back to America, because I wanted the baby to be born in America and I wanted my wife to have very good care. Even so, she lost the baby. We went back in 1951, again just for the summer. We had return tickets on the French Line for September twentieth, or something like that. A friend of mine, Peter Viertel, had an apartment in Paris, and he said, "We're going back to America for a couple of months, so why not use the apartment while we're gone?" That summer, Adam had been born, and we had a nurse [and a maid] with us, and I was enchanted with Paris then, in peacetime. So I said, "Fine." I switched my path. I've lived in Klosters, Switzerland, now for 26 years. Pure accident.

Giles: Viertel is a screenwriter, right?

Shaw: Screenwriter and novelist; he's written some good novels, too. . . . We met first before the war, playing tennis, and we became fast friends, and he kept telling me, "You've gotta learn how to ski." I was in Paris, at the time, and he said, "Come on up to Klosters"—he had a little house there, he and his wife. So I decided to go up for a month to learn how to ski. I fell in love with skiing: I became a fanatic. Well, that was an accident . . . And I loved the town, because that was the only place where I'd skied, you see? I came back, I fell more in love with the town, more in love with skiing, and finally built the house there. Now I'll finish the first draft on this new book [in Southampton] and the final draft, the real work, there [in Klosters]—it's a great place for me to work. It's quiet. People leave me alone. In the wintertime a lot of friends come through, but they know what my working hours are; they don't bother me. And the climate is great for working. It's cool in the summertime too. And it's very beautiful. People think that I'm going there to avoid taxes, which you can't do. By the way, if I *could* avoid taxes, I would. But if you're an American, you pay taxes the same as anybody else, even if you don't come *back* to America.

Giles: Did you stay away at first to any degree out of disgust with McCarthyism?

Shaw: Well, that made coming back to America a lot less attractive to me; because, naturally, I was among the people on the Left. [Almost inaudibly.] I was blacklisted. Luckily, the *New Yorker* didn't give a good Goddamn about it. And luckily, I had just published *The Young Lions*. So the publishers didn't give a Goddamn, and . . . and actually, the public didn't. And then, you know how I got off the blacklist? David Selznick, the producer, was asked to produce a show—the seventy-fifth anniversary of the invention of the electric light, a great big spectacular. President Eisenhower gave the opening address on television. Selznick wanted to do a short story of mine: "The Girls in Their Summer Dresses," but the powers that be said, "You can't have Shaw; he's blacklisted." But [Selznick] knew me very well. He said, "If he's a Communist, then I'm a Communist too. . . . If I can't have this story, get somebody else to do the program." [Within] ten minutes I was no longer blacklisted. [Laughs.] And you remember *that* kind of accident. But, by that time I didn't need the movies, I didn't need television or anything like that. I felt terribly sorry for my friends. And believe it or not, at that time three directors and producers out of Hollywood wanted to do *The Troubled Air*, which is so anticommunist, but the American Legion stopped me. So that's the sort of times we were living through. . . . I knew they wouldn't last anyway.

Giles: Why did you think they wouldn't [last]?

Shaw: Because I have that much faith in America. I showed that faith in the character of Michael Whitacre in *The Young Lions*. He's Middle America. He's slow to move. He gets dragged into doing some good things, reluctantly, but then he comes through. And that's the way I felt about America. Yeah. And it turned out I was right. You see?

Giles: You saw that as a period of short-term hysteria?

Shaw: Yeah. But there were people whose lives were broken—and remain broken. But, well, mine wasn't, but it *affected* me. I didn't like the fact that there were people going around trying to destroy me. I could see what they were doing. My phone was tapped. And everybody who had to go to Washington was asked about me.

Giles: Did you know Odets well?

Shaw: Yeah. Very well. [Strikes sharply at a match.] We were very good friends. He was a tragic figure.

Giles: Your politics then were, what—leftist?

Shaw: Left. But mostly because of the Spanish Civil War. The Communists were organizing money drives and sending kids there—the Abraham Lincoln Brigade and all that—so I gave them money and I supported them in print. But that's about as far as my leftism went. The funny part is that maybe it was good that Franco won, because otherwise Europe would have had a Communist Spain on the other side of France, instead of a democratic Spain.

Giles: Was any part of the blacklisting because of *Bury the Dead?*

Shaw: Yeah. There's no mention of communism there, but the play was done by a leftist company, I mean, they had political leanings toward communism. But I was 22 years old when I wrote that, and I didn't give a good Goddamn: if they wanted to do it, fine. They wanted to use me; I wanted to use them. . . . Odets was with Group Theatre. Odets, John Howard Lawson—a *wise* and outspoken Communist, and everybody knew it.

Giles: And he *really* got hurt in the blacklists.

Shaw: [Smoking hard, voice almost whispers.] Yeah. He couldn't work any more. And his politics ruined his talent too, [because] he began to write tracts instead of plays. He was a very talented man.

Giles: You had a lot of admiration for FDR, didn't you?

Shaw: I did, indeed. I never met him. I met Mrs. Roosevelt.

Giles: You don't blame him at all for our getting into the war too late?

Shaw: He did what he had to do. And the capitalists whose lives and fortunes he saved and made hated him. [Giles laughs.] Why, if it hadn't been for FDR, they'd have all gone under. Everybody would've gone bankrupt. But he was a consummate politician and he was farseeing. He knew what he wanted to preserve, but he took unusual measures to do it. Even lying to the American people.

Giles: Which he did occasionally.

Shaw: If you're gonna be president, you gotta lie.

II

Shaw: We were talking about the word *popular.* You have to remember that Dickens was the most popular writer of his time. Dostoyevski was enormously popular. Tolstoy was enormously popular. So I don't feel it's exactly derogatory to me, if I fall into that company.

Giles: Some *critics* mean the word in a derogatory way.

Shaw: Well, sure. They mean to *derogate* me. They warn. They use the words *popular* and *successful*, but they mean *false* or *grandstanding* or *cheaply entertaining*, or *sentimental*. *Popular* and *successful* are "crypt terms"—like fascist and cryptocommunist. They don't want to search their minds and see what they really have to say about me. And this whole sense that success is somehow corrupt—I don't think it is. I work as honestly and as well as I know how. I certainly believe in working well and not skimping on my work. And so *well-made* in any other profession is considered a compliment. Only in writing in the present day is that an epithet. And that shows a failure of the critic more than the writer. And so it doesn't bother me. . . . I've written for money. Very consciously. I've written radio scripts, and I've written movies. Those were compartments of my life that I had to enter. So that we'd be retrieved, my real books and my real places. But there's never been any blurring in my mind about what I was doing.

Giles: You have always known the distinction.

Shaw: Even when I was writing the junk, I knew it was junk, but I did it the best way I could. And I make no excuses for eating or feeding a family. I wouldn't have been able to write the novels if I hadn't found that freedom. Having found the freedom, I certainly wasn't gonna write junk. If I'd wanted to just make money, I'd have made a lot more money staying in the movies. You know, palaces all over and mistresses forever, and all that.

Giles: How would you react to a comparison of your career to that of Somerset Maugham?

Shaw: Well, a lot of people compare us, because he too wrote very carefully. And his stories are very well made. And . . . well, they're marvelous. The fact that he failed sometimes to stay up to his highest standard is the failure of every artist. I mean, you look at a painting Cézanne did one week and one that he did the next week, and they may be at the opposite ends of the spectrum. One is good, and one is not too good, but the intention when he started was always the same: to do as well as he could.

Giles: You respect Maugham, then.

Shaw: I certainly do. Anybody who reads his stuff has to respect him, I think. They say he's not Proust, but there's one Proust. There's one Joyce. I'll tell you something, a friend of mine, and he's a very keen critic who did three of my plays—Harold Clurman—he wrote me about a play that somebody had claimed was second-rate. And a friend of the playwright called him to ask, "What do you mean, second-rate?" "Well, if you consider that Shakespeare is first-rate, and Sophocles is first-rate, second-rate is pretty good." You have to put literature into its proper perspective. I mean, I'm not Shakespeare, and I'm not Sophocles. I make no pretensions. . . . And also, what your contemporaries say about you is never the last word. [Fitzgerald's] contemporaries killed [him] with their criticism. And now you see what they say about him. *Posterity* makes the judgment. Look, Hemingway never won a Pulitzer Prize.[1] He finally won a Nobel Prize.

Giles: Faulkner never won the Pulitzer until very late.

Shaw: Until very late. He was ignored, and he was starving. Then he suddenly got rich. Same with Hemingway. They became popular writers. Dumas never got into the French Academy, and his son, who wrote much worse, did. Flaubert was hauled into court for *Madame Bovary*. Joyce was considered a dirty old man and was on the Index. So . . . the judgment of your contemporaries is a very misleading thing. Proust couldn't get his books published, and he had to publish them himself. Stephen Crane . . . Fame and fortune is a dice game. When you win at the game, the guys who haven't won [will] likely say, "Well, he's cheating." Even though he's running a string of naturals. [Both laugh.]

Giles: Another basis of the Maugham comparison would be that he also wrote well in several genres.

Shaw: Yes. Except that he wrote successful plays, and I wrote flops.

Giles: Did *Gentle People* really flop?

Shaw: Well, no, it didn't flop, it was a mild success. But other plays of mine flopped. Ingloriously. *The Assassin* lasted for three weeks and closed.

Giles: That play was a source of controversy, wasn't it? Even before you wrote the denunciation of the theater [published in the preface to the book version of *The Assassin*].

Shaw: Yeah, well, yeah. Well, because of leftist politics. It's an overtly political play. I wrote it during the war. I started writing it in North Africa—I'd been in Algiers—and I finished it when I was waiting for D day in England. The army prevented it from going on in a war zone. Because I had to show it [to the army censors], you know. And they stopped it. Nobody knows that. This is the first time I've said it.

Giles: I can see why, though it's strange now, because the play does affirm America.

Shaw: With some guilt and some innocence. But it sure ends with an approbation. But the army doesn't want to hear "Boo!" because you're supposed to be these brave, reckless fellows. From a public relations point of view. They're all cowering pussycats.

Giles: Well, the Jordache books [*Rich Man, Poor Man* and *Beggarman, Thief*].

Shaw: Yeah, I was thinking about [that when] we were talking about the piece charging that I don't want to write about the proletariat any more. What about the Jordache family? The guy's a starving baker. Poor old woman can't stand on her feet behind the bakery. The kid delivers rolls at seven o'clock in the morning. Then the guy has to work as a seaman, as a bum prize-fighter, getting beat up for a couple of bucks. The whole cast is lower class, proletariat. Some of them rise above it, as it happens. That's one of the things I don't like about . . . movies that I otherwise like very much. For example, movies such as *Saturday Night and Sunday Morning* and *The Last Picture Show.* They never show anybody rising from that class, above the level of a kind of dumb brutality and resignation. The truth is that the men who wrote them, both those things, rose right above it. You see, there is a great mobility in modern democracies. People rise and fall. And you have to *show* that. I mean, if you just show utter desperation, you're not being truthful to the times or to the society in which you live. So, when you say that my cast of characters has changed so completely, it's not true.

Giles: Yeah. Let me mention another critical comment, if you don't mind. One fault of the Jordache books is that Tom is much more interesting than Rudolph, yet *Rich Man, Poor Man* focuses much more on Rudolph than on Tom.

Shaw: Well, that isn't true. You just count the pages, it isn't true. Well, you know, always from a schematic point of view, the rascal who wins your heart is bound to be more interesting than the decent citizen who rises and rises and rises and wins the rewards of his probity and his ambition, even within this system. That is, while there are many things in the system that I've denounced, I haven't come across a better system. People do get a chance to rise in it, and people can be decent here. Modern readers, the critics anyway, are crazy about people who are degenerate, neurotic, self-pitying, squeamish, unhappy, cruel. But I haven't found that to be true of everybody on balance.

Giles: I think Rudolph's a very interesting character; he's simply unable to express love, isn't he? At least not to a great degree.

Shaw: Well, that's true. He's stunted by ambition. And it's not a completely noble ambition. It's the ambition that everybody coming out of the Harvard Business School has: to get rich, to be respected by the community, to live well, and to be within the laws as much as possible; to take no chances. . . . But he gets trapped too. He winds up with a crazy, drunken wife. And then he ruins everything. That's why I made him rise so beautifully, because then the downfall, which is not his fault at all, comes more dramatically.

Giles: Wouldn't you call both the brothers fundamentally decent people?

Shaw: Yes, it comes out that way. And the women, too, Gretchen. [Long pause.] It's silly to defend your own books. . . . I just got a questionnaire sent out by the Screenwriters Guild about the plight of older writers. So I'm an older writer. So I didn't complain [in my answers] that my plight was terrible, of course. But one question amused me. It said, "When do you plan to . . . what would make you retire?" And I just wrote down one word: "Death." [Laughs.]

Giles: The last thing of yours I read, because I had a hard time getting it, was the 1962 play *Children from Their Games*.

Shaw: *Children from Their Games*. Yeah. That's so different from anything else I've done. That's a comic fantasy. It's very funny; it's black humor. [Pause.] It flopped.

Giles: Any conscious Molière influence there?

Shaw: Not that I know of.

Giles: I thought about that because the character is such a misanthrope, and . . .

Shaw: He is a misanthrope. That aspect, I would have to say, is like Molière. But, it's a kind of heartless play. . . . It's vicious satire on noise pollution and it came ahead of its time. Because it's about what we're doing to our environment. . . . And the noise is a symbol for all the irrelevant, damaging, polluting, bad thinking. As well as bad breathing, bad eating, bad work. So here's the noise, as a symbol for all those things. And so the man becomes misanthropic, because of the noise. The woman represents the grasping, materialistic side of our society. She has a long list of all the great things she's offered him. They're all the material things, you see. . . . Anyway, like all my plays, it's this much away from being a success. [Holds up hand with fingers slightly apart.]

Giles: Yeah. Martin Gabel played that.

Shaw: Yeah. Old friend of mine. We've had very bad luck together in the theater. Let's see. He directed two plays of mine—they were flops, *flops*, and he acted in one—it was a flop. So now we just remain friends. [Laughs.]

Giles: I like the play. The only difficulty I had with it is how much the daughter-in-law seems to change at the end. And I guess I don't quite see what would motivate that.

Shaw: Yes. Well, I want to say that she finally becomes a human being. She understands her father-in-law's problems and sympathizes. I might have glossed over a bit. And the play is a little bit like *Every Man in His Humor.*

Giles: It reminded me of an eighteenth-century play.

Shaw: Well, that's the kind of play it was. It's like *Volpone.*

Giles: Well, this probably seems crazy, but some of the lines of the main character reminded me of Groucho Marx.

Shaw: Yeah, yeah. They're supposed to be funny because they're extreme; they're surrealistic.

Giles: In the same way he was.

Shaw: Yeah. They seem like terrible non sequiturs. Right. Right. So much for realism. If that's a box of realism, so am I. [Laughs.]

Giles: Earlier, you referred to a kind of self-indulgent and confessional writing that's "in." Exactly what writers were you referring to?

Shaw: I can't say. Because the names are big names, and I don't want to. . . . You know, it's bad enough that the critics rap other writers. That's one of the reasons I quit being a drama critic. I couldn't stand writing bad reviews about people I knew were trying their best.

And I knew how tricky the theater is. If you got another cast, another director, it might be a great play. It's very hard to tell. If one of my books comes out at the wrong time, like *Tender Is the Night*, everybody jumps on it. If it comes out at the right time, like *Gentleman's Agreement*, everybody praises it to the skies. *The Man in the Grey Flannel Suit*, which isn't a good book, came out at just the right time and so it became a symbol forever.

Giles: You obviously read a lot.

Shaw: Oh yeah, I read a lot. But it's 67 years of reading. Well, I started reading when I was four years old; so it's 63 years of reading.

Giles: Mailer, I read somewhere, said that he thought that a writer needed to read less than a critic does. Do you think that's true?

Shaw: I don't think a critic has to read at all. [Both laugh.] That's a joke. Well, there was a period in the 1940s, amid [Alfred] Kazin's vogue when they said that we live in an age in which criticism is much more important than creative writing. Well, that's pure nonsense. The critics are living off the bones of the creative writer. People can't go on writing criticism of *Moby Dick* forever, you know, although it looks as though they will. And now Fitzgerald. And Hemingway. Imagine what they do to Victor Hugo in France. And Henry James, now.

Giles: And the Faulkner industry.

Shaw: That's a growing industry. Now, that's a real growth industry, as they say in the stock market. [Laughter, long pause.]

Giles: In the criticism of the Jordache books, the word *saga* comes up over and over again.

Shaw: Yeah, well, *saga*, again, is used as a derogatory term. But why it should be, I don't know. So it takes place over a period of 30 years. Many works of literature take place over such a period. We're not keeping to the Greek unities, wherein everything has to take place [within] 24 hours and in no more than one place. Now, why the Greeks thought of that idea, I have no idea. It appealed to their sense of order in some way. We've got a disorderly world. So sometimes it takes 30 years to tell your story. Sometimes it takes 30 years to write it. I have no feeling for structure in that sense. I have a very strong sense of structure in my own way. I don't follow any artificial rules.

Giles: One phrase that's appearing in criticism now is Barth's phrase, "the literature of exhaustion," which comes from Barth's theory that literature has already done virtually all it can, and now all it can do is imitate itself.

Shaw: That's sophomoric. I wrote the same thing when I was 18 years old in a creative writing class in Brooklyn College. And what I wrote is, "I'm sorry I wasn't an ancient Greek, [be]cause they said everything, and now, we'll just be repeating and embroidering." But I don't believe that. You believe it when you're 18 and pessimistic. I feel there's a great deal of vitality and variety in American literature. Look at what we have. Just look at some of the writers today. The vitality they have. Mailer. Bellow. Cheever. Barthelme. Myself. Styron. McMurtry. McGuane. Isaac Bashevis Singer, an American writer. Look how different they are, how vital they are, how far they range. Gore Vidal. And American vitality is running just as high as ever, even though we don't have Melville around, and so forth. Mark Twain. As I said, *second-rate* is very high praise when you consider. [Laughs.]

Giles: Yeah. Then one other phrase, and this is Malcolm Cowley's, . . . whose favorite period of American literature, of course, was—

Shaw: The Twenties.

Giles: Yeah. He says those people believed in a "religion of art." I guess he always cites "The Snows of Kilimanjaro" as best expressing that idea.

Shaw: Well, . . . I know the story very well, and it's a great story.

Giles: Cowley says that Harry is tainted like a priest who has been corrupted away from his religion by the things of the flesh. And that's what Hemingway was writing about.

Shaw: Well, maybe he was. I don't think he was. You know, I don't like his later books. I don't even like *Old Man and the Sea* as much as everybody else. It seems affected to me. . . . However, you know Cowley has the idea because he was young at that time, and he knew all those guys who were struggling to be writers. They kept talking about, "Gee, we gotta be writers and nothing else matters, and we let our families starve, and we dedicate ourselves, and that's all we have to do." And you know, they all go back to Florida, and say, "I've researched for a week for the mot juste." The guy could search for a week because he didn't have to work for a living. He had an income. You know, that's pretty easy, isn't it? And then you can make a religion out of laziness too. And a religion out of lack of discipline. But I believe I've led a moral life. I haven't hurt anybody much, not purposely; and I should be rewarded in heaven for the way I've lived. But I don't think I will be. Because I don't think there's a heaven.

Note

1. Hemingway did, of course win a Pulitzer Prize, in 1953 for *The Old Man and the Sea*. Still, Shaw was making a valid point. Hemingway did not win the Pulitzer for any of his earlier, better novels; and Fitzgerald, Dos Passos, and Thomas Wolfe never won a Pulitzer at all. Shaw also pointed out that, of the major American World War II novels, James Jones's *From Here to Eternity*, Mailer's *The Naked and the Dead*, and his own *The Young Lions* failed to win Pulitzers, whereas James A. Michener's *Tales of the South Pacific*, James Gould Cozzins's *Guard of Honor*, and John Hersey's *A Bell for Adano* received the prize. Shaw claimed that Michener, Cozzins, and Hersey all printed safe, "patriotic," "officer-class" pictures of the U. S. Army, whereas he, Jones, and Mailer were openly critical of the army and wrote from the enlisted man's perspective. It should be said that Shaw expressed admiration for much of Hersey's later work.

Part 3

THE CRITICS

Introduction

Other than reviews of his individual novels and short story collections, there is, as yet, a paucity of significant Shaw criticism. While frequently anthologized, his work has rarely been analyzed in any real depth. The critical materials that follow constitute the most perceptive investigations of Shaw's short fiction. In addition, they cumulatively illustrate the shifting consensus over the last forty years regarding his lasting importance and place in the canon of American literature.

William Peden's 1950 review of *Mixed Company* is an enthusiastic appreciation of the masterful craft and the rich diversity of theme and setting that characterize Shaw's short fiction. In his 1951 article, Bergen Evans focuses on Shaw's war novel, *The Young Lions*, but adds that the novelist "has produced some of the best short stories in contemporary literature."

The next three essays exemplify the largely negative critical reexamination of Shaw's work that began in the late 1950s and continued for almost three decades. Hubert Saal's 1957 review of *Tip on a Dead Jockey*, for instance, charges that Shaw's writing has lost its old moral edge largely as a result of the novelist's pursuit of the good life in Europe. Paradoxically, Chester E. Eisinger argues that Shaw could not transcend the moral indignation of his 1930s liberalism and that his fiction is marred by slickness and oversimplification.

In what is perhaps still the most balanced essay on Shaw, William Startt agrees that the novels are often superficial in vision and simplistic in execution, but maintains that the short stories are consistently honest, well-crafted portraits of society. Finally, Ross Wetzsteon's 1981 interview-essay, inspired by the appearance of the novel *Bread upon the Waters*, describes Shaw as an important and underrated writer of "moral fables" and persuasively calls for a reassessment of his work.

William Peden

In 1936 Irwin Shaw achieved sudden notoriety with "Bury the Dead," a savage antiwar play. Since then he has written several other plays, a best-selling novel, and three volumes of short stories. "Mixed Company" contains the best of these and several hitherto unpublished or uncollected stories. The collection is an important one. Mr. Shaw is probably the most artistic and articulate exponent of the socially-conscious short story writing today.

Among Mr. Shaw's best-known and most memorable stories are those directly or indirectly connected with war and the effect of war, violence, and intolerance: "Gunners' Passage," "Sailor Off the Bremen," "Act of Faith," "Walking Wounded." Of these and similar stories I like "Gunners' Passage" the best. Unlike some of Mr. Shaw's too-facile stories, it gains upon repeated readings and the inevitable changes of emotional climate frequently so destructive to "war" stories. Nothing much *happens* in this story of three enlisted men at an Air Force base in North Africa. The men simply talk and think about their past experiences and what lies ahead of them. Yet the work is eloquent in its simplicity and revealing in its understanding of simple men of good will in a violent world. Here Mr. Shaw's power lies in his ability to capture the essence of a character by the revealing statement, gesture, or thought.

In technically more ambitious stories, like "Sailor Off the Bremen," Mr. Shaw essays an allegorical study of the individual and national hatreds and tensions growing out of opposing ideologies. As the story of a politically naive American athlete who beats a Nazi to pieces, "Sailor Off the Bremen" precipitates the reader into a web of intrigue culminating in a shattering, brutal climax. All this is superbly handled. But as a study of opposing ideologies it is both confused and confusing. Whose, for example, is the real evil? Where does the real responsibility lie? I frequently feel, after rereading a story like this or "Act of Faith" or "Medal from Jerusalem," that Mr. Shaw stacks his cards too neatly,

From the "Best of Irwin Shaw," *Saturday Review*, 18 November 1950, 27–28. Reprinted by permission of Omni Publications International Ltd. and William Peden.

that he oversimplifies his moral, social, or political problems to fit the needs of a preconceived thesis.

In another group of stories, Mr. Shaw depicts with equal facility the manners and mores of American civilians during the Thirties and Forties: a disillusioned ex-football player whose life with an "intellectual" wife has been one of gradual disintegration ("80-yard Run"); a college professor victimized by nerves, that modern substitute for the medieval devil who undermines so many of Mr. Shaw's characters ("The Climate of Insomnia"); a charming phony who seeks to cover his own inadequacies by an unsuccessful search for an animate or inanimate scapegoat; a Garboesque dancer whose career is ruined by a bald man and an olive ("Welcome to the City").

Mr. Shaw's people seem wonderfully alive, even when the author descends to caricature and burlesque. Like Dickens, Mr. Shaw has created, prodigally, a crowded gallery of memorable people. Like Dickens, too, he handles scenes superbly; from the crummy atmosphere of a third-rate New York hotel to the oppressive heat of an Army newspaper office in Algiers, his stories are firmly anchored in time and space. And he communicates experience with a narrative felicity and sincerity which redeem even a frequently far-fetched, sentimental, or one-sided situation.

Bergen Evans

Irwin Shaw appeared on the American literary scene at the age of twenty-three when his playlet—for it was hardly more—*Bury the Dead* was produced at the Ethel Barrymore Theater in 1936. The action of the play was exceedingly simple. In "the second year of the war that is to begin tomorrow night" six dead soldiers refuse to be buried, on the grounds that they have never had a chance to live. Patriotism, religion, the pleas of their loved ones, the commands of their officers, and the threatened panic of society in general are all in vain, and they walk off the stage at the final curtain, followed by the men who had been ordered to bury them, with a vague but powerful suggestion that outraged nature will tolerate war no longer.

Hans Chlumberg, in his *Miracle at Verdun*, produced by the Theater Guild five years earlier, had also built a sensational play around a fantasy of the unburied dead. But Chlumberg's dead, finding the world no better for their sacrifice and themselves unwanted, had returned in despair to their graves. Shaw's play was more somber in its tone, his dead more passionate in their regrets, and the suggestion of hope in its conclusion, however vague and romantic, more exciting.

Pacifism of this particular kind, that attributed wars to the selfish machinations of an evil few and believed they could be ended by a refusal to take part in them, was not so popular in 1936 as it had been a few years earlier. Coming events were casting ominous shadows, and conscientious objectors merely added exasperation to the other tensions. But exasperation is vocal. *Bury the Dead* was too well written to be ignored, and Shaw was embarked upon a promising career.

The next year he produced another pacifist play, *Siege*, but this was not a success, and he has consistently omitted it from the list of his works.

In 1939 he had a second success with *The Gentle People*, a play which, because of its happy endings for the principal characters, is probably to be classified as a comedy. Two peace-loving men, a Jew and a

From "Irwin Shaw," *English Journal* 40 (November 1951):485–91. Reprinted by permission of the journal and the National Council of Teachers of English.

Greek, find what little happiness their lives afford in fishing from a small boat they own. Even this modest recreation is threatened, however, when they are terrorized by a racketeer who extorts "protection" money from them. They appeal to the law only to find the judge in league with the racketeer. Bold with desperation, they lure their oppressor on board their boat, knock him on the head, throw him overboard, and return, having rifled his pockets and regained their money, to the tranquil life.

In 1940 Shaw ventured directly into comedy with *Retreat to Pleasure*, wherein a blonde is pursued through Florida by a manufacturer of valves, a playboy, and a philosophical liberal. There are minor eccentrics—a polite, punch-drunk prizefighter and an inebriated lady who from time to time shrieks, "Tear the tattered ensign down"—but, despite all they could add, the play left the critics lukewarm and the audiences elsewhere. This, too, is quietly omitted from the list of his works.

Three years later he produced another serious play, *Sons and Soldiers*. In this play a young married woman in the year 1912, warned by her physician that it would be dangerous for her to bear the child with which she is pregnant, has a vision in which she sees the future down to 1942. She sees that she will bear two sons. One will be killed in World War II and the other will be going off to that war, as a pilot, in that year. She awakens from the vision and, remembering that her son had told her in the vision that he was content to die if he had to, refuses to have the abortion, resolved to go on with life at whatever cost.

Shaw's last play to date is *The Assassin*, a dramatization of the assassination of Admiral Darlan, written while he himself was in uniform, though not actually produced until he had been mustered out. It was unfavorably reviewed and closed after a short run. Shaw published it with a vigorous preface in which he trounced dramatic critics and, while he was about it, took a few swipes at audiences, actors, censors, sceneshifters, electricians, and anyone else connected with the stage he could think of. It was probably this outburst (which was not without merit) that led the *New Republic* to employ him as their dramatic critic from September, 1947, to March, 1948. His work as a critic was certainly above the average and distinguished by an effort to analyze the plays he reviewed as co-operative productions of author, designer, director, and cast.

In 1948 he published his first novel, *The Young Lions*. In this he traced the careers of three soldiers, two Americans and a German, from

New Year's Eve, 1938, to the end of the war in Europe. The Americans are Noah Ackerman, a lonely young Jew who is just beginning to find a meaning in his life in a happy marriage, and Michael Whitacre, a director, whose marriage is dissolving in the futile atmosphere of Hollywood and Broadway. Both enter the army reluctantly, though both feel that they ought to do something. The German, Christian Diestl, an Austrian ski instructor and a former Communist, has joined the Nazi party and enters with enthusiasm into what he sees as a crusade. Yet, as the war goes on, Ackerman and Whitacre find increasing strength and purpose (Whitacre later and to a lesser extent than Ackerman), while Diestl degenerates. The three of them come together at the end of the book in a wood outside of a concentration camp which the Americans have just liberated. Diestl kills Ackerman wantonly from ambush and is himself killed by Whitacre, who only at that moment becomes a full soldier.

In making an enemy a central figure in his novel, Shaw had set himself an artistic challenge, and he met it, as might have been expected, by leaning over backward. The German Army is pictured as being definitely superior, in morale and discipline, to the American army. Lieutenant Hardenburg, the fanatical Nazi who serves as Diestl's mentor, is so romantically depicted, in his titanic single-mindedness, that Goebbels himself would have applauded the presentation. And Diestl comes close to being the most sympathetic character in the story. It is true that he imbrutes as the action progresses, but this is due to the fact that his side is losing. Shaw may not have intended to support Machiavelli and Hitler in their assertions that there can be no virtue in a defeated state, but he does so nonetheless.

Ackerman is meant to be the chief recipient of our sympathies, but, except for the delineation of his aimlessness and rootlessness at the beginning, he is not made credible. On one occasion, persecuted because he is a Jew, he challenges the ten largest men in his company—positive giants, while he weighs only one hundred and thirty-five pounds and is tuberculous—to fist fights and insists on fighting them one after the other. He has four teeth knocked out, his nose is broken, two ribs are cracked, and his larynx is split, but he doggedly persists. His later heroism under fire is more believable, but even so his military career comes close to being one of those boyish dreams of glory that Steig celebrates in his cartoons. And the strengthening of his character under fire, his finding of "an inner balance, a thoughtful quiet maturity," tolerance, resignation, and a hope for a better world, is too much like the sentimental propaganda dished out during the first World War (the propaganda that, presumably, enraged the author of *Bury the Dead*) to be accepted without uneasiness.

The best of the book is its graphic presentation of the war itself—the induction center, the barracks, a road block in a leafy wood, death in dappled shadows, Rommel's retreat (worthy to stand beside Hemingway's account of the rout of the Italians at Caporetto), an ambush at a bridge over a dry ravine in North Africa, the landing on the Normandy beaches, and the growing demoralization of the defeated Germans. Whatever faults may be found with the book's "message," it remains a good, perhaps a great, war book.

But it is certainly not a pacifistic book. Indeed, it is hard to believe that Shaw was ever seriously a pacifist. *Bury the Dead* merely reflected an intellectual fashion. In so far as it had anything to say, it was the assurance, hardly new in the world, that the light is sweet and that it is a pleasant thing for the eyes to behold the sun. As a matter of fact, its author's solution for most of mankind's ills is naïvely *un*pacifistic. If soldiers are unhappy, let them mutiny. If the gentle people of the world are oppressed by gangsters, let them murder the gangsters. If tyrants threaten liberty, let some peace-loving young man assassinate them. The treatment for Nazi ruffians is to lure them up a dark street and beat them to a bloody pulp ("Sailor Off the Bremen") or if, made humble by defeat, they ask what atonement they can make, advise them to cut their throats ("Retreat"). After the Americans have liberated the concentration camp in *The Young Lions*, a rabbi asks permission to hold Jewish religious exercises in public. The American commanding officer, Captain Green, who has been represented as a model officer and in whose kind, we are specifically told, lies the hope of the future, grants the permission. An Albanian Fascist protests that it might be unwise to inflame the populace by such a spectacle; whereupon the captain says that he will put machine guns on the surrounding roofs and shoot down anyone who attempts to interfere. And when, in Shaw's latest book, the hero finds that he has been ruined by a Communist friend, he assures the friend that "if it comes to it, I swear to God I'll pick up a gun and kill you."

Whatever the merits of these suggestions, they hardly reflect a pacifistic mind, and Shaw himself has renounced his early reputation. In 1950 he withdrew *Bury the Dead* lest it be exploited by the Communists, who were then holding out the Stockholm Peace Pledge with one hand and egging on North Koreans and Chinese "volunteers" with the other. He did not wish, he said, for "the forlorn longings and illusions of 1935 to be used as ammunition for the killers of 1950."

Far more serious than his concern with pacifism is his concern with the uncertain liberal, the man who wants to do the right thing but is not sure what the right thing is and even less sure of how to go about doing it and, even when he is sure on both counts, is restrained by conflicting sympathies or enervated by his ability to see the opposing point of view. For he is essentially a master of episode. He has published approximately fifty short stories, in three separate volumes, collected from the various magazines in which they first appeared, chiefly the *New Yorker*. And it is in the short story, of all narrative forms the closest to the drama, that his talents have found their most congenial scope.

Many of his stories deal with Jews. Some relate their sufferings in pogroms and concentration camps, their aspirations and agonies in Palestine. The better ones, as stories, deal with their everyday life in America. "The Boss" is a somber tale of an inept, slow-witted tailor who goes mad under his greedy wife's oppression. In "God on Friday Night" a Jewish boy who has left the ways of orthodoxy begs his mother to light candles and say the traditional prayers on Friday night, so that his wife, long sterile but now pregnant, will bear a child. "The Lament of Madame Rechevsky" is a wonderful monologue in which a spoiled woman, fallen on evil days in her widowhood, goes to her husband's grave to lament but ends by reproaching the dead man for her present hardships and demanding that he provide for her as he used to. Sadness and a sort of amused tenderness give some of these stories a fine quality of pity, but in others Shaw is overcome with indignation which, however excusable, defeats his artistic purposes.

He has some pictures of dire poverty ("Second Mortgage") in which the main concern is with the bare necessities of life, but he is more interested in the maintenance or loss of dignity, the beginnings or endings of love, the struggle to preserve those things by which, more than by bread alone, men must live. "The Monument" is a fine story of a barkeeper who regards the good reputation of his bar as a personal monument and threatens to quit when the owner proposes to buy an inferior brand of whiskey to use in cocktails. In "Preach on the Dusty Roads" (a reworking of a brief incident in *Sons and Soldiers*), a businessman saying goodbye to his soldier-son wishes with passionate despair that he had devoted his life to wild protest, preaching as a fanatic along dusty roads—anything so that at this moment he might feel that he had at least tried to prevent what was happening. "The Dry Rock," one of Shaw's bitterest and best, is a story of a man's humiliation for lack of courage. A man and his wife on their way to a dinner party to which she attaches great importance are involved in a traffic accident in the course of which their taxi-driver, "a little gray man," is abused and beaten. His only chance for justice lies in the willingness of the passengers to serve as witnesses. The man feels they ought to go through with it. He knows that it will be a sordid, tedious, and even, perhaps, a dangerous thing to do, for the aggressor turns out to be a minor gangster; but he also knows that it is tremendously important, that half the evil of the world exists because men of good will aren't willing to act. But he reneges under his wife's scorn and hates her and himself for his weakness.

Most of Shaw's men are goaded and destroyed by their women or find that they are not equal to them. In "Return to Kansas City" a young bride married to a second-rate prize-fighter longs to escape from the boredom of New York to the familiar delights of Kansas City. To get the money for the visit, she nags her husband into agreeing to a bout that is certain to ruin him. In "[The] Girls in Their Summer Dresses" a wife's senseless jealousy spoils what had started as a happy day. In "Mixed Doubles" a woman playing tennis as her husband's partner is annoyed by his response to the wiles of a younger woman who is playing opposite them. She suddenly perceives that all the faults of his life are exemplified in the faults of his game and for the first time begins to think of a divorce.

Many of the stories are deliberately funny ("No Jury Would Convict," "Lemkau, Pogran and Blaufox," "My Green Flower," etc.), but where the intention is too obvious the effect is not always successful. He has a great deal of humor, but his humor is best when it only highlights absurdity or adds a touch of the ludicrous or pathetic. In addition, there is a Saroyanesque exuberance, an overflowing of sheer vitality and good humor, that informs some of his best stories with a pure delight in being. In "The Indian in Depth of Night" a late wanderer in Central Park is "suffused with benevolence and delight" when a holdup man identifies himself as a Creek Indian and threatens to report him to the police when he insists that he has nothing to hand over. Perhaps the best of this kind is "Welcome to the City," a story of the wonder of love as it comes to a lonely young man in a verminous hotel when a mendacious young woman with bad teeth returns his affection.

Shaw's material is fresh. His people come in off the streets; they are not literary derivatives. His emotional restraint often makes them seem superficial and reduces their griefs and tragedies to an indiscriminate misery. But, where his pity overcomes his self-restraint and still evades his indignation, he has produced some of the best short stories in contemporary literature.

Hubert Saal

Irwin Shaw's high place among contemporary writers rests largely on his short stories. From the time he began to publish in the Thirties, Shaw roamed easily between comedy and tragedy, with an endless variety of themes about rich and poor, happy and sad, strong and weak. Sturdiness was his trademark. Not for him the peripheral insight, the passionless emotion, the tenuous motivation, the fragile plotless probing that was no story at all. He was that rare thing, a short story writer who was a storyteller. Whether he treated, as in "Girls in Their Summer Dresses" what was hardly more than a telling insight, or, as in "Sailor Off the Bremen" active brutality, or, as in "The City is in Total Darkness," "Act of Faith," and most of his other stories, the darker questions of being and becoming, he sounded a sturdy major chord.

Did any writer of that prewar time have a better eye and ear for what went on around him? Shaw cared, and his characters cared, about politics and injustice and loneliness and love and growing up and growing old. They (and clearly he) believed fiercely in what Faulkner was later to spell out, "that man will not merely endure: he will prevail."

More than anything else, what gave strength and substance to Shaw's enormous facility was his sense of life's tragic possibilities. His stories show him to be a man of moral values, aware of evil wherever he found it, aware of all the injustices and discrepancies within man or without him which cause him to suffer. Against wrong, Shaw spoke up. Again and again, with true tragic dignity, his characters rose up at the last, refused to submit, protested, did something.

Between these stories and Shaw's new collection, *Tip on a Dead Jockey,* is a gap that cannot be measured by time alone. The new stories are all of a piece in tone and theme and character. Each of them is humorless, unhappy, concerned with failure. For Shaw the salt seems to have lost its savor. For the most part, he here is writing about Americans in Europe where Shaw himself has been living for the past few

From "Disenchanted Men," *Saturday Review*, 3 August 1957, 12–13. Reprinted by permission of Omni Publications International Ltd. and Hubert Saal.

years. But Europe is only a picture postcard backdrop before which his escapist Americans trail out thin and dreary lives.

The title story [from the collection *Tip on a Dead Jockey*] sets the pace for almost every one that follows. Its chief character, Barber, is an ex-pilot trying to forget his ex-wife. (There are a lot of ex's: ex-lovers, ex-soldiers, ex-husbands, ex-wives, and expatriates.) Barber is broke and when he's offered a chance to make a bagful of money by illegally flying a planeful of gold past customs, he gets a hunch, and declines. A lesser man of little sense accepts and comes out rich and Barber sadly returns to a lonely hotel room.

Barber is a weak man but we have no pity for him for he wouldn't take the risk and could only compound his fear by regretting, once someone else had done the job, that it hadn't been he. What is astonishing for Shaw is the amorality of the story. Not for a moment does Barber decline the opportunity because it's dishonest. He's afraid to die.

Barber appears again, under the alias of Beddoes in "In the French Style." Beddoes too is a wanderer in Europe, who refused to commit himself to anything or anyone ("he made a point of never pleading for anything") and he loses his girl to a nondescript American tourist. After a feckless attempt to talk her back he too goes off to loneliness.

Two of the stories are very good, indeed. "A Wicked Story" is reminiscent of Shaw's most acid vein. "And Then There Were Three" is as good as his very best. It's the one story in which Shaw allows Europe an integral part, shows what it can mean to Americans, in this case two best friends and a girl. The better boy loses the girl, his friend, Europe and youth, but his failure is through strength not weakness.

But almost everywhere else Shaw leads through weakness, not strength. He has given us petty, selfish, disenchanted men and women, motivated by flimsy hunches and superstitions, incapable of action, without any sort of values, without dignity. Technically, the stories are effortlessly able. But they used to be planes peeling off at high altitudes for a sheer dive toward the ground, to be pulled out only at the last split second, and all the excitement and thrill of "how would it come out" rode with them. In most of these stories Shaw levels off too soon, before the issue is in doubt and not only communicates the indifference of his characters but his own.

What caused the change in Shaw? The clue it seems to me is in his brilliant story, "The Climate of Insomnia," published a few years ago.

Part III

The hero, Cahill, is an insomniac who awakens in the night, remembers a telephone message to call his best friend, and begins to worry what it could be about. Cahill catalogues marriage, children, friendship, job, political affiliation one by one, like a dentist who can only find which is the diseased tooth by pulling hard on them all. They all hurt. And Cahill is Everyman today, frightened out of his wits by real or imagined fears from every quarter. He reflects on the possible suicide of mankind through the atomic bomb, and thinks, "a man must keep himself from speculating on these matters. . . . When he'd come home in 1945 he'd thought all that was behind him. My limit, he always said . . . is one war."

It sounds like Shaw's limit too. He is a victim, like his characters, not of the war that ended in 1945, but of the Cold War since and of the prospect that it might get hotter. Shaw the artist, the man who always dared to raise his voice, has found himself, in Cahill's words, caught "in the massive tide of events beyond his control." I cannot believe that a book like *Tip on a Dead Jockey* is Shaw's final answer. I count on him to live up to the tradition of the tragic hero, the man who licks his wounds and Joblike asks, Why? why? why? and then, although he gets no satisfactory answers, sallies forth again.

William Startt

> Once, on the set, a young actor had come up to Carrington and
> had asked him to tell him, in just a short sentence, what the
> secret was of being a good actor. Carrington had pretended to
> be thinking deeply, had rubbed the big, impressive nose judi-
> ciously and had answered, "Be delighted, my boy, be de-
> lighted."—Irwin Shaw, *Two Weeks in Another Town*.

Although his tone is still one of resentment and his style still vigorously
aggressive, Irwin Shaw today is no longer the idealistic "moral writer
who conceives moral problems simply, feels them deeply, and dramatizes them with often terrifying historical relevance" (Diana Trilling,
Nation, September 20, 1946). Shaw first achieved recognition in the
late 1930's with his plays (*Bury the Dead*, 1936, and *The Gentle People*,
1939), and later with his *New Yorker* stories, both of which managed to
capture the almost intangible mood of post-depression America. While
he was never a proletarian writer in the sense that Steinbeck and Dos
Passos were, Shaw's stories had a strong sociological overtone; in spite
of his toughness and youthful bitterness, however, most of them were
well-laced with a gentleness and a restrained optimism which urged
the reader to look forward, more in hope than in expectancy, to a better
world. The best of these early stories have a humanitarian glow about
them which in spite of the youthfulness of the author suggests neither
immaturity nor naivety. Never a thematic writer, Shaw so thoroughly
absorbed the *zeitgeist* of the late 1930's that even today his early stories
have an immediacy and a reality usually not found in his novels.

It is my premise that Shaw is essentially a dramatist and short story
writer whose talent, however admirable, thins out and becomes flat
when applied to the longer and more integrated genre of the novel. A
short story writer is not necessarily an embryonic novelist. In the novel,
Shaw no longer can rely solely upon impressions and mood; he must

From "Irwin Shaw: An Extended Talent," *Midwest Quarterly* 2 (Summer 1961): 325–
37. Reprinted by permission of Dr. James B. M. Shick, editor-in-chief, *Midwest
Quarterly*.

plot and contrive extensively; consequently, the best sections of his novels are those self-contained, well-honed scenes and episodes where the hand of the experienced writer of shorter fiction is still visible. But, invariably, these isolated scenes are strung together by a manufactured, frequently melodramatic, and often unconvincing plot. Still, Shaw the writer, rather than Shaw the novelist, makes excellent reading. If Shaw the man has lost those convictions which lent such compassion and eloquence to his early fiction, Shaw the writer is still a master craftsman. The right word and the apt phrase appear to come easily to him; as a narrative artist he has few peers on the contemporary American scene. By examining Shaw's fiction, and by concentrating on the arguments presented in his latest novel, *Two Weeks in Another Town* (1960), we shall see how the author has come to terms with the problem of the writer who relies on craft and technique more than on art.

Shaw's first novel, *The Young Lions* (1948), was a commercially successful failure. Ecstatically touted by advance reviews as the great American novel of World War II, the book was so structurally deficient and so sprawling in organization that even Shaw's more enthusiastic admirers could recognize only the author's narrative excellence in a series of brief scenes which added a much-needed dramatic luster to an at times tedious book. Had Shaw stuck to one story—that of Noah Ackerman—he might have written an effective, tightly organized novel, but the Ackerman story was interspersed with the adventures of two other figures, Christian Diestl and Michael Whitacre. It is only Ackerman who emerges as a genuinely convincing character. The gentle young Jewish boy suffers a virtual martyrdom through no fault of his own. Here Shaw is standing on firm ground. He examines Ackerman's plight with the same compassion found in his play, *The Gentle People*, and in the best of his stories. With only minor revision, one scene in particular, in which Ackerman challenges a group of soldiers who have been tormenting him, could be reprinted as a well-made short story. (My only reservation here is that I feel Shaw has overstressed the theme of anti-Semitism.)

Less successful is the story of Christian Diestl, who, first against his will and later in an almost anesthetized state of indifference, falls in with the Nazi philosophy. Many of Diestl's type may have been swept along in the inexorable flood of racial and nationalistic philosophy (inertia is strong and, often, the will is weak), but Shaw makes no attempt—or at best an unsuccessful one—to show us why this has happened. Diestl is a negative hero, a protagonist who goes from good to bad without really coming to life in the reader's mind. Moreover, it is here, as well as in the story of Michael Whitacre, that Shaw begins to use the techniques of the highly skilled popular writer. The Diestl episode, with its authentic descriptions of desert warfare in North Africa, suffers from the introduction of a love affair between Diestl and his captain's wife. This is the stuff that popular fiction is made of, and as presented by a quality writer it is all too obvious that the whole incident was created for effect—an effect never achieved.

Michael Whitacre is a familiar type, a glamorous but cynical Broadway-Hollywood figure, who may have been designed to brighten the story. In spite of the fact that Shaw probably drew on his own experience as a dramatist and scenarist, Whitacre never becomes any more than an animated cardboard prop. Too cynical for his own good, Whitacre, disgusted with the neon glitter of the entertainment world, entered the army as a private almost with relief. Caught midway between idealism and opportunism, he can only flounder fecklessly and drift with the inertia of the war. Ironically, it is Whitacre, not Ackerman, who survives.

Had Shaw wished, he could have fashioned an excellent short story out of the Whitacre material; had he been more analytic and more objective, Diestl would have made a fascinating protagonist for a novel about Nazi Germany, but as these characters are handled in *The Young Lions*, one can only conclude that Noah Ackerman deserved better company. . . . Shaw's most recent collection of short stories, *Tip on a Dead Jockey* (1957), is as skillfully written as any of his earlier ones. Almost any one of them would serve as a good model for a class in creative writing, but the old intimate glow and the compassionate analysis of people and themes familiar to both the author and his readers are gone, for Shaw is now writing for a popular audience. Instead of capitalizing on his ability to create mood and atmosphere, he frequently resorts to a highly cinematic plot (*Tip on a Dead Jockey* was successfully filmed by Metro-Goldwyn-Mayer two years ago). Often passages in his stories sound more like *ersatz* Hemingway than Shaw. The final paragraph in *Tip on a Dead Jockey* reads as follows:

> He walked back to the hotel because he was through with taxis, and went up and sat on the edge of his bed in his room, in the dark, without taking his coat off. I better get out of here, he thought, rubbing the wet off the end of his nose with the back of his hand. This continent is not for me.

For all that it has a familiar ring, this is good professional writing. This staccato eloquence is even more evident in an early scene in *Two Weeks in Another Town* when Andrus is leaving his family at the airport.

> "Daddy"—the boy turned away from the window toward his father—"were you ever in a plane that caught fire?"
> "Yes," Jack said.
> "What happened?"
> "They put the fire out."
> "That was lucky," the boy said.
> "Yes."

This excerpt is almost *too* tough and clipped; still, I suppose any American writer living in Paris and writing about other expatriate Americans should be permitted a few Hemingwayisms (generally speaking, Shaw is not a Hemingway imitator). The main fault I find with this kind of writing is that it is too bad to praise and too good to criticize. Even if one recognizes an all too familiar style, he is loathe to carp if it is brilliantly handled. Shaw might be using more technique, *per se*, than he formerly did, and he might consciously be relying more on plot and on contrivance than on his impressions, but the writing itself is still excellent, and from the point of view of style one feels that Shaw is still delighted (if not completely satisfied) with his own work.

But the theme which recurs again and again in *Two Weeks in Another Town* is what is the position in the world of art of the creative artist who is reduced to mere manipulation of technique and self-imitation. What should the writer do when he ceases to be delighted with his own performance? Self-delusion acts only as a temporary narcotic; there are those awful moments when the artist is forced to compare himself as he now is to what he once was.

On his first night in Rome, Delaney takes Andrus to see a revival of a post-war film which they had made together. Both men sit together in a semi-deserted theater and watch the work which they were capable of doing two decades ago.

> When the lights came up, he sat, silently for a moment. Then he shook his head to clear away the past. He turned to Delaney who was slumped in his seat, his hand up to the earpiece of his glasses, looking tough and bitter, like an old catcher who has just lost a close game.

"Maurice," he said gently, loving him, and meaning what he said, "you're a great man."

Delaney sat without stirring, almost as if he hadn't heard Jack. He took off the heavy, thick-rimmed glasses and stared down at them, symbol of pride outraged, vanity at bay, of vision clouded and distorted by age.

"I was a great man," he said harshly. "Let's get out of here."

Later, when his attempts at dubbing are going poorly, Andrus faces the problem honestly.

"Wait a minute Maurice," Jack said. "Maybe this isn't going to work. Maybe it's been too long and I've lost the gift. If I ever had it."

"You had it, you had it," Delaney said impatiently.

"Anyway," Jack said, "if you want to get somebody else, I'll bow out right now. Before we waste any more of your time and my time. I'll get on the afternoon plane to Paris and maybe everybody'll be a lot happier."

"Don't be in such a goddamn hurry to give up," Delaney said. "After one hour. What the hell's wrong with you? Where do you think I'd be today if I quit like that?"

"I just wanted to let you know that you're not stuck with me, if you don't want to be," Jack said.

"Now Jack . . ." Maurice smiled at him winningly, warmly, "you're not going to turn sensitive on me, are you?"

But moments of honest self-recognition are rare with Delaney. He is an egocentric who thrives on adulation; he can exist only by deluding himself and others into believing that his is still a vital talent. He must be surrounded by admirers who reassure him of his own genius. Without praise, however hollow and meaningless it might be, he is nothing. Alone, the realization of his failure begins to gnaw at him like a soul-destroying malignancy for which there is no remedy. He has a serious accident while horseback riding in Rome and must absent himself from the studio for at least six weeks. In a state of mild delirium he admits that his recent films have been mere artistic facsimiles of his early productions. He begs Andrus to supervise production during his absence and remembers a script by the young scenarist, Bresach, which he has read.

"Get that kid . . . what's his name?"

"Bresach."

"Get him to help you. Call him the dialogue director or your assistant or whatever. I read his script . . ."

"But you told me you hadn't," Jack said.

Delaney smiled weakly against the pillow.

"I wanted to sound him out first. The script's too damned good for a kid that age. I didn't want to praise him from the beginning. They're tricks in every trade, Jack . . . I have a hunch about that kid. He's hot. He's got the movies in his blood. He'll come up with a lot of ideas. Use him . . ."

Use him, Jack thought.

"Listen to him. Pick his brain," Delaney went on, gasping. "Maybe this is just what this picture needs. I have a hunch about him. That's the way I was at that age. Maybe this picture'll start me all over again. Jack, you promise . . . you promise, don't you? I need you . . ."

But Bresach proves to be even better than Delaney had hoped. After a few days on the set it is obvious that the finished product will be unmistakably his and not Delaney's. When the producer suggests that Delaney take a prolonged recuperative vacation and let Bresach direct his next film, the old director's vanity reasserts itself, and he uses his authority to have Andrus and Bresach banned from the set.

Delaney sighed. "Jack ," he said flatly, "if I hear you're anywhere near that set tomorrow I'm going to get out of bed and come down and get behind the camera myself."

"Maurice," Jack said, "this may be the last chance I get to talk to you—maybe the last chance anybody'll get to talk to you—so you'll have to listen to the truth for once. You've ruined yourself out of vanity, Maurice . . . You're a man teetering on the edge of a cliff and everybody knows it. Everybody but you. Maurice, I've done everything I can to pull you back—there's still a chance you can be saved—there's still a lot to be saved . . . Don't throw it away."

"Get out of town, Jack," Delaney whispered. "Fast."

As presented, Delaney is a figure more deserving of pity than contempt. His pretenses are pathetic, and ultimately he succeeds in fooling no one, not even himself. He symbolizes the danger of living in the past, and Shaw seems to say that an artist who refuses to move with the times and adapt his talent accordingly will eventually fall victim to self-imitation. Just as yesterday's news makes stale journalism, the superficially manipulated events, themes, and techniques of twenty years ago make for specious, imitative art.

This is the moral issue which Shaw has examined in *Two Weeks in Another Town,* and while the novel lacks the concentrated impact that we find in his best stories, one gets the feeling that Shaw feels this problem deeply and had dramatized it to the best of his ability. Though his best writing is undoubtedly found in his pre-war stories, he has tried (successfully, I believe) to avoid repetition or self-imitation. Now essentially a novelist rather than a short story writer, Shaw's talent is still best suited to descriptions of mood and atmosphere. When he expands this talent and writes a novel on the grand, popular scale, one feels the strain, but at the same time one senses an honest effort. His style is still remarkable for its rhetorical fluidity. He does not wallow nostalgically in the past, and in every novel he attempts to say something as well as to entertain. He is, then, an honest professional.

If Shaw could expand his talent into a short novel and avoid the insertion of superfluous plot and contrivance, he might produce something comparable in quality to the best of his early stories. If not, one can only hope that he continue to find delight in his ability to write well.

Chester E. Eisinger

Irwin Shaw resembles Schulberg in some significant ways. The most striking is not their shared incapacity to free themselves from the thirties but the adulteration of the liberal heritage in the work of both by the idols of respectability and success. Shaw can resist neither the deadly lure of what passes for metropolitan sophistication nor the comfortable corruption of bourgeois materialism. These forces have seriously disrupted the integrity of the value system he purports to believe in. They have given his work that patina of slickness and sentimentality which vitiates so much of it. They have been in part responsible for a literary opportunism which, to confine the matter to the forties, seized upon antifascism, the war, and the McCarthy era attack upon the entire left as timely subjects for books. He is, however, a more finished writer than Schulberg, and his prose is sometimes smooth instead of slick. He is generally competent in the techniques of the short story, and when not dogged by the inner contradictions of thought and impulse that I have noted, he can write a moving and effective story. He is of inestimable value, without regard for the quality of his fiction, for the close way he works with the surface of his society and gives us so much of the range of its manners. He does not penetrate to its heart, but he knows its surface tensions and the ready conversational currency it exchanges for ideas.

The preoccupations and attitudes that Shaw learned in the thirties he brought into the next decade, largely untouched except for the pacifism of *Bury The Dead*. The liberal antinaziism that showed up in the title-story of *Sailor off the Bremen and Other Stories* (1939)[1] remains a constant in his work. The liberal attack on anti-Semitism, a virus Shaw sees on the domestic scene as well as in the ideology of fascism, is almost truculently advanced in his pages. The pressures imposed by money, which Shaw felt as a result of the depression, were expressed in the forties as the multifarious demands of middle-class life. And an

From "Fiction and the Liberal Reassessment," in *Fiction of the Forties* (Chicago: University of Chicago Press, 1963), 86–113. Reprinted by permission of the University of Chicago Press and Chester E. Eisinger.

affinity for the general propositions of democracy, summed up perhaps in the idea of the value and dignity of man, marks every phase of his fiction.

But intertwined with this heritage from the thirties is a fascination with the color and things of middle-class America. Shaw admires the attractive people who might stroll down Fifth Avenue to Washington Square, who breakfast at the Brevoort or eat at home on the terrace at glass and wrought-iron tables. Shaw is enamored of these appurtenances of the middle-class life, which appear in his work as status symbols. When, in one of his stories, the old lady pleads with her impoverished tenants for her rent money because she needs it to buy food, we can feel a legitimate desperation at the shared poverty which makes the poor the prey of the poor. But where, in a story like "Main Currents in American Thought," the harried writer has to find the money for expensive piano lessons or party dresses, the value of these desiderata does not seem to justify the constant tension the writer must live with. Or in "Weep in Years to Come" we may accept the antifascist theme, but it is difficult to escape the conclusion that the man in this story is fighting against Hitler in order to preserve no more than the highest standard of living in the world.

Shaw is more successful when he is content to write a tract for the Aspirin Age. He is as sensitive as the journalist or the hostess to the vital topic of the moment. He knows about the high cost of living, the problems of juvenile delinquency, the threat of atomic and germ warfare, the conflict of loyalties raised by friends who dare to dissent, the security neuroses of the organization man. He has ready at hand a collection of horrors to stock the modern man's nightmare, as he shows us in "The Climate of Insomnia." In his best moments he knows the miserable insignificance of men who are unable to rise to any imaginative grasp of the meaning of great events, as he shows in "The City Was in Total Darkness."

Shaw is also successful when his stories demand a straightforward and obvious treatment of emotions. He has no talent for the handling of ideas and no real appetite for them. In "Residents of Other Cities," a story about a pogrom in Kiev, the sixteen-year-old Jewish protagonist says, "My father was always at the side of God and he neglected life." The boy rejects his father's way when he takes a gun and kills the men who have raped his aunt and his sister. This statement and the boy's action suggest to me the activistic, antispiritual, and essentially anti-intellectual creed that is typical of Shaw. It helps to explain his addiction to violence and his joyful acceptance of the Hebraic law of an eye for an eye. The relationship in Shaw between a fierce loyalty to Jews and Jewishness and the application of violence as an instrument of justice arises from his rejection of the traditional passivity of the ghetto Jews, people of the Book, who could not and would not fight back against their oppressors, even to save their lives. Shaw seems at pains to make many of his Jewish characters basic and physically aggressive types. In this way he hopes to combat anti-Semitism, warning that the Jew will fight back against it. And he hopes, furthermore, to establish a place for the Jew in American society where active physical resistance to social ills, where recourse to violence, is a part of the cultural pattern. The Jew who shares in this pattern identifies himself as an American.

Shaw also believes that violence is forced upon good men by their resistance to naziism. Fascism has made the kind of world in which the only possible response is to maim or to kill, to exchange brutality for brutality. Shaw does not seem to be concerned with the degeneration of character that might follow when good men resort to such brutality, although he is quick to point out the evil effects upon bad men. Again he celebrates the Jewish reply in kind to the Nazi policy of exterminating the Jews. When a German major in one of Shaw's stories confesses his guilt to a Jew and cries out, how can I wash my hands, the Jew replies, "You can cut your throat . . . and see if the blood will take the stain out." In Shaw, the way to deal with the bully, whether he lives in Germany or around the corner, is to fight him with fists or gun.

Another obvious emotion in Shaw is hatred. He is a vigorous and implacable hater. He writes about the Germans as though he were cutting them to pieces, systematically and joyfully. No reconciliation is possible, in his view, with the German mind. The Germans are obsessed with war, and already planning to try for world conquest a third time. The only good German is a dead German. While the reader may be carried along by the vigor of Shaw's emotion and even by an acquiescence in the anti-Nazi bias, which might lead for a while to a suspension of critical intelligence, it does not take long to see that Shaw's phobia against the Germans represents a race theory not unlike the one the Germans had so crudely used. The danger for the writer in relying upon the blood and the viscera instead of the mind lies in his falling into such a trap as this, to find himself supporting at one extreme what he so loudly decries at the other.

Shaw is not so primitive as to rely always upon the exploitation of undiluted, primary emotions. The athlete who takes such satisfaction in breaking up the Nazi off the Bremen may be contrasted with the athlete whose life is a long decline into stagnation from the high moment when he made his eighty-yard run. The appetitive and activistic values that Shaw often admires are in the latter case seen as unable to provide the emotional and intellectual maturity necessary for adult life. I should say in passing, however, that Shaw's notion of maturity involves a knowledge of modern painting and the theater, of politics and labor, but does not include a profound knowledge of the human heart.

In dealing with the war and the Jew, Shaw is often guilty of stopping short with the easy answer when the harder lay beyond or of finding the pleasant solution when the demands of his story make disaster imperative. I have spoken of saints and of rhetoric in connection with the war novel. Shaw's war stories, as well as his war novel, flow from a hagiographical impulse and a sense of mission. These are stories in which the camaraderie of men at arms is good to see, and everyone rejoices when the emergency operation at sea is successful or the lost plane finally comes in. They end well, in a schmaltzy blaze. And the Jew at war is also sentimentalized. Shaw sees him as a victim whom the world must rescue. And he sees the world's resentment because it must fight a war to save the Jew. But in the end, men will come together in brotherhood and mutual trust. This is the moral of "Act of Faith," when the Jewish soldier, with every reason to take his pistol home in order to fight off anti-Semites, decides instead to trust his comrades and the future, sells his pistol and provides them all with money for a leave in Paris. Here Shaw yields up his belief in violence to the kind of easy affirmation that marks him as an old-fashioned liberal. He has not developed the scepticism and the provisionalism of the new liberalism. He has not stared unblinkingly at the power of evil, but has turned his back upon its magnitude.

In addition to the four volumes of short stories that Shaw published between 1939 and 1950, he wrote two novels in the period, a form in which he is less at ease than in shorter fiction. The novels rose directly out of the experience of his time, *The Young Lions* (1948) being about the war and *The Troubled Air* (1951) dealing with the anticommunism of the postwar years. Shaw wrote a novel about the war despite the fact that in 1945 he had said he was suspicious of novels about the war. He wrote it, he has said, to make the fundamental point that the soldier must kill with a sense of sin and tragedy. It is a point that emerges, but obscurely, from the novel. He wrote it also, I suspect, in obedience to that impulse in him to make a record of what his generation believed and how it acted. The same impulse embedded in the same political context had been at work in the short stories that preceded the novel, as Shaw has made clear in speaking of the years when Americans were coming slowly to an understanding of what a growing fascism meant in Europe: "I think I was recording in my short stories what we, our age, felt then." For Shaw these motives for writing made a design for the novel in which democracy would be set against fascism, democracy representing growth of spirit culminating in the realization of one's humanity and fascism representing degeneration to total barbarism and bestiality. The structure of the novel is contained in the polarized themes. The triumph of Noah the American is in his mature recognition of the American ideal: the quiet, decent, competent, pragmatic, humane man. The complete disintegration of Christian the Nazi follows logically from the premises of fascism: the love of war and killing, the cultivation of the predatory and egotistic elements in man, the unrestrained lust, the utilization of treachery, the belief, as Shaw himself has put it, that the end justifies the means. Between them stands the liberal dilettante who wavers between the ideal of service and the opportunism of self-service. Noah's example and his death bring the liberal also to maturity. The war is a purgation when the liberal finally accepts the commitment to it that makes him a responsible human being. The chief problem of the novel lies in the logic of its structure, which demands unbroken parallel lines, one ascending in growth and one descending in disintegration. As a diagram these lines have the appeal of simplicity, which is precisely what is wrong with this conception as the foundation for a novel. Nothing of the unpredictability of human behavior and no sense of the ambiguity of human motive can be permitted to disrupt the smooth flow of these lines. This structure, and the conception of human nature and political ideologies which it assumes, satisfies the demands of rhetoric but does not satisfy any sense of the complex texture of experience.

Shaw treats the problem of the Jew in this novel by identifying Noah Ackerman with the American ideal. He brings Noah to a fulfilment of a personality pattern which, in its virility, its activism, its self-reliance, is the American type as Shaw defined it. Shaw's concern for the Jew, then, turns out to be, not a hope that the Jew might exist in the United States as a unique person with his own culture who embodies an idea of Jewishness, but a hope that the Jew will assimilate himself to the dominant culture and become like everybody else.

The sensitive and sophisticated liberal of this novel becomes the protagonist of *The Troubled Air,* under a different name still confused, still a victim of forces more decisive than any he can command. The producer and director of a radio show, the liberal is faced with a crisis when a hate sheet accuses five members of his cast of being Communists or Red sympathizers, and the agency handling the program demands that they be fired. The book may very well draw upon the activities of a newsletter called *Counterattack,* which was established in 1947 by a group of former FBI men, according to Alan Barth. Under its auspices, *Red Channels,* a formal index for the purge of leftists and dissidents in radio and television, was published in 1950. But it is not necessary to establish a specific source for this book. What Shaw wants to do is to show the havoc that stems from the witch-hunt hysteria that had possessed a large part of the articulate American public in the postwar years. He wants to dramatize the vicious character of reactionary forces as they try to eliminate from American life the possibility of dissent. He wants to show how fear eats away at the lives of men who must live in an atmosphere of universal distrust. He wants to convey his complete disillusionment with the Communists, whose treachery he makes palpable in this book. Earlier in his work Shaw had pleaded for understanding and tolerance with respect to Russia and the Communists, but this novel clearly repudiates them. This novel is different also in that its liberal is left at the end a ruined man with no more than the decency and good will he had at the beginning. Shaw had been willing before this only infrequently to admit the tangible effects of evil as real and lasting. He found no easy answer this time. But the purpose of the liberal's self-immolation is cloudy. He is certainly the victim of sobering events, but he gives no evidence that he has learned from them or that he will change his social-political orientation. As the book ends he is poised on the edge of nothing, with nothing to look forward to. To this the old liberalism had brought him.[2]

It is something, however, that at least Shaw should recognize the limitations of liberalism's faith and optimism. It is worth remarking that he had done so once before, in his short story "The Passion of Lance Corporal Hawkins." In fact, he views sceptically in this story the entire complex of liberal ideas that stem from H. G. Wells. Doubt is cast on the idea that reason will prevail in human affairs, that man's social condition will get better and better, that socialism will be an improvement on what has preceded it. The horrors of the war and the peace, and the plight of the Jews, especially in their struggle to establish and hold Israel, seem to have brought Shaw to the beginning of a sober reassessment of his views. The title and action of this story, suggesting a connection with the passion of Christ, is perhaps Shaw's acknowledgement that men must suffer bitterly, must even die, if they are to endure the ironies of history or seek the knowledge that saves.

Notes

1. Shaw subsequently published three other volumes of short stories in our period: *Welcome to the City and Other Stories* (1942), *An Act of Faith and Other Stories* (1946), and *Mixed Company* (1950).

2. Another ad hoc novel, in a related area, is *The Sure Thing* (1949), by Merle Miller. It also contains unexamined liberal assumptions. It is addressed to the problems of loyalty and security and built around a dismissal from the State Department on the grounds of Communist sympathies.

Ross Wetzsteon

"I'm still surprised when people pay me for what I write." Irwin Shaw slouches in his chair, both hands around a glass of Jack Daniels in his lap, smiling like a tired Jewish Buddha. "When I was a kid in Brooklyn, I told this guy I'd take $50 a week for the rest of my life if I could just write what I wanted and he could keep the rest." He leans back, rubs his cheek with a meaty hand, and lets out a long rumpled laugh. "I'm sure as hell glad he didn't take me up on it!"

Irwin Shaw has made money—lots of it. But it's a literary axiom that commercial success is inversely proportional to critical acclaim: As sales mount, reputations decline (an occasional *Ragtime* only recalls another axiom—the one about the proof of rules). Pondering the best-seller list, critics analyze what went wrong: What middlebrow nerve was touched? What drugstore fantasy was pandered to? And if the author has previously published finely crafted but modestly read novels, where is the betrayal of talent? So with 10 of his 11 novels having appeared on the best-seller list, and with his new novel, *Bread upon the Waters*, headed there in the fall (it has a 100,000 first printing and is the main Book-of-the-Month Club selection for September), Irwin Shaw has come to represent big bucks and bad books.

The unexamined consensus among the quality controllers of American literature is that Shaw was an exceptionally gifted short-story writer who published a promising first novel and then betrayed his promise. According to the official line, with his laconically pointed dialogue, his controlled tough-guy lyricism, and his anti-rhetorical skepticism, he could have been the heir to Hemingway. Instead, by turning increasingly to beautiful-people potboilers, full of sex and violence, set against the cardboard backdrops of Hollywood and Cannes, he did little more than provide source material for TV mini-series starring washed-

From "Irwin Shaw: The Conflict between Big Bucks and Good Books," *Saturday Review* 8 (August 1981):12–17. Reprinted by permission of Omni Publications International Ltd. and Ross Wetzsteon.

up ladies' men and failed Charlie's Angels. Ten pages into one of his novels and you can hear the cameras dollying in.

And yet *Bread upon the Waters*, with its unadorned moral severity, casts an arc of light back over his entire career. Some aspects of his work that once seemed vague and unclear become brilliantly illuminated, while others that once stood out brightly become lost in shadows. In fact, his new novel—arguably his best yet—in paring away everything extraneous to his vision, forces us to reconsider the consensus. Perhaps we have been misreading Shaw all along.

Allen Strand, the hero of *Bread upon the Waters*, belongs to the world of ordinary rather than beautiful people. His adventures take place not in the opulent resorts of the jet set but in the quiet thoughts of a contemplative man. Superficially unlike Shaw, he's superficially unlike a Shaw protagonist as well—to such an extent that *Bread upon the Waters* will be universally characterized as an uncharacteristic Shaw novel, a new departure, a different direction. To some readers, it may signal a decline in narrative vigor. To more, I hope, it will indicate a clarification of moral rigor.

Strand teaches high school history, relaxes by strolling in Central Park, sleeps only with his wife. Pity the publisher's blurb writer: What can he say about a 50-year-old teacher with a wife and three children whose only story is that he suffers a mild heart attack and stoically watches as his family slowly drifts apart? One evening, just as Strand and his family are sitting down for dinner in their West Side apartment, their youngest daughter comes through the door, supporting an elderly gentleman. He's just been mugged in Central Park and she's frightened off his attackers with her tennis racquet. It turns out that the elderly gentleman is a mysteriously wealthy lawyer, and out of gratitude he gradually insinuates himself into the lives of the Strand family. Just concert tickets at first, then a weekend at his estate in the Hamptons, then. . . . There's something ominous about his generosity, something disruptive about his attentions. . . . But Shaw resists histrionics; the twists of the plot involve only the ordinary decisions of Strand's daily life. And yet by the end of the novel these decisions test and virtually destroy the family.

Like many of Shaw's characters, Allen Strand is suffering "a mid-life crisis." But the crises come in unanswered phone calls rather than blown deals, small family deceits rather than steamy adulteries, daily disappointments rather than soap-opera revelations—an erosion of the familiar so slow Strand can hardly see it happening until it's over. The moral choices of everyday life, the quiet victories and defeats of a decent man—this, then, is a novel of conscience, and it can only end with the protagonist alone.

Unfortunately, in keeping with Strand's character, the novel has more than its share of vacuous platitudes ("We're like two people in the water, in different currents, slowly being pulled away from each other"). But there's also an elegaic note Shaw has rarely sounded before:

> What changes a year, not even a year had made, what uprootings, blows, sad discoveries, defections. The rumble of the ocean oppressed him, the waves rolling in implacably, eroding beaches, undermining foundations, menacing, changing the contours of the land with each new season. Old harbors silted over, once thriving seaports lay deserted, the cries of gulls over the shifting waters plaintive, melancholy, complaining harshly of hunger and flight and the wreckage of time.

Has Irwin Shaw mellowed? Or have we been misreading him all along? In fact, *Bread upon the Waters*, reflecting its serene biblical title, reveals that for all the glamour of his settings, Shaw is always concerned with decency of character; that for all the adventures of his stories, he is always obsessed with virtuous behavior. Far from uncharacteristic, then, this novel suggests that his other books too are all moral fables.

"The decline of Irwin Shaw" is a myth, and like all myths has its purpose. For while middlebrow taste has a strong stake in the standard American success story, highbrow taste has just as strong a commitment to its opposite—that the standard American success story is inevitably a story of moral corruption. (That this is to some degree the story Shaw himself tells in his novels only compounds the irony.)

Not that Shaw hasn't handed his critics enough weapons—several hundred thousand of his millions of words are indistinguishable from the computer printouts of Robbins, Wallace, Sheldon, and Susann. But the point is that, especially when re-read in light of *Bread upon the Waters*, his early novels, while full of promise, are hardly masterpieces of modern literature, and his later novels, while full of compromise, are hardly the epitome of drugstore trash. Put another way, his strengths and weaknesses have been there all along, in each and every novel.

212

Shaw's strengths as a novelist are those of another century—relentlessly fluid narrative, dramatically focused set pieces, and sharp, incisive dialogue—which help account for both his critical disfavor (the current canon stresses narrative fragmentation, inconclusive confrontation, and failed communication) and his commercial success (in the age of 90-minute electronic media, the public can turn only to the popular novel for sprawling saga). In short, Shaw is that most contemptible of contemporary writers—a believer in *stories*.

On the other hand, Shaw frequently suffers from the short-story writer's inability to form a coherent whole out of brilliant sequences. Furthermore, his work is too often cheapened by factitious glamour, shallow characterizations, and pompous attitudinizing, to say nothing of centerfold sex and gung ho violence. Worst of all, the antirhetorical inheritance from Hemingway, laconically exposing the pious platitudes of the day, occasionally turns into a kind of sentimental cynicism.

But all the time, in every novel, sometimes embedded in the narrative structure itself, sometimes barely glimpsed through the smoke of post-coital cigarettes, we can now see that the key to his novels is moral choice. Yes, in Irwin Shaw's novels, one has to make moral choices even in Cannes! If one expects something more from the heir to Hemingway, one expects far less from the peer of Robbins.

In re-reading *The Young Lions*, for instance, published in 1948, one can see why many readers still regard it as his finest novel, but one can also find passages, scenes, and characters indistinguishable from those in novels regarded as his worst. What remains of enduring value, of course, are the demythologizing of the war (a sympathetic Nazi character; unflinching reminders of American anti-Semitism; a scorn for patriotic homilies); the shattering set pieces (the desert massacre of the English company; the white-maned preacher at Dover; Christian cutting the throat of the concentration camp commandant); and the unique Shaw voice ("She's the kind of girl who's always saying she doesn't like your shirts. Know that kind?"—what other writer has struck precisely that tone?).

But the same writer who could so brilliantly deromanticize ideology was also capable of romanticizing the glibbest cynicism. ("Same songs, same uniforms, same enemies, same defeats. Only new graves.") In fact, the lapses for which Shaw has been so severely castigated were there from the beginning: adolescent posing ("He loved the war because in no other way could a man be truly tested"); ponderous moralizing ("She was Roger's girl, and . . . it was inconceivable that he,

Noah, could repay the generous acts of friendship even by the hidden duplicity of unspoken desire"); and preposterous "creative writing" ("Outside the room he heard the murmur of seven million people walking through the streets and corridors of the city"). When we read prose like this, how can we talk of a subsequent "decline"? Yet for all its passages of brilliance and banality, we can now see that at the heart of the novel are the moral choices made by its three central characters.

While *The Young Lions* was forgiven for its lapses, *Rich Man, Poor Man* (1969) wasn't credited with its virtues. There's no need to dwell on its flaws—the papier-mâché characters, the paperback prose, the cheap macho irony. Instead, it must be acknowledged that Shaw's narrative drive remains unflagging, and that the novel contains far more incisive dialogue (" 'There's nothing like a failing marriage,' she said, 'to bring out flights of rhetoric' "), concise characterization (" 'They're nobody's friends,' Gretchen said. 'They're drinkers' "), and sharp insight ("He had old-fashioned manners and up-to-date hatreds") than any mere hack entertainer could hope to achieve in a lifetime. More to the point, all three of the novel's major characters struggle to become better people.

Re-read the other novels too, and discover neither Hemingway nor Robbins but the last of the tough old pros, halfway between the two. Behind *la dolce vita* of Rome's international film colony in *Two Weeks in Another Town* (1960) is the story of a man who looks back at the bright promise of his youth, and who attempts to salvage some decency and honor from the compromises and betrayals into which he fell. Or re-read *Evening in Byzantium* (1973), the story of a man attempting to retain his integrity in a tabloid world. Or still another example, *Beggarman, Thief* (1977), a story about the struggle, in short, to become a better man.

The story Irwin Shaw has told again and again, "the story of a man who looks back at the bright promise of his youth, and who attempts to salvage some decency and honor from the compromises and betrayals into which he fell"—this is also the story told of Irwin Shaw's career. Only his critics leave out the second half.

Born in the Bronx in 1913, Shaw spent most of his childhood in Brooklyn. "We lived down at Brighton Beach," he recalled once, "which was a wild place then. In front of our house there was a mile of just wasteland to the beach. There was nothing else. They were still farming there, they had creeks where ya swam, ya fished, ya canoed."

He read Hemingway, of course, and Fitzgerald, also Joyce, Shaw, and Chekhov. "But ya know? If ya wanna read prose that just flows in endless invention, ya gotta go back to Dumas—*Three Musketeers, Twenty Years After, The Count of Monte Cristo.*"

After graduating from Brooklyn College, where he played quarterback on the varsity football team, he began his professional writing career in 1934, turning out scripts for radio serials. In 1936, at the age of 23, his play *Bury the Dead* was a Broadway success, and shortly afterward he began writing short stories for the *New Yorker* that some critics still regard as his greatest claim to literary renown. "My parents tried to dissuade me from this absurd profession," he once said. "They'd get all their most important friends t'say, ya know, nobody's a writer. Learn to be a schoolteacher, a lawyer, a doctor. No, I'm gonna be a writer. This was when I was 14, 15 years old. And my mother used to call them *bubbermeisers*, ya know, grandmothers' tales. She denies it now. She tells everybody, 'we always encouraged him!'"

During World War II, he wrote for *Stars and Stripes* and *Yank*, then was assigned to direct films of combat for the Signal Corps. Out of this experience came *The Young Lions* in 1948, at once the beginning of his fame and of his "decline." "That got great reviews," he once complained, "and that was a big best seller. And from that time on, I couldn't *buy* a good review. I'd become a best seller. And people got on me sayin' I was writing for money. . . . For a long time, I haven't been taken seriously by the critics, ya see? They don't even review me, for example, in the *New York Review of Books*. There are several reasons. Part of the reason is that myth, ya know, that I live out of the country and I'm a, ya know, a success. An automatic success. A money machine. That's part of it. And it's ridiculous."

Ridiculous? Then what makes Irwin run? Not money, certainly—both his books and his conversation are studded with contempt for a culture obsessed with wealth and admiration for individuals scornful of its corruptions. Not fame—in the age of the talk-show writer, he resolutely turns down nearly all requests for interviews. And in a society in which notoriety too often replaces talent as the measure of an artist's achievement, he lives a quiet, semi-reclusive life, half the year in the small Swiss town of Klosters, half the year in a secluded area of Southampton—far from gossip columns, literary feuds, and cameo appearances in *People*. Not glamorous sex, either—though he is rumored to have a roving eye, he was married to the same woman for nearly 20 years, and he began living with her again seven years after their divorce

215

in the late Sixties. They are still together. He has never been romantically linked with media sex symbols.

Perhaps a clue to Shaw's drives can be found where most clues are located—in childhood. Irwin Shaw's father was a real estate salesman who was wiped out in the crash of 1929. This gave Shaw an early burden of financial responsibility, which must have weighed heavily on a 16-year-old boy entering the Depression. The most obvious way of escaping the lower-middle-class (a frequent preoccupation of his characters) is through making money (a frequent mistake of his characters). But an even quicker route is through fantasy, through daydreams, through imagination (remember, too, how many of his characters are artists).

Even today, in his thick accent straight off the docks, he speaks of the writer as a kind of elitist—"once you buy a typewriter you're no longer one of the masses." And his novels have a curious ambivalence—while on the one hand they're contemptuous of money, on the other they're enamored of glamour, and the hero's struggle is often an attempt to resolve this dilemma. What better way than to make an honorable profession out of the vicarious, than to make a lucrative living through honest fictions? Rich man, poor man—Shaw, of course, is referring to both pocket and spirit. It seems possible, then, that what drives Irwin Shaw—and this would certainly help account for his enormous popularity with the reading public—is the desire to escape the economic constrictions of the lower-middle-class while at the same time retaining its moral values.

Irwin Shaw pulls himself out of his chair and slouches to the bar of his Southampton home to refill his glass. "I can't work this morning. I'm drinking because I'm so angry at what they did to my stories on TV last night. 'The Girls in Their Summer Dresses,' those other two—they completely ruined them. Just like the movie of *The Young Lions*—a complete betrayal of what I wrote."

He moves slowly back across the room, his hand pressed against his hip, and with a painful stooping movement eases himself back into his chair. "I've become a bionic man," he grumbles in his Brooklyn accent. "I used ta be an athlete until I had ta get this goddamn fake hip. The body remembers. . . ." He sips from his glass. "Erosion! Age!" he suddenly exclaims with a beaming grin.

Shaw settles deeper into his chair, crosses his hands on his belly, and lets out a grunt of pleasure. "I don't care if I make money when I'm writing. If I do, fine. If not, that's fine too." He sips from his glass. "Actually, I seem to have sailed into an area of calm at last—though it's taken me 67-and-a-half years to get there."

He rubs his mouth with his forearm, rumples his hair, coughs. "I've long since given up trying to figure out what book is going to be commercially successful. This book now—there's been more pre-publication enthusiasm than for any of my books since *The Young Lions*." He gives a who-the-hell-knows shrug. "You figure it out. There's no sex, no violence, everybody behaves honorably, there's nothing but stringent moral problems. When people out here found out parts of the book take place in the Hamptons, they were afraid I was going to spill the beans—who's screwing who, that kind of thing." He shifts in his chair, crosses his legs, winces. "That's of no importance to me. Damned hip is killing me. Stringent moral problems."

A photographer arrives. She tells Shaw her doctor has a message for him. "Yeah?" "He told me to tell you, you should win the Nobel Prize." He coughs again, skeptical. "I have several ailments," he says. "What are his specialties?" "He's my gynecologist." "Oh Christ!" he laughs uproariously, slapping his belly and rocking back and forth. "Oh Christ! Well, tell the good doctor thanks anyway."

He picks up an envelope. "I just heard my publisher has taken out insurance on me for my next book. Twice my advance. Hell, they'd make more money on me if I died. I'm not Garbo, you know." he grumbles amiably at the photographer. "You don't have to worry about getting my good side."

Critics? "I'd be lying if I said they don't bug me," he says. "Even when they say good things it's never the same as the image you have of yourself. You, for instance, I don't know what you're going to write, but I do know one thing"—he wags his forefinger and grins, but he's not kidding—"whatever you write, I'm gonna be annoyed."

Talking to Shaw's friends, the one thing you hear over and over is his anger at the accusation from critics that he's "gone commercial." "That's crap," he says, "I wish I *did* know how to write for money. But nobody'd write a book like *Bread upon the Waters* if all he wanted was to make money.

"Actually, I dreamed this book," he says. "It was in Switzerland. I woke up in the middle of the night—something about a king and a noble beggar. I remembered what happened to Coleridge, you know, that 'Kubla Khan' thing, how he forgot it. So I got outta bed in the middle of the night and typed up two or three single-spaced pages—it had a beginning, a middle, an end, everything—then I went back to bed. And in the morning, I realized I had the makings of a book. I saw this whole family, every one of them.

"All of literature comes out of the family—Oedipus, Hamlet—even Genesis is a family story. Storytellers always revert to the family—the people we're born from and the people born to us. It's impossible to exhaust." He reaches across his chest and scratches his shoulder. "I guess it's a conservative book—in ways I've always been conservative—honesty, courage, fidelity."

His hero's name: Strand—like a road?

He looks up and smiles. "I didn't think about it, it just came out that way."

Strand—like alone?

Irwin Shaw shakes his head. "Like a road. The road he has to take." He thinks for a moment, leaning forward, his chin in his hand, then says quietly, "Knows who he is, what he stands for, what he has to do. Not romantic, not mentally clouded, not over-optimistic or over-pessimistic. Just sane and clear-eyed and decent. Survives that way."

He pauses, looks up, suddenly leans back in his chair, slaps his belly, and laughs like a longshoreman. "Well, we can try!"

Chronology

1913   Irwin Shaw born 27 February in New York City, son of William and Rose (Tompkins) Shaw.

1934   Graduates from Brooklyn College with B.A. Ends career as Brooklyn College varsity quarterback.

1936   Play, *Bury the Dead*, produced in New York.

1939   Marries Marian Edwards, 13 October. Play, *The Gentle People*, produced in New York. *Sailor off the Bremen* (short story collection).

1942–1945   In U. S. Army serves in North Africa and Europe. Present at liberation of Paris. Attains rank of warrant officer.

1942   *Welcome to the City* (short story collection).

1944   Play, *Sons and Soldiers*, produced in New York. O. Henry Memorial Award First Prize for "Walking Wounded."

1945   Play, *The Assassin*, produced in New York. Book version, with different third act and with preface denouncing cowardice and mediocrity of the Broadway theater, published following year. O. Henry Memorial Award Second Prize for "Gunners' Passage."

1946   *Act of Faith and Other Stories* (short story collection).

1948   *The Young Lions* (novel).

1950   *Mixed Company* (short story collection). *Report from Israel* (nonfiction with camera studies by Robert Capa). Son, Adam, born.

1951   Moves to Paris, begins his expatriate years. *The Troubled Air* (novel).

1956   *Lucy Crown* (novel).

1957   *Tip on a Dead Jockey* (short story collection).

1958   Film version of *The Young Lions*.

1960   *Two Weeks in Another Town* (novel).

219

1961   *Selected Short Stories* published by Modern Library.

1963   Play, *Children from Their Games,* produced in New York. Writes and produces the film *In the French Style,* based on two stories, "A Year to Learn the Language" and "In the French Style."

1964   *In the Company of Dolphins* (travel book).

1965   *Voices of a Summer Day* (novel). *Love on a Dark Street* (short story collection).

1966   *Short Stories of Irwin Shaw* published by Random House.

1970   *Rich Man, Poor Man* (novel).

1973   *Evening in Byazntium* (novel). *God Was Here but He Left Early* (short story collection).

1975   *Nightwork* (novel).

1976   Leaves Paris after 25 years. Begins dual residence on Long Island and in Klosters, Switzerland.

1976–1977   *Paris! Paris!* (memoir with Ronald Searle).

1977   *Beggarman, Thief* (novel).

1978   *Short Stories: Five Decades* published by Delacorte.

1979   *The Top of the Hill* (novel).

1981   *Bread upon the Waters* (novel).

1982   *Acceptable Losses* (novel).

1984   Dies 16 May in Davos, Switzerland.

Selected Bibliography

Primary Works

Short Story Collections

Act of Faith and Other Stories. New York: Random House, 1946. "Preach on the Dusty Roads," "Faith at Sea," "Gunners' Passage," "Walking Wounded," "Hamlets of the World," "Retreat," "Part in a Play," "The Priest," "Night in Algiers," "Medal from Jerusalem," "The Veterans Reflect," "Act of Faith."

God Was Here but He Left Early. New York: Anchor Books, Doubleday, 1973. Part 1: "God Was Here but He Left Early," "Where All Things Wise and Fair Descend"; part 2: "Whispers in Bedlam," "The Mannichon Solution," "Small Saturday."

Love on a Dark Street. New York: Delacorte, 1965. "The Man Who Married a French Wife," "The Inhabitants of Venus," "Noises in the City," "A Year to Learn the Language," "Love on a Dark Street," "Once, in Aleppo," "Circle of Light," "Wistful, Delicately Gay," "Tune Every Heart and Every Voice," "Goldilocks at Graveside."

Mixed Company. New York: Random House, 1950. Contains previously collected and uncollected stories. "The Girls in Their Summer Dresses," "The Eighty-Yard Run," "Act of Faith," "Main Currents of American Thought," "Strawberry Ice Cream Soda," "Material Witness," Sailor off the Bremen," "The Climate of Insomnia," "God on Friday Night," "Triumph of Justice," "The City Was in Total Darkness," "The Monument," "Return to Kansas City," "The Lament of Madame Rechevsky," "Night, Birth and Opinion," "It Happened in Rochester," "Borough of Cemeteries," "The Passion of Lance Corporal Hawkins," "Welcome to the City," "Widows' Meeting," "Gunners' Passage," "Mixed Doubles," "Little Henry Irving," "Hamlets of the World," "The Indian in Depth of Night," "Weep in Years to Come," "The Priest," "Lemkau, Pogran and Blaufox," "The Man with One Arm," "Walking Wounded," "The Dry Rock," "Faith at Sea," "Search through the Streets of the City," "Night in Algiers," "Preach on the Dusty Roads," "The Green Nude."

Sailor off the Bremen and Other Stories. New York: Random House, 1939. "Sailor off the Bremen," "I Stand by Dempsey," "The Girls in Their Summer Dresses," "Return to Kansas City," "The Deputy Sheriff," "Second Mortgage," "March, March on down the Field," "Walk along the Charles

River," "No Jury Would Convict," "Santa Claus," "The Monument,"
"The Greek General," "My Green Flower," "Strawberry Ice Cream
Soda," "The Boss," "Little Henry Irving," "Stop Pushing, Rocky," "Res-
idents of Other Cities," "Weep in Years to Come," "Borough of
Cemeteries."

Selected Short Stories of Irwin Shaw. New York: Modern Library, 1961. "The
Eighty-Yard Run," "Main Currents of American Thought," "The Girls in
Their Summer Dresses," "Sailor off the Bremen," "Welcome to the City,"
"Weep in Years to Come," "Search through the Streets of the City,"
"Night, Birth and Opinion," "The City Was in Total Darkness," "Ham-
lets of the World," "Walking Wounded," "Gunners' Passage," "Medal
from Jerusalem," "Act of Faith," "Age of Reason, "Mixed Doubles,"
"The Climate of Insomnia," "The Green Nude," "Tip on a Dead
Jockey," "In the French Style," "Voyage Out, Voyage Home," "The
Sunny Banks of the River Lethe," "Then We Were Three."

Short Stories: Five Decades. New York: Delacorte, 1978. "The Eighty-Yard
Run," "Borough of Cemeteries," "Main Currents of American Thought,"
"Second Mortgage," "Sailor off the Bremen," "Strawberry Ice Cream
Soda," "Welcome to the City," "The Girls in Their Summer Dresses,"
"Search through the Streets of the City," "The Monument," "I Stand by
Dempsey," "God on Friday Night," "Return to Kansas City," "Triumph
of Justice," "No Jury Would Convict," "The Lament of Madame Re-
chevsky," "The Deputy Sheriff," "Stop Pushing, Rocky," "March, March
on down the Field," "Free Conscience, Void of Offence," "Weep in Years
to Come," "The City Was in Total Darkness," "Night, Birth and Opin-
ion," "Preach on the Dusty Roads," "Hamlets of the World," "Medal
from Jerusalem," "Walking Wounded," "Night in Algiers," "Gunners'
Passage," "Retreat," "Act of Faith," "The Man with One Arm," "The
Passion of Lance Corporal Hawkins," "The Dry Rock," "Noises in the
City," "The Indian in Depth of Night," "Material Witness," "Little
Henry Irving," "The House of Pain," "A Year to Learn the Language,"
"The Greek General," "The Green Nude," "The Climate of Insomnia,"
"Goldilocks at Graveside," "Mixed Doubles," "A Wicked Story," "Age
of Reason," "Peter Two," "The Sunny Banks of the River Lethe," "The
Man Who Married a French Wife," "Voyage Out, Voyage Home," "Tip
on a Dead Jockey," "The Inhabitants of Venus," "In the French Style,"
"Then We Were Three," "God Was Here but He Left Early," "Love on
a Dark Street," "Small Saturday," "Pattern of Love," "Whispers in Bed-
lam," "Where All Things Wise and Fair Descend," "Full Many a
Flower," "Circle of Light."

Short Stories of Irwin Shaw. New York: Random House, 1966. "Sailor off the
Bremen," "I Stand by Dempsey," "The Girls in Their Summer Dresses,"
"Return to Kansas City," "The Deputy Sheriff," "Second Mortgage,"

"March, March on down the Field," "Walk along the Charles River," "No Jury Would Convict," "Santa Claus," "The Monument," "The Greek General," "My Green Flower," "Strawberry Ice Cream Soda," "The Boss," "Little Henry Irving," "Stop Pushing, Rocky," "Residents of Other Cities," "Weep in Years to Come," "Borough of Cemeteries," "The Eighty-Yard Run," "Main Currents of American Thought," "Welcome to the City," "Search through the Streets of the City," "Night, Birth and Opinion," "The City Was in Total Darkness," "Hamlets of the World," "Walking Wounded," "Gunners' Passage," "Medal from Jerusalem," "Act of Faith," "Age of Reason," "Mixed Doubles," "The Climate of Insomnia," "The Green Nude," "Tip on a Dead Jockey," "In the French Style," "Voyage Out, Voyage Home," "The Sunny Banks of the River Lethe," "Then We Were Three," "A Wicked Story," "Peter Two," "The Kiss at Croton Falls," "The Wedding of a Friend," "God on Friday Night," "Free Conscience, Void of Offence," "Material Witness," "The House of Pain," "Triumph of Justice," "Select Clientele," "The Indian in Depth of Night," "It Happened in Rochester," "The Dry Rock," "Prize for Promise," "Lemkau, Pogran and Blaufox," "Dinner in a Good Restaurant," "The Lament of Madame Rechevsky," "Pattern of Love," "Preach on the Dusty Roads," "Faith at Sea," "Retreat," "Part in a Play," "The Priest," "Night in Algiers," "The Veterans Reflect," "The Passion of Lance Corporal Hawkins," "Widows' Meeting," "The Man with One Arm."

Tip on a Dead Jockey and Other Stories. New York: Random House, 1957. "Tip on a Dead Jockey," "A Wicked Story," "In the French Style," "Peter Two," "Age of Reason," "The Kiss at Croton Falls," "Then We Were Three," "The Sunny Banks of the River Lethe," "The Wedding of a Friend," "Voyage Out, Voyage Home."

Welcome to the City and Other Stories. New York: Random House, 1942. "The City Was in Total Darkness," "Main Currents of American Thought," "God on Friday Night," "The Eighty-Yard Run," "Welcome to the City," "Free Conscience, Void of Offence," "Material Witness," "The House of Pain," "Triumph of Justice," "Night, Birth and Opinion," "Search through the Streets of the City," "Select Clientele," "The Indian in Depth of Night," "It Happened in Rochester," "The Dry Rock," "Prize for Promise," "Lemkau, Pogran and Blaufox," "Dinner in a Good Restaurant," "The Lament of Madame Rechevsky," "Pattern of Love."

Novels

Acceptable Losses. New York: Delacorte, 1982.
Beggarman, Thief. New York: Delacorte, 1977.
Bread upon the Waters. New York: Delacorte, 1981.

Evening in Byzantium. New York: Delacorte, 1973.
Lucy Crown. New York: Random House, 1956.
Nightwork. New York: Delacorte, 1975.
Rich Man, Poor Man. New York: Delacorte, 1970.
The Top of the Hill. New York: Delacorte, 1979.
The Troubled Air. New York: Random House, 1951.
Two Weeks in Another Town. New York: Random House, 1960.
Voices of a Summer Day. New York: Dial, 1965.
The Young Lions. New York: Random House, 1948. Modern Library edition
   published in 1958.

Plays

The Assassin. New York: Random House, 1946.
Bury the Dead. New York: Random House, 1939. Reprinted in John Gassner,
   ed. *20 Best Plays of the Modern American Theater,* 1930–1939. New York:
   Crown, 1939.
Children from Their Games. London: Samuel French, 1962.
The Gentle People. New York: Random House, 1939.
Sons and Soldiers. New York: Random House, 1944.

Nonfiction

In the Company of Dolphins. New York: Bernard Geis Associates, 1964.
Paris! Paris! New York: Harcourt, Brace, Jovanovich, 1976, 1977. With Ronald
   Searle.
Report on Israel. New York: Simon & Schuster, 1950. With Robert Capa.

Secondary Works

Biographical Essays

Alpert, Hollis. "The Joys of Uncertainty." *Saturday Review* 45 (December
   1962): 16–17.
"Shaw Strikes Back," *Newsweek* 5 (November 1961): 109–11.
Brierre, Annie. "Pourquoi Préférez-vous Paris?" *Nouvelles Littéraires* (19 Feb-
   ruary 1959): 1, 4.
Commins, Dorothy. *What Is an Editor? Saxe Commins at Work.* Chicago: Uni-
   versity of Chicago Press, 1978.
Salter, James. "Winter of the Lion." *Esquire* 112 (July 1989): 69–76.
Shnayerson, Michael. *Irwin Shaw: A Biography.* New York: Putnam's, 1989.

Critical Studies

Aldridge, John W. "Mailer, Burns, and Shaw: The Naked Zero." In *After the Lost Generation*, 133–56. New York: Noonday, 1951.

Baird, Joe L., and Ralph Grejada. "A Shaw Story and Brooks and Warren." *CEA Critic* 28 (February 1966): 1, 3–4.

Berke, Jacqueline. "Further Observations on a Shaw Story and Brooks and Warren." *CEA Critic* 33 (November 1970): 28–29.

Brooks, Cleanth, and Robert Penn Warren. *Understanding Fiction*. 2d ed. New York: Appleton-Century–Crofts, 1959. An analysis of "The Girls in Their Summer Dresses," pp. 84–90.

Eisinger, Chester E. "Fiction and the Liberal Reassessment." In *Fiction of the Forties*, 86–145. Chicago: University of Chicago Press, 1963.

Evans, Bergen. "Irwin Shaw." *English Journal* 40 (November 1951): 485–91.

Fiedler, Leslie A. "Irwin Shaw: Adultery, the Last Politics." *Commentary* 22 (July 1956): 71–74.

Giles, James R. *Irwin Shaw*. Boston: Twayne, 1983.

———. "Irwin Shaw's Original Prologue to *The Young Lions*." *Resources for American Literary Study* 11 (Spring 1981): 115–19.

Grana, Gianni. "Due opere di schietta narrative: Irwin Shaw e Robert Ruark." *Fiera Letteraria* no. 2 (1965): 5.

Healey, Robert C. "Novelists of the War: A Bunch of Dispossessed." In *Fifty Years of the American Novel: A Christian Appraisal*, ed. Harold C. Gardiner, S. J., 257–71. New York: Scribner's, 1951.

Jones, Peter G. "Sexuality and Violence in the War Novel." In *War and the Novelist: Appraising the American War Novel*, 113–61. Columbia: University of Missouri Press, 1976.

Krutch, Joseph Wood. "Over Most of These Stations." *Nation* 15 (May 1943): 714–16.

Kuznetsov, Vladimir. "To the Memory of Irwin Shaw." *Soviet Literature* 10 (1984): 168–70.

Moorhead, Michael. "Hemingway's 'The Short Happy Life of Francis Macomber' and Shaw's 'The Deputy Sheriff.'" *Explicator* 44 (Winter 1986): 42–43.

Peden, William. "Best of Irwin Shaw." *Saturday Review* 33 (18 November 1950): 27–28.

Saal, Hubert. "Disenchanted Men." *Saturday Review* 40 (3 August 1957): 12–13.

Startt, William. "Irwin Shaw: An Extended Talent." *Midwest Quarterly* 2 (Summer 1961): 325–37.

Trilling, Diana. "Fiction in Review." *Nation* 9 (October 1948): 409–10.

Trilling, Lionel. "Some Are Gentle, Some Are Not." *Saturday Review* 34 (9 June 1951): 8–9.

Wetzsteon, Ross. "Irwin Shaw: "The Conflict between Big Bucks and Good Books." *Saturday Review* 8 (August 1981): 12–17.

Young, Stark. "Assorted Murders." *New Republic* 113 (29 October 1945): 573.

———. "Current Slapping." *New Republic* 114 (8 April 1946): 479–80.

———. "The Great Doom's Image." *New Republic* 87 (13 May 1936): 21.

Interviews

"The Art of Fiction IV: Irwin Shaw," in *Writers at Work: The Paris Review Interviews, Fifth Series*, edited by George Plimpton. Interviews by John Phillips and George Plimpton and by Willie Morris and Lucas Matthiessen. Middlesex, England, and New York: Penguin, 1981.

Index

229

The Author

James R. Giles is professor of English at Northern Illinois University. The author of Twayne's United States Authors Series volumes on Claude McKay, James Jones, and Irwin Shaw, he has also published *Confronting the Horror: The Novels of Nelson Algren* (1989). His journal articles focus primarily on twentieth-century American fiction, black American writing, and the evolution of American naturalism.

The Editor

Gordon Weaver earned his Ph.D. in English and creative writing at the University of Denver in 1970. He is professor of English at Oklahoma State University. He is the author of several novels, including *Count a Lonely Cadence, Give Him a Stone, Circling Byzantium*, and most recently *The Eight Corners of the World*. His short stories are collected in *The Entombed Man of Thule, Such Waltzing Was Not Easy, Getting Serious, Morality Play*, and *A World Quite Round*. Recognition of his fiction includes the St. Lawrence Award for Fiction (1973), two National Endowment for the Arts fellowships (1974 and 1989), and the O. Henry First Prize (1979). He edited *The American Short Story, 1945–1980: A Critical History* and is currently editor of the *Cimarron Review*. Married and the father of three daughters, he lives in Stillwater, Oklahoma.